East New Jersey Land Records 1719 – 1727

Books C-2 and D-2

Richard S. Hutchinson

Colonial Roots
Millsboro, Delaware
2015

Colonial
Roots

Helping you grow your family tree

ISBN 978-1-68034-034-1

CONTENTS

Introduction v

Abbreviations vii

East New Jersey Land Records, Book C-2 1

East New Jersey Land Records, Book D-2 53

Index 106

INTRODUCTION

New Jersey was divided into two provinces in 1676, East New Jersey and West New Jersey. The division line ran from the east side of Little Egg Harbor to a point on the Delaware River where it was intersected by the old partition line between New York and New Jersey. Referring to today's boundaries, it ran from the dividing lines between Burlington and Ocean Counties, and Somerset and Hunterdon Counties. Thus what is known today as North Jersey was then called East Jersey and governed first by Sir George Carteret and later by a board of 24 proprietors. The present South Jersey was known as West Jersey, and came under the rule of William Penn and other Quaker leaders. Consequently, West Jersey was largely settled by Quakers from England, notably at Burlington, Gloucester, Newton, Rancocas, Willingsburgh, and Pyne Poynte (now Camden). In 1701/2 the two provinces were united under the Governor of New York. In 1738 New Jersey acquired its own royal governor, the last being William Franklin, son of the famous Benjamin Franklin.

As sole proprietor of East New Jersey, Sir George Carteret died in 1679/80, leaving a will under the terms of which the province was to be sold to pay his debts. It was conveyed to William Penn and eleven associates. The majority of this first board of proprietors resided in or near London. The original board soon expanded to 24 members in order to cover the enormous cost (at that time) of £3400. Each of the twenty-four shares were later divided into quarters making the total number of rights outstanding 96. These shares came to be known as "full quarter shares."

The earliest sales of land were by the proprietors of East and West Jersey. The Land Act of 1785 ordered the recording of deeds by the counties; prior to this time land conveyances (after the initial grants from the proprietors) were recorded in the East and West New Jersey capitals, Perth Amboy and Burlington. The Secretary of State's Office continued recording deeds in the East and West Jersey books begun by the proprietors and provincial secretaries in Perth Amboy and Burlington.

This volume represents abstracts of Books C-2 and D-2. The period of these books, 1719 to 1723/4 and 1722 to 1727 is the general period of recording, not the date of the actual transaction (land sales, conveyances, mortgages, powers of attorney, etc.) which oft times predated 1719 – in these books the earliest entry is from1682. During this period of recordation East Jersey consisted of the original four East New Jersey counties of Bergen, Essex, Middlesex,

Monmouth; and also Somerset County (which was formed out of Middlesex County in 1688).

County courthouses hold copies of the recorded deeds beginning in 1785; in some cases earlier. The Bergen County deed books start in 1715 and contain records from the 1740s to the 1750s. The Essex County Deed Book A began in the late 1600s but was destroyed by fire. Essex County Deed Book B begins in 1728 overlapping the Proprietary records. The county filings of Middlesex and Somerset start in 1785. Monmouth County also recorded some deeds much earlier than the 1785 time line but seems to have ceased doing so in 1745 with some exceptions.

Early deeds and associated records for East and West Jersey were published in 1890 by the state of New Jersey as *Patents and Deeds and other Early Records of New Jersey, 1664-1703*, originally as volume 21 of New Jersey Archives, 1st Series - Edited by William Nelson

The importance of these records to the genealogist is obvious. Of special interest are the relationships revealed in these records. Often the first name of the grantor's spouse is recorded. One is also able to follow ownership of land from parents to their children and their children's spouses in many of the conveyances. Descendancy of the land and the parallel descendancy of the heirs is not always apparent. It has been estimated that about 1/4 of the colonial land transfers were recorded.

Earlier works by the author include *Burlington County, New Jersey, Deed Abstracts: Books A, B and C*; *Middlesex County, New Jersey Deed Abstract Book 1*; and *Monmouth County Deed Books A, B, C & D*.

F. Edward Wright
Lewes, Delaware
2007

ABBREVIATIONS

a. – acre, acres
absd. – abovesaid
abt. – about
ackn. - acknowledge
adj. - adjoining
Admin. – administration, administrator, administratrix
afsd. – aforesaid
apprd. - appeared
atty. – attorney, attorneys
bef. – before
beg.- begins, beginning
betw. - between
bnd. - bound
bot. – bought
Co. – county
crk. – creek
dau. – daughter
d. – died, dead
daus. – daughters
dec'd. – deceased
e. – east
Esqr. - Esquire
exec. – executor, executors, executrix
excep. – except, excepting
[FNU] – First Name Unknown
form. – formerly
Gent. – gentleman
[LNU] - Last Name Unknown
n. – north
pt. - part
pt/o. – part of
recr'd. – record, recorded
s. – south
sd. – said
tr. – tract
Twp. – township
w. – west

wch.- which
wits.- witness, witnesses
w/o. - without

Book C-2 – East New Jersey Land Records
1719-1723/4

Earliest Dated Deed – 1682
Also, contains the 1721, NY will of Albert Terhunen; and a grantee
who lost his deed after being taken by Pirates.

Pg 1. 6 Nov 1719. Abraham Drake, of Piscataway Twp., Middlesex Co., East NJ, carpenter, and his wife, Deliverance, sells to Peter Vanneste, Sen. of Raritan, Middlesex Co., East NJ, yeoman, for £50, all those tr. of land & meadow, being 20 a. & 20 chains by 10 chains, bnd. e. & w. by 2 highways, s. by Isaac Smalley's town lot, and n. by land that was George Jewels. ALSO, 6 a. of meadow in Woodbridge Meadows, bnd. w. by Isaac Tappin, s. by John Bloomfield, n. by Samuel Hale, and part by Joseph Worth, and e. by John Worth. ALSO, a house lot of 10 a., beg. at a corner that was Michael Seymonds lot now Samuel Potter's. ALSO, a tr. of land of 15 a. of upland, beg. by a highway then by a swamp, and then several courses to beg.; bnd. s. by Benjamin Hull, n. by John Langstaff now Samuel Potter's, e. & w. by highways. However, if sd. Drake pays unto sd. Vanneste £50 on 6 Nov 1724 and the rent money, then the deed of sale shall be null & void. WHEREAS, John Borrowe, of Piscataway Town, of the afsd. place, became seized, by a deed from William Hodgson, of Amboy, of the afsd.. place, bricklayer, dated 28 Feb 1717, for certain tr. of upland in Piscataway Town, and also 6 a. of meadow in Woodbridge Meadows. AND, WHEREAS, John Borrowe by a deed on 4 Jan 1717 conveyed unto sd. Drake all of the absd. tr. and meadow. Wits.: Samll. Walker, Robert Hay, Alex. Mackdowall. Signed: Abraham Drake, Deliverance Drake. Ackn.: 14 May 1720, Alexander Mackdowall apprd. bef. John Parker, Majesty's Council .

Pg 5. 1 Feb 1719. Henry Taylor, of Woodbridge, Middlesex Co., East NJ., turner, leases to Walter Thong, of NY City, merchant, for £1, a tr. of land in Woodbridge Twp., being 30 a., by transferring uses into possessions, and is in the actual possession of same, wch. is one half of a First Division lot, beg. at the n.w. corner of the lot and then several courses to the beg.; being Lot 16 in the second tier. ALSO, a tr. of woodland in Woodbridge Town of 60 a., being a First Division lot, # 17. Wits.: Edward Pennant, James Woods. Signed: Henry Taylor made his mark. Ackn.: 6 Feb 1719/1720, sd. Pennant and Woods apprd. bef. David Jamison, Esqr., Chief Justice.

Pg 7. 2 Feb 1719. Henry Taylor, of Woodbridge, Middlesex Co., East NJ., turner, leases to Walter Thong, of NY City, merchant, for £103, [for the same land in the deed above – Pg. 5 per transferring uses into possessions.] Wits.:

Edward Pennant, James Woods. Signed: Henry Taylor made his mark. Ackn.: 6 Feb 1719/1720, sd. Pennant and Woods apprd. bef. David Jamison, Esqr., Chief Justice.

Pg 11. 2 Jun 1719. Bef. Richard Wises, Notary, apprd. Mrs. Elizabeth Prince, of London, widow, one of the legatees and late mother of Henry Prince, late of East NJ, merchant, dec'd, authorizes Edward Vaughan, of Elizabeth Town in East NJ and Patrick Macknight, of NY, merchant, her lawful attorney to act on her behalf on all matters in America pertaining to her. Wits.: Paul Richard, Benj. Francurt, Junr. Signed: Elizabeth Prince. 4 Oct 1720, Paul Richards testified bef. David Jamison, Esqr., Chief Justice, that he saw sd. Elizabeth Prince sign same.

Pg 14. 12 Feb 1717. Noah Bishop, of Woodbridge, Middlesex Co., NJ, blacksmith, for £33, paid by Henry Taylor, turner, of the absd. place, does discharge the sd. Taylor and sd. Bishop conveyed to sd. Henry Taylor a tr. of land in Woodbridge Twp., of 30 a., being half of a First Division lot in Woodbridge Commons, wch. was a one-third lot in the Second Tier, #6, bot. by sd. Noah from John Kinsey and Thomas Pike, Exec. of the will of William Ellison, of sd,. Woodbridge. Wits.: Daniel Britten, Thomas Pike. Signed: Noah Bishop. Ackn.: 6 Apr 1720, Noah Bishop apprd. bef. John Parker, Majesty's Council.

Pg 17. 26 Sep 1718. I, Samuel Moore, of Woodbridge, Middlesex Co., NJ, Gent., for £50, sells to Henry Taylor, of the afsd. place, turner, a tr. of land in Woodbridge Twp., being 60 a., and one of the First Division lots in Woodbridge Commons (in Right of his grandfather, Samuel Moore, form. of Woodbridge, dec'd) being the fourth lot of the Second Tier, #17, beg. by a highway that runs betw. the first & second tier lots and then a few courses to the beg. AND, Mary Moore, does freely give up her Right to dowry and Power of Thirds unto the sd. premises. Wits.: Mary Moore, Wm. Rogers. Signed: Samll. Moore, Mary Moore made her mark. Ackn.: 5 Apr 1720, Samuel Moore and Mary Moore apprd. bef. John Parker, Majesty's Council.

Pg 20. 16 Nov 1719. John Vanmater, of Somerset Co., NJ, yeoman, and his wife Margaret, sell to Henry Miller, of the afsd. place, yeoman, for a competent sum of money a tr. of land on the w. side of the South Branch of the Raritan River, Somerset Co., now in possession of sd. Miller, beg. on the bank of the South Branch and then several courses to the beg.; bnd. s.e. by the river, s.w. by land form. of John Campbell, dec'd, n.w. by land of John Vanmater, n.e. by land late belonging to John Drummond, of Lundie. Wits.: Lewis Morris, George Willocks. Signed: John Vanmetere, Margaret Vanmetre made her mark. On 23 Nov 1709[1719] received of Henry Miller the consideration. Ackn.: 7 Nov 1719, George Willocks apprd. bef. Thos. Gordon, Majesty's Council.

Pg 24. 28 Jan 1719. George Willocks, of Perth Amboy, Middlesex Co., Gent., sells to Peter Runion, of Piscataqua, of the afsd. place, yeoman, for 5 shillings, 30 a. in East NJ, to be taken up and surveyed in East NJ, as belonging to the Proprietors and amongst whom the sd. Willocks stands lawfully seized, by transferring uses into possessions. Wits.: John Harrison, Richard Sutton. Signed: George Willocks. Ackn.: 21 May 1720, George Willocks apprd. bef. William Eire, Esqr., Judge, Middlesex Co.

Pg 25. 29 January 1719. George Willocks, of Perth Amboy, Middlesex Co., Gent., sells to Peter Runion, of Piscataqua, of the afsd. place, yeoman, for lawful money 30 a. in East NJ [being the land in the absd. deed – Page 24], being part of 200 a. bot. from John Harrison & James Alexander, of Perth Amboy by an indenture dated 1 & 2 inst. January. Wits.: John Harrison, Richard Sutton. Signed: George Willocks. Ackn.: 23 May 1720, George Willocks apprd. bef. William Eire, Esqr., Judge, Middlesex Co.

Pg 28. 23 Nov 1719. Andrew Johnston, of Perth Amboy, Middlesex Co., NJ, merchant, and his wife Catherine, sells to James Alexander, of the afsd. place, Gent., for 5 shillings, a lot of land in Perth Amboy; bnd. n. by lot of sd. Johnston, e. by Water Street, and s.e. by lot of John Barclay, being five-eights of an acre, under transferring uses into possession. Wits.: George Willocks, John Watson. Signed: Andrew Johnston, Katherine Johnston. Ackn.: 7 Dec 1719, Andrew & Katherine Johnston apprd. bef. William Eire, Esqr., Judge, Middlesex Co.

Pg 29. 24 Nov 1719. Andrew Johnston, of Perth Amboy, Middlesex Co., NJ, merchant, and his wife Catherine, sells to James Alexander, of the afsd. place, Gent., for a competent sum of money, [the land in the absd. deed – Page 28]. Wits.: George Willocks, John Watson. Signed: Andrew Johnston, Katherine Johnston. Ackn.: 7 Dec 1719, George Willocks apprd. bef. William Eire, Esqr., Judge, Middlesex Co.

Pg 32. 15 Mar 1719. George Willocks, of Perth Amboy, Middlesex Co., Gent., sells to John Barclay, of the afsd. place, Gent., for £24, a lot of land in Perth Amboy on the w. side of Willocks' Lane wch. leads out of the n. side of Smith Street, beg. by the n.e. corner of land form. sold by sd. Willocks and now in possession of John Luffborrow, Junr., wch. corner is 212 feet from Smith Street running along the afsd. lane, and then several courses to the beg. Wits.: Andrew Johnston, John Watson. Signed: George Willocks. Ackn.: 23 Mar 1719, George Willocks apprd. bef. John Hamilton, Esqr., Majesty's Council.

Pg 34. 15 Mar 1719. George Willocks, of Perth Amboy, Middlesex Co., NJ, Gent., sells to Adam Hudd, of Woodbridge, in afsd. place, Gent., for £54, for a lot in Perth Amboy on the w. side of Willocks' Lane wch. leads out of the n. side of Smith Street, beg. by the n.e. corner of land form. sold by sd. Willocks to

John Barclay of sd. city, Gent., by a deed dated this date, wch. sd. n.e. corner is from Smith Street 252 feet and running along the sd. lane, and then several courses to the sd. lot of John Barclay and along same to the beg. Wits.: Andrew Johnston, John Watson, John West, Senr. Signed: George Willocks. Ackn.: 23 Mar 1719, George Willocks apprd. bef. John Hamilton, Esqr., Majesty's Council.

Pg 37. 13 Apr 1720. Thomas Gordon, of Perth Amboy, Middlesex Co., NJ, Esqr., sells to Samuell Leonard of the afsd. place, Esqr., for a competent sum of money, a tr. of land on the n. side of Tennant's Creek, beg. on the s side of the crk., 2 chains above where Fly Brook falls into Tennant's Creek above where the Post Road crosses the n. side of sd. crk. and then several courses to the beg. Wits.: Thomas Gordon, Junr., Margaret Gordon. Signed: Thomas Gordon. Ackn.: 16 Aug 1720, Thomas Gordon, Esqr., apprd. bef. Adam Hude, Esqr., Judge, Middlesex Co.

Pg 39. 20 Apr 1720. John Hamilton & James Alexander, Esqr., sell to Capt. John Morris, of Newark, for £14, 18 shillings, 9 pence, 39.5 a. of land in common (to be returned to ye sd. Capt. Morris for 41.5 a), wch. is part of 1,500 a. of land belonging to them in East NJ, lately bot. of Isabella Daves, heir of Gawen Lawrie, dec'd, by deeds of lease & release, dated 3 & 4 April 1719, to be taken up and surveyed & Patented in East NJ. Wits.: Wm. Deare[?], John Parker. Signed: John Hamilton, James Alexander. Ackn.: 13 May 1720, John Hamilton & James Alexander apprd. bef. Wm. Eier.

Pg 40. 13 Apr 1720. Thomas Gordon, of Perth Amboy, Middlesex Co., NJ, Esqr., for diverse causes has forever quit claimed unto Samuel Leonard of the afsd, place, Esqr., a tr. of land Lying on the e. side of South River within the bnds. of Perth Amboy, on Tennant's Creek, bnd. & betw. land form. Patented to David Vilant and that Patented to Thomas Gordon. Wits.: Thomas Gordon, Junr., Margaret Gordon. Signed; Thomas Gordon. Ackn.: 16 Aug 1720. Thomas Gordon apprd. bef. Adam Hude, Esqr., Judge, Middlesex Co.

Pg 42. 10 Dec 1714. Joseph Morgan, of Freehold, Monmouth Co., NJ, clerk, sells to Jacobus Romeyn, of the afsd. place, for £200, a tr. of land in Freehold on the s. of land of James Johnston's (now John Craig's), beg. where sd. Johnston's line crosses the middle brook, and then along sd. Craig's line, then up North Brook and then several courses to the beg. ALSO, another tr. of upland and meadow in sd. county, form. of Thomas Foreman and sold to John Campbell, as by Forman's deed to sd. Campbell, dated 1698; beg. where a small run comes into Spotswood's middle brook below James Miler's corner and then down sd. brook, being 4 a. of long meadow; bnd. s. by middle brook, n. by Craig's land & North Brook, e. by barrens. All sd. lands were form. lands of John Campbell as by his deeds and by him sold unto Joseph Morgan, dated 6 Feb 1709, and all of the estate title that was granted to sd. Morgan by Patent, dated 5 July 1695. Wits.: Gerret Schenck, Joseph Vandorn, Peter Wyckoff. Signed: Joseph Morgan. Ackn.: 25 May 1720, Joseph Morgan apprd. bef. John Reid.

Pg 44. 18 Nov 1718. David Harriott, Junr., of Woodbridge, Middlesex Co., NJ, cooper, for £20 & other diverse causes, sell to James Lockhert, of the afsd. place, yeoman, a tr. of upland of 10 a., in Woodbridge Twp. that form. belonged to Wm. Compton, of sd. Woodbridge, dec'd, and bot. by Gawen Lockhert, the natural father of the sd. James Lockhert, as by deed dated 6 Feb 1691, being 10 a., but since it came into possession of the sd. Gawen Lockhert, 2 a. were taken off the s. end by the surveyors of highways, and the land came from the Commons as in the Town Book, beg. at a corner of Stephen Kent, Junr.'s house lot & addition, bnd. e. by sd. house lot, s. by absd. highway and w. by land in common, being abt. 50 rods by 30 rods. Wits.: John Smith, Thos. Petis[?]. Signed: David Harriott, Junr. Ackn.: 9 Dec 1718. David Harriott apprd. bef. Adam Hude, Esqr., Judge, Middlesex Co.

Pg 46. 1 Jul 1710. John Johnston, of NY City, NY, Esqr., for 5 shillings and the natural affection and love I bear unto my son, John Johnston, Junr., of Monmouth Co., NJ, grant & sell a tr. of land on the w. side of the North Branch of Raritan River, Somerset Co., NJ, being 133 a., beg. by the North Branch at the upper end of a tr. form. of Lord Neil Campbell, dec'd, , and then n.w. 7 n. to land form. sold to Matthias D' Night and then along his land back to the sd. Branch and then down same to the beg. ALSO, an island abt. one-half mile further up the sd. Branch opposite the lands of D' Night; being abt. 14 a. Wits.: Tho. Ffarmer, Geo. Willocks. Signed: John Johnston. Ackn.: 2 Apr 1720, George Willocks apprd. bef. John Hamilton, Esqr., Majesty's Council.

Pg 47. 22 Jul 1720. John Smith, of Middlesex Co., NJ, yeoman, sells to George Elmore, of the afsd. place, carpenter, and Union, his wife, for £17, a tr. of land in Middlesex Co., beg. with clear fields joining Piscataway road, being 10 a. with a piece of woodland; bnd. w. & s. by land of Henry Alord, e. by Slangtale brook, n. on Metuchen Road, and in all being 20 a. Wits.: Joseph Leigh, Desior Smith. Signed: John Smith. Ackn.: 6 Sep 1720, Joseph Leigh apprd. bef. Adam Hude, Judge, Middlesex Co.

Pg 50. 22 July 1720. Articles of Agreement. I, John Smith am obligated by these articles of agreement to pay George Elmore, and his wife, Union, for all building that shall be on this place when it is returned unto me or to my heirs being praised by the workman to have ye value further more than I bind my self to make satisfaction for them likewise and to find him as many apple trees as he shall for cause to set out on the place. Wits.: Joseph Leigh, Desior Smith. Signed: John Smith. Ackn.: 6 Sep 1720, Joseph Leigh apprd. bef. Adam Hude, Judge, Middlesex Co.

Pg 50. 14 Nov 1712. John Robinson, of Duck Creek, PA, weaver, sells unto James Moore, of Woodbridge, Middlesex Co., NJ, yeoman, for "One _____ and _____ £20, for a piece of salt marsh now belonging to John Robinson, being 15 a., being in the bounds of Woodbridge or amongst the Raritan Meadows, and on both sides of the Great Creek ; beg. by the Parsonage Meadow, and then w. to meadow of Stephen Kent, then s. to the meadow form. of Robert Rogers, dec'd, e. by meadow now of late of Henry Lathenby and part of meadow of James Moore and then to the beg., wch. said meadow descended unto John Robinson, as heir to his late father, John Robinson, dec'd. Wits.: Henry Brotherton, Shobal Smith, John Lynn. Signed: John Robinson. Ackn.: 2 Jul 1720, Henry Brotherton apprd. bef. Adam Hude, Judge, Middlesex Co.

Pg 53. 23 Aug 1720. Richard Soaper, Woodbridge, Middlesex Co., NJ, yeoman, and Elizabeth, his wife, sell to James Moores, of the afsd. place, yeoman, for £92, for a tr. of land in Woodbridge Twp., being 60 a., beg. at a marked tree along the n. side of the Raritan River, and then to a spring comes out of the bank and runs into the sd. river, and then several courses to land of Jekabods Smith and then to the beg. Wits.: John Samuel Moore, John Warden, John Harrison[?]. Signed: Richard Soper & Elizabeth Soper both made their marks. Ackn.: 24 Aug 1720, Richard & Elizabeth Soper apprd. bef. Adam Hude, Judge, Middlesex Co.

Pg 57. 24 Mar 1716/17. John Compton, of Woodbridge, Middlesex Co., East NJ, blacksmith, and wife, Elizabeth, sell to James Robbenson, of the afsd. place, yeoman, for £11, 5 shillings, for several tr. of land in Woodbridge, being 10 a. that was surveyed & laid out for Thomas Pike, Wm. Isleay, Richard Jones, George Brown, with the FIRST, beg. at the s.e. corner of Richard Jones' house lot, then s. w. & w. of a road to Piscataway, then to sd. Robbenson's ,and bot. of John Clarkson, then to the line of Richard Jones and then to the beg. ALSO, land betw. James Robinson and Richard Jones, being 34 rods by 20 rods, bnd. on the s. by sd. Robbenson, n. by sd. Jones, w. by Common land. ALSO, a small piece w. of sd. Robbenson beg. at the n.w. corner of his land and then by the sd. road, then e. as it runs to the s.w. corner of James Robinson' land being 10 a. Wits.: John Vail, Tobias Hatch, Sam. Smith. Signed: John Compton. Ackn.: 7 Apr 1719, John Compton apprd. bef. Adam Hude, Judge, Middlesex Co.

Pg 60. 25 May 1720. Jacobus Romine, of Freehold, Monmouth Co., East NJ, yeoman, and Mary, his wife, sell to Archibald Craig, of the afsd. place, yeoman, for £240, for a tr. of land in sd. county on s.e. side of land wch. was James Johnston's now John Craig's, beg. where James Johnston's line crosses Middle Brook, then to the North Brook and then up same to sd. Johnston's middle brook and then to the beg. ALSO, another tr. of upland and meadow in sd. county beg. where a small run comes into Spotswood's middle brook below James Miller's corner running down sd. brook, being 4 a. of long meadow with all bnd. s.w. by middle brook, n.w. by sd. Craig's land, n.e. by North Brook, & e. by the Barrens; wch. land was conveyed to sd. Romine by deed from Joseph Morgan, 10 Dec 1714. Wits.: Francis Pierce, Timothy Loyd, Thomas Mount. Signed: Jacobus Romine made his mark. Ackn.: 25 May 1720, Jacobus Romine apprd. bef. John Reid.

Pg 63. 2 Mar 1716. Isabella Davis, of NY City, widow of Wm. Davis, late of sd. city, Gent., dec'd, the only surviving dau. & heir at law of James Lawrie, the eldest son of Gawen Lawrie, Esqr., dec'd, late Gov. and Proprietor of East NJ, sells to John Johnston, of NY City, Esqr., for £60, leases for one year the 600 a. tr. below, under transferring uses into possessions. WHEREAS, the Proprietors of East NJ in 1690 surveyed & laid out land for the use of Gawen Lawrie, including a tr. of upland & meadow at Barnegat, Monmouth Co., being 600 a., and they Patented on 24 May 1690 and confirmed unto Miles Forster, of NY City, merchant in the right of Gawen Lawrie, Esqr., dec'd, a tr. of land at Barnegat on Muscato Creek, beg. on the s. side of sd. crk., and several courses to the Bay; bnd. n. by sd. Creek, e. by the Bay, s. & w. by unsurveyed land, with upland and meadow being 600 a. AND, whereas sd. Forster on 3 Mar 1703 endorsed on the back side of the Patent for 5 shillings, did grant unto Wm. Davis and Isabella, his wife, who by right of inheritance as well as heir at law of her grandfather, the afsd. Gawen Lawrie, dec'd, as well as heir of her father, James Lawrie, dec'd, is possessed of the afsd. tr. of 600 a. Wits.: Francis[?] Harison, Henry Lane. Signed: Isabella Davis. Ackn.: 4 Mar 1716/7, Isabella Davis apprd. bef. John Hamilton, Esqr., Majesty's Council.

Pg 70. 1 Mar 1716. Isabella Davis, of NY City, widow of Wm. Davis, late of sd. city, Gent., dec'd, the only surviving dau. & heir at law of James Lawrie, the eldest son of Gawen Lawrie, Esqr., dec'd, late Gov. and Proprietor of East NJ, sells to John Johnston, of NY City, Esqr., for 10 shillings [for the land in the absd. deed – Page 63.] Wits.: Fra. Harison, Henry Lane. Signed: Isabella Davies. Ackn.: 4 May 1716/7, Isabella Davis apprd. bef. John Hamilton, Esqr., Majesty's Council.

Pg 73. 13 Aug 1711. George Willocks, of Perth Amboy, Middlesex Co., NJ, merchant; John Harrison and heir of John Harrison of Raritan River, merchant, dec'd; Cornelius Longfield of sd. River, Gent.; and Michael Hawdon, of NY, Gent. by a deed of release, dated 22 Feb 1702, released and forever quit claimed unto John Johnston, of Monmouth Co., NJ, Esqr., several tr. of land abutted together and with another tr. wch. will make him up to a full one-fifth part to be divided into five parts in all the tr. of land. AND, WHEREAS, John Reid, Surveyor General together with William Lawrence, another surveyor surveyed & divided the several tr., returned unto John Johnston, his just & equal one-fifth part. The whole five equal parts to be divided being 1,477 a. as follows. FIRST, all the tr. on the e. side of Matchaponix River, beg. at the mouth of fly brook where it empties into sd. River and then down same to said fly brook and then down it to the beg. ALSO, all the boggy meadow at the head of fly brook above the upper corner of the tr. last mentioned. ALSO, a tr. on the w. side of sd. River beg. where the fly brook empties in sd. River and the several courses to sd. River and down same to beg. ALSO a tr. on the e. side of Manalapan River, beg. where the great bog run falls into the Manalapan, then sever courses back to the Manalapan and to the beg., as by the Return given by sd. Reid & Lawrence, surveyors, dated 28 Oct 1710. NOW BY THIS INDENTURE, the absd. grantors forever quit claim unto John Johnston, for several good causes, now in his possession, being the 1,477 a. Wits.: Wm. Anderson, H. Lane, Jas. Reginer, David Lyell, John Barclay. Signed: Mich. Howdon, Cornelius Longfield, John Harrison, Geo. Willocks. Ackn.: 19 Feb 1716, Henry Lane, merchant, and David Lyell, goldsmith, apprd. bef. Lewis Morris, Esqr., Majesty's Council.

Pg 77. 19 Sept 1713. Martha Barker, of London, widow of Thomas Barker, late of London, merchant, dec'd, releases unto John Harrison, of Somerset Co., NJ, for £1,160, paid to John Estaugh, late of Rotherrith, Co. of Surry, Great Britain, now of Gloucester Co., NJ, Gent., her attorney, land now in Harrison's possession re: transferring uses into possessions, being on half of an undivided twenty-fourth part of land in East NJ. Wits.: John Kay, Geo. Willocks. Signed: Martha Barker by her attorney John Estaugh. Ackn.: 15 Oct 1713, George Willocks apprd. bef. Thomas Gordon, Majesty's Council.

Pg 83. 8 Mar1713. William Robinson, of Elizabeth, Essex Co., NJ, Gent., and Deborah, his wife, sell to John Tremble, of the afsd. place, yeoman, for £55, for one-sixteenth of one-eighth of one-twenty-fourth of the East NJ. Wits.: Richard Harker, Robt. Howen[?], Joannah [LNU]. Signed: William Robinson, Deborah Robinson. Ackn.: 27 Oct 1720, Robt. Howen[?], apprd. bef. Isaac Whitehead.

Pg 85. 28 Oct 1720. James Alexander, of NJ, Gent., sells to Henry Rolfe, of Rahway, Essex Co., Esqr., for a competent sum of money, 200 a. to be taken up and surveyed in East NJ, being part of 300 a. belonging to sd. Alexander, wch. he bot. of Donald Cameron, of Lockiel. Wits.: John Hendrick, John Ieiley[?]. Signed James Alexander. Ackn.: 29 Oct 1720, John Hendricks apprd. bef. Isaac Whitehead, Judge, Essex Co.

Pg 86. 22 Nov. 1712. Nathaniel Fitz Randolph, Stephen Kent, John Compton, Thomas Martin, LowranceVangalen, Thomas Pike, Peter Elston, John Griffith, Richard Jons, Ephraim Andrews, Moses Rolph, Richard Soper, Samuel Slon, John Loofburrow, Thomas Pursele, Timothy Blumfield, John Ayres, Goven Lockhart, John Noks, John Pike, Joseph Conger, John Jacques, William Bun, Edward Crowel, Benjamin Crumwel, George Brown, Obediah Ayers, William Kelsy, John Worth, Thomas Coler, Ichabod Smith, James Clarkson, William Bingla, Adam Hude, Elisha Parker, & John Bishop, all being of the town of Woodbridge, Middlesex Co., NJ, freeholders of the sd. town, have made choice of three of their number – John Bishop, Thomas Pike, and Adam Hude - to sell & convey so much of the land that lays in Common within the bounds of sd. Woodbridge as will pay £40 to the High Sheriff, John Campbell, Esqr., of sd. county or to John Pike, of Woodbridge, for the charge of a law suit carried on in John Pike's name, in defense against paying quit rents by virtue of the power under the hands of the sd. freeholders entered in the freeholder book records. NOW, KNOW YE, that the sd. John Bishop, Thomas Pike, & Adam Hude by the power given by sd. Dead[deed?] to discharge the Trusts in us reposed, we, the sd. Trustees for £31, 4 shillings to John Pike, paid according to Agreement of the sd. freeholders bef. the delivery of these Presents by Elisha Parker, of sd. town, merchant, the Trustees do hereby acknowledge and have confirmed unto sd. Parker forever by a deed, dated 22 Sep last past, 39 a. within the bnds. of Woodbridge in Rahway Neck; bnd. as follows: adjoining the n. side of two Second Division lots wch. sd. Parker bot. of John Ayres & William Iselsey, s. by sd. two lots, e. by Common Land, n. by a Second Division lot, wch. sd. Parker bot. of John Worth & w. by John Conger's Second division lot in part & part by land in common; together with small slips of land at the w. end, wch. in whole is 39.5 a. Wits.: Samuel Fitz Randolph, Edward Crowell. Signed: John Bishop, Thos. Pike, Adam Hude. Ackn.: 6 Jun 1718, Edward Crowell apprd. bef. Adam Hude, Judge, Middlesex Co. & Somerset.

Pg 87. 4 Dec 1701. Robert Webster, of East NJ, yeoman, and his wife [unnamed] sells to Gabriel Le Boyleaula, of the sd. Province, for £210, a tr. of land in Middlesex on the Raritan River, being 144 a.; bnd. by land form. of John Langstaff[?] but now William Bensortis[?], s.w. by sd. River, n.w. by John Pondix, n.e. by land unsurveyed. Wits.: John Barclay, Thomas Gordon. Signed: Robert Webster. Ackn.: 6 Oct 1720, John Barclay apprd. bef. Wm. Eire, Judge, Middlesex Co.

Pg 89. 14 Sep 1713. New Barbados. I, solemnly promise that as soon as Capt. Edmund Kingsland, and Mary, his wife, have duly executed according to law a certain conveyance (grant by them to me, dated 20 Apr 1710, for a certain tr. of land and meadow on N. Barbadoes Neck as in such conveyance is set forth) by signing same bef. of the members of her Majesty's Council & entered into the public records within 6 months according to law, I shall surrender renounce and release and deliver unto Capt. Edmund Kingsland a certain Bond of Performance under penalty of £2,000, dated 20 Apr 1710, as afsd. Wits.: J. Arents, Jn. Conrad Codwiss. Signed: Arent Schuyler. Ackn.: 16 Feb 1720, Jacob Arents apprd. bef. Isaac Whitehead, Judge, Essex Co.

Pg 90. 28 Jun 1711. Joseph Stevens, of NJ, yeoman, am firmly bnd. unto George Hale, of sd. Province, yeoman, for £1,000. The condition of this obligation is such that the sd. Hale did on 23 Jun 1709 bot. of Mary Campbell, who as well for herself as attorney to her son, John Campbell, convey a piece of land, being 1,040 a. in NJ on the Raritan River btw. the lands of Thomas Hale &

John Dubries. And, whereas, sd. Hale on the day of the absd. date conveyed
unto bounden Joseph Stevens one-half of sd. lands according to the division
made in a map annexed to sd. deed. NOW, sd. bounden Stevens is ejected out
of sd. lands he now possesses, shall convey unto sd. Hale one-half of the lands
and if they he may so happen loose, the obligation is to remain in full force.
Wits.: John Cock, Abraham Governeur. Signed: Joseph Stevens made his mark.
Ackn.: 11 May 1721, John Cock apprd. bef. David Jamison, Chief Justice, NJ.

Pg 91. 3 Nov 1705. Jonathan Jaquish, of Woodbridge, Middlesex Co., East NJ,
planter, and his wife, Ruth, sell £42, to his brother, John Jaquish, of the afsd.
place, planter, for a tr. of upland within Woodbridge, it being a part of the shares
of the farm that was form. belonged to his grandfather, Henry Jaquish, dec'd,
and being 40 a. , beg. at the n.w. corner of his division and then running severl
courses to John Steward and part on [FNU] Courtland's line and then to the
beg.; bnd. n. by sd. Steward and Courtland, s. by brother John's land & w. & e.
on my own land. Wits.: William Robinson, John Bishop. Signed: Jonathan &
Ruth Jaquish both mark their marks. Ackn.: 12 Nov 1705, Jonathan & Ruth
Jaquish apprd. bef. Samuel Hale, Justice. And, on 11 Jan 1720/1, John Bishop
apprd. bef. Adam Hude, Judge, Middlesex Co.

Pg 92. 16 Dec 1710. Jonathan Jaquish, of Woodbridge, Middlesex Co., East
NJ, yeoman, sells to John Jaquish, of the afsd. place, yeoman, for £98, for a tr.
of land within Woodbridge on Rahawack, Middlesex Co., East NJ, being 30 a.,
being bnd. s. by my brother, John, , w. by 10 a. I form. sold to John Allen, n. by
[FNU] Hogeland, e. part by Hogeland & part by my own fresh meadow and part
by a highway running through sd. land. ALSO, 4 a. of fresh meadow, w. joining
the sd. land, n. by Hogeland, e. by Rahawaugh River, s. by brother John's land,
along with 10 a. of salt meadow in Rahawaugh Meadows; bnd. n. by sd.
Meadows, e. by John Dolly and s. by brother John, e. by John Alston. Wits.:
Joseph Gillman, John Skiner, Benjamin Drewitt. Signed: Jonathan Jaquias,
Ackn.: 9 Jan 1720/1, John Skinner apprd. bef. Adam Hude, Judge, Middlesex
Co.

Pg 94. 14 Mar 1710/11. Jonathan Jaquish, of Woodbridge, Middlesex Co., East
NJ, laborer, sells to John Jaquish, for [can't read] of the afsd. place, a certain tr.
of upland wch. I [can't read] John Alston, of the afsd. place, being 10 a.; bnd. n.
by Richard Hoagland & [FNU] Courtland, s. by brother John, e. by my own
land. Wits.: Jno. Alston, John Bishop. Signed: Jonathan Jaquish made his
mark. Ackn.: 11 Jan 1720/21, John Bishop apprd. bef. Adam Hude, Judge,
Middlesex Co.

Pg 95. 25 May 1720. John Jaquish, of Woodbridge, Middlesex Co., East NJ,
sells to Richard Skinner, of the afsd. place, for £100, for land in Woodbridge
Twp., beg. at the s.w. corner of Ezekiel Bloomfield's land, and then down
Courtland's line and partially upon land of Hoagland to the highway and as it

runs to my own land and on the line betw. that I bot. from my brother Jonathan and then to the beg. Wits.: Israel Thornell, Tobias Hatch. Signed: John Jaques. Ackn.: 10 Jan 1720/21, Israel Thornell apprd. bef. Adam Hude, Judge, Middlesex Co.

Pg 96. 11 Sep 1720. Stephen Jacques, the son & lawful heir & Exec. of Henry Jaques, dec'd, of Newbury, Essex Co., in Massachusetts Bay, New England, carpenter, for the natural love & affection I bear unto my kinsman, John Jaques, of Woodbridge, East NJ, yeoman, have quit claimed unto sd. John Jaques, all my Right in every parcel of land now in his possession and any other lands in East NJ in Woodbridge but exempt whatsoever Rights do belong to Jonathan Jaques or the heirs of Henry Jaques, dec'd, in these late divisions although possessed by you. Wits.: Benjamin Force, Joseph Moullon. Signed: Stephen Jaques. Ackn.: 11 Sep 1720, Stephen Jaques apprd. bef. Joseph Woodbridge, Majesty's Council, Massachusetts Bay.

Pg 97. 1 Jul 1721. William Robison, of Elizabeth Town, Essex Co., NJ, Gent., and Deborah, his wife, sell to John Hallinbeck, Albany Co., NY, yeoman, for £300, for a tr. of land in Essex Co., on the n. side of Rahway River, the w. branch known as Robison's Branch, and the tr. known as Robison's Plantation, beg. at the s.w corner of Edward Frazier's land, on the n. side of sd. branch on a direct line to sd. Robison's house and from the house along Frazier's line to John Reynoe's line and then along same and then several courses to sd. Robison's Branch and then down same to the beg., being 199 a.; (excep. one acre sold to Robert Border on the e. side of the road.) ALSO, I confirm unto sd. John Hallinbeck another tr. wch. was bot. from Robert Burnet, beg. at the n.e. corner of the land I sold to William Sandford and then several courses to the beg., being 50 a. ALSO, a lot of land on the s. side of sd. Branch beg. at the brook by the w. side of the road near the wooden bridge by the house of William Robison, then along the road to Woodbridge line, and then several other courses to the beg., being one acre. Wits.: Bister Van Boscerkt, George Johnston, Alex. Macdowall. Signed: Wm. Robison, Deborah Robison. Ackn.: 10 Jul 1721, William Robison apprd. bef. William Eier, Judge, Essex Co.

Pg 99. 1 Aug 1715. [H]umphry Wall, son of Garret Wall, dec'd, of Middletown, Monmouth Co., NJ, yeoman, sells to John Whitelock, of Freehold, in the afsd. place, yeoman, for £10, for 100 a. in the Second Division and addition to the Second Division land of my father's share of the proprietary, wch. was devised to me by his will, to be laid out & surveyed, to have the 100 a. & the premises. Wits.: Thomas Whitlock, William Walling made his mark. Signed: Humphry Wall. Ackn.: 5 Sep 1715, Thomas Whitlock apprd. bef. John Reid. On 28 Apr 1721, Humphry Wall, being of full age of 21 do confirm the within written deed of sale to all intents and purposes according to the contents thereof as written. Wit.: Wal. Wall, Thomas Smith, cordwainer.

Pg 100. 1 Aug 1715. John Wall, son of Garret Wall, dec'd, of Middletown, Monmouth Co., NJ, yeoman, sells to John Whitlock, of Freehold, in the afsd. place, yeoman, for a competent sum of money, a one-third part of a one-seventh part of a forty-eight part of a full undivided part of East NJ, wch. was conveyed to me amongst other shares by deed of my father, dated 7 Mar 1710. Wits.: Humphry Wall, Thomas Whitlock. Signed: John Wall. Ackn.: 5 Sep 1715, Thomas Whitlock apprd. bef. John Reid.

Pg 101. Jun 1721. Joseph Meeker, Junr., of Elizabeth Town, Essex Co., NJ, Esqr., sells to Elijah Davis, of the afsd. place, cordwainer, and John Dagworthy, of the same place, for 40 shillings, for one acre of land, being part of land in East NJ that I bot. of James Alexander, to be taken up and surveyed in East NJ. Wits.: Moses Shepard, Wm. Williamson. Signed: Jos. Meeker, Junr. Ackn.: None.

Pg 102. 6 May 1718/9. John Bowne, of Monmouth Co., NJ, cordwainer, sells to James Alexander, of NJ, Gent., for a competent sum of money, for a one-twentieth part of a one-twenty fourth part of East NJ, reserving to sd. Bowne the first, second and addition to the Second Division of land wch. I have Patented or Surveyed of laid out, being 875 a. to sd. Alexander, wch. form. belonged to Robert Turner. Wits.: J. Bass, Tho. Kearny. Signed: John Bowne. Ackn.: Perth Amboy, 18 Aug 1721, Jeremiah Bass, Esqr. apprd. bef. William Eire, Esqr., Majesty's Council.

Pg 103. 23 Sep 1720. Donald Cameron, of Lockhiel, Scotland sells by Evan Drummond, of the same place, Gent., and his attorney, sells to James Alexander, of NJ, Gent., for £36, for 300 a. of land in common belonging to sd. Cameron in East NJ, in right of the Second Division, lately belonging to Sir Eugeniois Cameron, of Lockhiel, dec'd, to be taken up and surveyed in the unappropriated lands of East NJ. Wits.: Wm. Eier, Richard Bishop. Signed: Donald Cameron by his attorney. Ackn.: [No date] Evan Drummond apprd. bef. William Eier, Mayor of Perth Amboy & Judge, Middlesex Co.

Pg 104. 24 Sep 1720. Donald Cameron, of Lockhiel, and Evan Drummond, his attorney, of Scotland, merchant sells to James Alexander, for £32, for a town lot of Wickatunk, Monmouth Co., known by the name of Lockhiel's town lot, 18 chains by 9 chains, bnd. s. by highway, e. by lot of Thomas Barker, n. by John Baker, e. by lot of the Earl of Perth. Wits.: Wm. Eier, Andrew Keruohaun[?]. Signed: Donald Cameron by his attorney. Ackn.: [No date] Evan Drummond apprd. bef. William Eier, Judge, Middlesex Co.

Pg 105. 4 Feb 1708. Thomas Gordon, of Perth Amboy, Middlesex Co., NJ, sells to John Johnstone, of NJ, for a competent sum of money, for a tr. of land in Middlesex Co., beg. at the s.w. corner of land of sd. Johnstone on a run that leads to Cranberry Brook to the plantation of sd. Johnstone, then to Peter

Sonman's land, then along [FNU] Forman's land, being 400 a. ALSO, another tr. at Barnegat, beg. at Margaret Wonder's land, then to the Bay. ALSO, a small piece of land in Perth Amboy lying at the n.e. side of Dock; bnd. n. by street, e. by Water Street, and several other courses. Wits.: [Rest can't be read].

Pg 107. 30 Jun 1716. John Sharp, of Perth Amboy, Middlesex Co., NJ, carpenter, for diverse causes and the natural love for my son, John Sharp, Junr. now residing with me, have freely granted and released unto him, my house & lot of land whereon I now dwell in Perth Amboy, beg. at the n. corner of my lot and w.n.w. along the lines of the lot of land form. Patented to Samuel Gibson now possessed by Thomas Hind, then to High Street and along same along the great marsh or intended dock and then to the beg.; bnd. n. by sd. Gibson's lot, e. & w. by the mentioned streets and s. by the remainder of my lot of land [bot.] from George Willocks, Gent., by deed dated 7 Jun 1710. Wits.: David Herriot, John Brown. Signed: John Sharp made his mark. Ackn.: John Sharp apprd. bef. Adam Hude, Judge, Middlesex Co.

Pg 108. 25 Oct 1711. John Reid, of Hortencie, Monmouth Co., East NJ, sell to John Bartow, of West Chester, NY, for £151, 2 shillings, for those tr. of land in Monmouth Co, being a tr. of meadow & upland at Barnaget Beach e. of Fresh Creek and then several courses to the Bay and then along the Bay and meadow edge to the creek where it beg.; bnd. s. by William Bingley's land, e. by the Bay, n. by the Sandy Hamocks, & w. by unsurveyed land by deed of Andrew Burnett amongst others, dated 12 Oct 1700. ALSO, a tr. of land on Manasquan River, beg. where long brook falls into sd. River and along sd. river, then across sd. river to long brook and to the beg.; by Patent, dated 7 Oct 1700. ALSO, a tr. of land on Manalapan River beg. at the head of Mount brook, then several courses by my land to the land late of Robert Barclay, then to the river, and several courses to land to beg., part by deed of Robert Barclay, dated 4 Nov 1699 & part by Patent, dated 7 Jun 1701. ALSO, all that land in Middlesex Co., on South River, beg. at s. end of Roundabout meadow and several courses to land late of Charles Gordon, dec'd, then to river and down same to beg. ALSO, a tr, of meadow by the River at the upper corner of meadow late of David Mudie, dec'd, and up sd. river several courses to the beg., by deed of Andrew Burnett, dated 12 Oct 1700. Wits.: John Jackson, Will. Bradford, Senr. Signed: John Reid. Ackn.: New York – 16 Jul 1712, William Bradford apprd. bef. David Jamison, Esqr., Chief Justice, NJ.

Pg 110. 2[?] May 1721. John Hamilton & James Alexander sell to John Walls, [can't read] for 110 a. of land to be taken up & surveyed in the unappropriated lands of East NJ (wch. is part of 1,500 a. of land in East NJ bot from Isabella Davis, grand-daughter & heir of Gawen Lawie, Proprietor, dec'd)Wits.: Israel Stuckey, John Provost. Signed John Hamilton by James Alexander, his attorney, and James Alexander. Ackn.: 27 May 1721, returned 100 a. to John

Walls, by James Alexander, Surveyor General. John Hamilton & James Alexander apprd. bef. William Eire, Mayor of Perth Amboy.

Pg 111. 13 May 1721. John Hamilton & James Alexander sell to John Walls, of Newark, house carpenter, for £49, for 120 a. of land to be taken up & surveyed in the unappropriated lands of East NJ, wch. is part of 1,500 a. held in common and purchased from Isabella Davis, grand daughter of Gawen Lawrie, Proprietor, dec'd. Wits.: John Anderson, Peter Bard. Signed: John Hamilton, Ja. Alexander. 20 May, returned to Jno. Walls 116.25 a. and on 27 May another 3.75 a. with deed. Signed: Ja. Alexander, Surveyor General. Ackn.: John Hamilton & James Alexander apprd. bef. William Eier, Mayor, Perth Amboy.

Pg 113. 4 Jul 1721. John Parker, Esqr., sells to John Walls, of Newark, house carpenter, for £49, for 120 a. of land to be taken up & surveyed in the unappropriated lands of East NJ, wch. is part of 400 a., purchased by sd. Parker from Daniel Hollinshead, who is vested with one-quarter of a Proprietary by deeds from Walter Benthall. Wits.: William Eier, Peter Savery. Signed: John Parker. Ackn.: 24 Jul 1721, John Parker apprd. bef. William Eier, Judge, Middlesex Co.

Pg 114. 13 May 1721. Daniel Hollinshead, Gent., sells to John Walls, of Newark, house carpenter, for £49, for 120 a. of land to be taken up & surveyed in the unappropriated lands of East NJ, wch. is part of 1,500 a. held in common and purchased by sd. Hollinshead, of one-quarter of a Proprietary from Walter Benthall, upon the Third Dividend or in addition to the Second Dividend. Wits.: John Rudyard, Ja. Alexander. Signed: Daniel Hollinshead. Ackn.: 13 May 1721, Daniel Hollinshead apprd. bef. William Eier, Mayor, Perth Amboy and on 27 May 1721, Returned to John Walls 84.25 a. by deed from James Alexander, Surveyor General.

Pg 115. 15 Dec 1719. John Bishop, of Woodbridge, Middlesex Co., East NJ, Esqr., for the fatherly love & affection he bears toward his son, John Bishop, Junr., of the afsd. place, have given and granted to him a piece of land within Woodbridge being part of my farm at Rahway, beg. at the n.e. corner of Daniel Brittain's orchard, then n.e. along the highway, then s. to the beg.; bnd. e. by highway, n. by my own land, w. & s. by John Elston's & Daniel Brittain. Wits.: Daniel Brittain, Timothy Tuttle. Signed: 8 Feb 1720/21, John Bishop. Ackn.: John Bishop apprd. bef. Adam Hude, Judge, Middlesex Co.

Pg 115. 1 Jul 1720. John Bishop of Woodbridge, Middlesex Co., East NJ, Esqr., for the fatherly love & affection he bears toward his son, John Bishop, Junr., of the afsd. place, have given and granted to him a piece of land and tenement within Woodbridge commonly known as Pepiak Neck together with my Second Division lot in the great neck and also a parcel & meadow on the e. side of the road from Rahway to the town commonly known as Fresh Meadow;

bnd. on the highway, s. by Daniel Brittain's & John Moore's, e. & n. by my brother, Noah. ALSO, 6 a. of salt meadow on the island adjoining the Sound and the great creek. ALSO, a [?] Right in the bounds of Woodbridge. Wits.: Noah Bishop, John Alston. Signed: John Bishop. Ackn.: 8 Feb 1720/21, John Bishop apprd. bef. Adam Hude, Judge, Middlesex Co.

Pg 116. 11 Apr 1720. John Bishop, Junr., of Woodbridge, Middlesex Co., East NJ, yeoman, and his wife, Freelove, sell to Daniel Brittain, of the afsd. place, cordwainer, for £29, a tr. of land in Woodbridge, beg. at sd. Brittain's n.e. corner of his house lot by the highway and then several courses to the land of John Elstone's and along the line to a corner of my own land and sd. Elstone's and then to the beg., being 14.5 a.; bnd. e. by highway, n. by my father's land, w. by sd. Elstone's land and s. by sd. Brittain's land. Wits.: John Cooper, Timothy Tuttle. Signed: John Bishop, Junr., Freelove Bishop. Ackn.: 8 Feb 1720/21, John Bishop, Junr. apprd. bef. Adam Hude, Judge, Middlesex Co.

Pg 118. 15 Nov 1720. John Bishop, Junr., of Woodbridge, Middlesex Co., East NJ, yeoman, and his wife, Freelove, sell to Daniel Brittain, of the afsd. place, cordwainer, for £40, a tr. of land in Woodbridge, commonly known as Fresh Meadows, being 17.75 a., beg. at the highway to Woodbridge at the corner of sd. Brittain's mowing ground, then e. along the line dividing the land and sd. Brittain's land and that of John Moore's, then several courses to the highway and then to the beg.; bnd. s. by Brittain's & Moore's land, e. by Noah Bishop, and w. part by sd. Bishop and part by highway. Wits.: John Bishop, Moses Bishop[?], Elizabeth Wright made her mark. Signed: John Bishop, Junr., Freelove Bishop. Ackn.: 8 Feb 1720/21, John Bishop apprd. bef. Adam Hude, Judge, Middlesex Co.

Pg 119. 24 Aug 1721. Michael Kearny, of Perth Amboy, Gent., sells to Arent Suyler [Schuyler], of Barbadoes Neck, Bergen Co., East NJ, Gent. for a competent sum of money, for 200 a. to be taken up & surveyed in the unappropriated lands of East NJ, being part of 400 a. wch. sd. Kearny bot. of the NJ Society as an indenture dated 4 Jul 1715. Wits.: Wm. Verplanck, John King. Signed: Michll. Kearny. Ackn.: 30 Oct 1721, Michael Kearny apprd. bef. William Eier, Judge, Middlesex Co.

Pg 120. 22 Oct 1720. Thomas Lyon, of Newark, Essex Co., East NJ, yeoman, and Hannah, his wife, sell to Samuel Williams, of the afsd. place, carpenter, for £90, for a tr. of land in Newark, beg. at the corner of James Clizle[?] land by highway, then to the corner of Henry Lyons; bnd. by James Clizle [?] & Henry Lyon, n. by highway, e. by common land, being 28 a. Wits.: John Burwell, Amos Robards. Signed: Thomas Lyon, Hannah Lyon made her mark. Ackn.: 19 May 1721, John Burrell apprd. bef. Joseph Harrison, Judge, Essex Co.

Pg 122. 9 May 1718. [Hard to read] Thomas Lyon, of Newark, Essex Co., East NJ, yeoman, gives to Amos Williams, of the afsd. place, carpenter, for various good causes, his land, goods, chattels, and premises. Wits.: Jedediah Buckingham, Jonathan Jordan. Signed: None. Ackn.: 11 Feb 1718/19, Jonathan Jordan apprd. bef. Isaac Whitehead, Judge, Essex Co.

Pg 123. 13 Jul 1721. John Longstaffe, of Piscataway, Middlesex Co., NJ, yeoman, for various considerations and the love and affection I bear unto my daughter, Sarah Longstaffe, of the afsd. place, grant & confirm unto her a parcel of land within Piscataway bounds, beg. at a tree and then along Samuel Potter's & Thomas Higgins land, dec'd, and then several courses to the beg.; bnd. n. by a small brook, e. by a highway, w. by Thomas Suttun, s. by a small spring. Wits.: Samuel Walker, Thomas Sutton made his mark, Benj. Hull. Signed: John Langstaffe. Ackn.: 23 Nov 1721, Samuel Walker apprd. bef. Adam Hude, Judge, Middlesex Co.

Pg 124. 7 Oct 1707. Walter Riddell, of the Parish of St. John's Clarkenwale, County of Middlesex, Gent., by a lease & release, dated 21 & 22 of March last past, made betw. William Aikman, son & heir of William Aikman, of Scotland, dec'd, and the afsd. Riddell, for a competent sum, a one full equal tenth part of a forty-eighth part of East NJ. ALSO, one full and equal one-tenth part of a forty-eighth part. NOW KNOW that sd. Riddell for diverse considerations put and authorize my kinsman and well beloved friend, John Johnston, of East NJ, Esqr., in America, and doctor of physick, to be my lawful attorney to act in my name in the land in East NJ in America. Wits.: J.D. Peyster, W. Laurier. Signed: Walter Riddell. Ackn.: NY, 20 Aug 1708, William Lourier apprd. bef. Roger Mompesson, Esqr. Chief Justice, NY.

Pg 126. 22 Mar 1706. William Aikman, son and heir of William Aikman, of Scotland, Advonel[?], dec'd leases to Walter Riddell, of the Parish of St. John's Clarkennellen, County of Middlesex, Gent., for a competent sum of money, land now in his possession, by an indenture dated the day bef. re: transferring uses to possessions, being a full one-tenth part of one-forty-eighth part of land in East NJ. AND, WHEREAS, sd. Aikman is possessed of a one-tenth share of a forty-eighth of a joint flock in goods & effects in East NJ, wch sd. Aikman sets over to sd. Riddell. Wits.: John Hamilton, Walter Pringle, Richard Holden. Signed: William Aikman. Ackn.: NY - 30 Aug 1708, John Hamilton apprd. bef. Roger Monpesson, Esqr., Chief Justice, NY.

Pg 129. 13 May 1718. Walter Riddell of Great Britain, sells to Adam Hude, of Woodbridge, Middlesex Co., East NJ, Esqr., for 75 ounces of plate, 100 a. of land & premises to be taken up & surveyed in the unappropriated lands in East NJ. Wits.: Eugham Johnston, Eupham Johnston, Junr. Signed: Walter Riddell by his attorney, John Johnston. Ackn.: 20 Nov 1721, John Johnston, attorney for sd. Riddell, apprd. bef. John Parker, Majesty's Council.

Pg. 129. 23 Nov 1682. The proprietors of East NJ, in America of the one part, sell to John Reid, Gairdiner, of Shank, Scotland, County of Eding, of the other part, for £14, for 10 a. of 1,500 a. to be set out by the Surveyor General. WHEREAS, the Proprietors have designed & divided 1,500 a. on Amboy Point in sd. Province into 150 lots to consist of 10 a. each lot. NOW, BY THIS INDENTURE, the Proprietors confirm unto sd. Reid 10 a. of upland and if sd. Reid does not bef. 25 Dec 1683, record a memorandum there in the public record on this land, or if sd. Reid shall not within 3 years from the date of these Presents clear 3 a. of the 10 a. of upland and build a dwelling home in that place designed to be set out for a town on Ambo Point, then the Proprietors shall take back possession of the above sd. 10 a. and pay sd. Reid £15. Wits.: James Young, writer, Mary Young, Ja. Kinkaid. 31 Jul 1721 - Then returned to John Reid 10 a. in Amboy upon the within deed. James Alexander, Surveyor General. Recorded – 5 Dec 1721.

Pg 131. 17 Feb 1720. John Hamilton, of Perth Amboy, Middlesex Co., NJ, Esqr.,., forever quit claims unto John Reid, of Hortencie, Monmouth Co., NJ, Gent., 10 a. and any Right he had to them. WHEREAS, John Reid by an instrument from the Proprietors of East NJ, dated 23 Nov 1682, became entitled to 10 a. within Perth Amboy. ALSO, sd. Reid, by an instrument from them, dated 24 Jun 1688, obtained a tr. of land within Perth Amboy, beg. at the head of Division Creek the supposed outer bnd. of Perth Amboy next to the Sound, and then several courses again to the mouth of sd. crk. and then to the beg.; bnd. e. by the Sound or river, s. by Thomas Gordon's land, n. by Monvele's land, & w. by unappropriated lands, and the absd. 10 a. was intended to be vested in John Hamilton. AND, WHEREAS, it now appears that the 10 a. in Perth Amboy for sd. Reid by the absd. instrument is now with 60 a. of land within the bnd. of Woodbridge, form. granted in the name of John Barkely[?], Baron of [?] & George Carteret, Knight, Lords Proprietors, by seal dated 31 [?] 1670 to one Henry Lesenby, of Woodbridge, planter, and wch. sd. 60 a. is now vested by various indentures in the estate of George Willocks, of Perth Amboy, Gent. THEREFORE, to prevent controversies betw. the parties, prejudiced by the mistake of locating John Reid's Right to 10 a. form. granted to Henry Lesenby , the parties have agreed that the sd. John Hamilton for a competent sum relinquishes his intentions on the 10 a. to John Reid. Wits.: George Willocks, Andrew Johnston. Signed.: John Hamilton. Ackn.: 11 Mar 1720, George Willocks apprd. bef. Thomas Gordon, Majesty's Council.

Pg 133. 28 Nov 1721. Walter Riddell, of Great Britain, Esqr., one of the Proprietors of East NJ, sells to Andrew Johnston, of Perth Amboy, merchant, for £70, 15 shillings, for 96 a. to be taken up and surveyed in the unappropriated lands of East NJ. Wits.: Geo. Leslie, Jennet Parker. Signed: Walter Riddell by his attorney, John Johnston. Ackn.: 7 Dec 1721, Walter Riddell by his attorney, John Johnston apprd. bef. John Parker, Majesty's Council.

Pg 134. 10 Feb 1720. Michael Kearny, of Perth Amboy, Gent., sells to Thomas Pearson, of Newark, Essex Co., NJ, yeoman, for a competent sum of money, 57 a., to be taken up and surveyed in the unappropriated lands of East NJ, being part of the 400 a. that sd. Kearny bot. of the NJ Society, on 1 July 1715. Wits.: John Vail, Zachari Weeks. Signed: Michael Kearny. Ackn.: 7 Dec 1721, Michael Kearny apprd. bef. William Eier, Judge, Middlesex Co.

Pg 135. 13 Jan 1720. Thomas Warne, of Amboy, Middlesex Co., NJ, yeoman, sells to Jacob Arents, of Newark, Essex Co., Phisitian, for a competent sum, for 600 a., being part of my Proprietary, to be taken up and surveyed in the unappropriated lands of East NJ. Wits.: Robt. Carhartt, Thomas Brown. Signed: Tho. Warne. Ackn.: 31 Jan 1720, Robert Carhart apprd. bef. Thomas Gordon.

Pg 136. 1 Oct 1716. John Harrison, of Somerset Co., East NJ, Esqr., sells to Isaac Van Nuyse, of New Vybrecnt, Kings Co., Nassau Island, NY, yeoman, for £200, for a parcel of land in Somerset Co., East NJ, being 200 a., beg. at the n.w. corner of John Van Dyk's land at the road to John Harrison's Mill, then s. along sd. Van Dyk's line and then several courses to the sd. road and then along same to the beg.; bnd. n. & e. by John Van Dyk's land, s. by sd. Harrison's land, & w. by Thomas Yates' land and n. by sd. road. Wits.: William Janson, Thos. Yates. Signed: John Harrison. Ackn.: 9 Oct 1720, William Janson apprd. bef. Adam Hude, Judge, Middlesex Co.

Pg 138. 11 Dec 1721. Edward Vaughan, of Elizabeth Town, Essex Co., NJ, Rev[?], and Mary, his wife, late Mary Emott, relict & Exec. of the will of James Emott, late of NY, Gent., dec'd, for £30, a tr. of land on the e. side of South River, being 100 a.; bnd. n. by Charles Gooden's line, w. by the river, s. & e. By unsurveyed land. WHEREAS, the late James Emott on 3 Oct 1709, made his will, named his then wife Mary, now Mary Vaughan, party to these Presents, Exec. and gave power to his wife to dispose of his lands, and sd. Mary proved the sd. will in the Prerogative offices of NY and afterwards intermarried with afsd. Edward Vaughan. Wits.: Daniel Price, John Barclay. Signed: James Emott, Mary Emott. Ackn.: Perth Amboy – 4 Jan 1721, John Barclay apprd. bef. William Eier, Judge, Middlesex Co.

Pg 140. 25 Feb 1720. Mary Rescarrick, widow of George Rescarrick, lately dec'd, confirms unto George Rescarrick, her son, lawfully begotten betw. sd. George, her late husband, dec'd, and the sd. Mary, for the natural love & affection wch. she bears unto her son, the tr. of land on s. side of Cranberry Brook described below and the one-half of the lots in Perth Amboy as described below; excep. all the rents and profits of the sd. tr. of land on the s. side of Cranberry Brook and above sd. lots to be hers during her natural life. WHEREAS, the Proprietors of East NJ granted by their Patent to the late George

Rescarrick, dec'd and sd. Mary, his wife, dated 27 Sep 1700, all that tr. at Cranberry brook, Middlesex, beg. on the s. side of Cranberry Brook by the Great Road above the bridge and e. up the brook, and then several courses back to sd. brook where it beg. AND, WHEREAS, George Willocks, of Perth Amboy, Middlesex Co., merchant, by deed sold unto sd. George Rescarrick, dec'd, and Mary, 2 lots of land in Perth Amboy being 9 chains by 2 chains; bnd. n. by Dock Street, s. by Smith Street, e. by a lot of James Dundas, dec'd, and w. by a lot of David Campbell, dec'd, by deed dated 18 Sep 1708. AND WHEREAS, sd. George Rescarrick, dec'd, by his will, dated 21 Mar 1714, bequeathed unto sd. Mary, his wife, one-half, and to their son, George, the other half part of all of his land and worldly materials. Wits.: Anthony Ward, Andrew Gordon. Signed: Mary Rescarrick. Ackn.: 25 Feb 1720, Mary Rescarrick apprd. bef. Thomas Gordon, Majesty's Council.

Pg 143. 8 Jun 1716. Capt. Samuel Leonard, Of Middlesex Co., NJ, and Anne, his wife, sell to Alexander Scobie, of the afsd. place, yeoman, for £40, for 100 a. of landing the sd. county, beg. at the s.w. corner of sd. Scobie's landand along his line, and then to the s.e. corner of sd. Leonard's land, and then several courses to the beg, wch. 100 a. was conveyed to Samuel Leonard in Right of Robert Burnet's addition to the Second Dividend, by deed of his Exec., dated 2 Apr 1715. Wits.: John Leonard, Henry Hurle. Signed.: Samll. Leonard, Anne Leonard. Ackn.: 27 Feb 1721, John Leonard apprd. bef. John Johnston, Junr., Majesty's Council.

Pg 145. 7 Jun 1721. James Alexander sells to John Budd, of Philadelphia, PA, for £146, 2 shillings, for 365.25 a. to be taken up and surveyed in the unappropriated lands of East NJ, in the remainder of James Alexander's half of 1,500 a. purchased in common with John Hamilton from Isabella Davis, heir of Gawen Lawrie, one of the Proprietors. Wits.: Fenw. Lyell, Isaac Stuckey. Signed: James Alexander. Ackn.: 254 Feb 1721, James Alexander apprd. bef William Eier, Mayor of Perth Amboy.

Pg 147. [Ink is faded] 7 Jun ??. Major William Drummond, eldest brother & heir of Captain Robert Drummond, late Commander of the ship *Caledonia*, dec'd, & Elizabeth Drummond, widow & relict, and Admin., of sd. Robert Drummond, sells to John Budd, of Philadelphia, PA. WITNESSETH, the sd. William & Elizabeth Drummond by their attorney, James Alexander, for £ 46,17,2 pence, released unto John Budd 234.33 a. to be taken up and surveyed in the unappropriated lands of East NJ and the Second and addition to the Second Dividend, belonging to the two-thirtieth parts of a Proprietary form. bot by sd. Capt. Robert Drummond from John Dobie. Wits.: Fen. Lyell, Isaac Stuckey. Signed: William Drummond, Elizabeth Drummond. Ackn.: 24 Feb 1721, James Alexander apprd. bef. William Eier, Mayor of Perth Amboy.

Pg 148. 24 Oct 1719. William Marsh, of Jamaica , Queens Co., Long Island (Nassau Island), mariner, son & heir of Jonathan Marsh, late of Rhode Island, mariner, dec'd, sells to John Budd, of Philadelphia, PA, Gent., for £24, 158 a., to be taken up & surveyed, in the unappropriated lands of East NJ; wch. land is part of one-sixteenth of a Proprietary, wch. Jonathan Marsh bot. of Robert Turner, late of Philadelphia, dec'd. Wits.: Cornelius Van Brunt, Lawrance, Silkes, George Hiton. Signed: William Marsh. Ackn.: 17 Mar 1721, Lawrence Silkes apprd. bef. William Eier, Mayor of Perth Amboy.

Pg 150. 16 Feb 1719. Thomas Warne, of Middlesex Co., East NJ, Gent., sells to Jacob Arents, of Newark, Essex Co., NJ, Phisitian, for £20, for a tr. of land in Elizabeth Town, beg. at the n.w. corner of the orchard near the small brook in the Division line that parts Newark from Elizabeth, then along sd. line, to the north mountains, then around rocky end of the sd. mountain, and then to a deep gutter that runs into the w. branch of the Rahway River, then down same and several courses to the beg., being 136 a.; bnd. n. by sd. Division line and land around the s. end of the north mountain, w. by w. branch of the sd. River, s.e. by unappropriated lands and part by highway from the w. to the e. branch of Rahway River, and e. by land of his own, and n.e. by a final run. Wits.: Thomas Elison, Seth Elison. Signed: Thos. Warne. Ackn.: 26 Sep 1720, Thomas Elison apprd. bef. Joseph Harrison[?], Judge, Essex Co.

Pg 151. 6 Dec 1697. John Baker, of Elizabeth Town, Essex Co., East NJ, Gent., for diverse, good considerations and £19, sells to Ephraim Clarke, of the afsd. place, planter, for a tr. of upland at a place commonly known by the name [can't read] Riggoz, being 40 a.; bnd. n.w. by John Baker, e. by land of Thos. Johnson, and John Hind, and land of Charles Tooker, s. by a small brook called peach garden brook. Wits.: Andrew Hamton, Samuel Whitehead. Signed: John Baker, Agnes Baker. Ackn.: 8 Mar 1721, John Baker apprd. bef. Samuel Whitehead, Judge, Essex Co. 12 Feb 1703, Samuel Whitehead and Andrew Hamton apprd. bef. Benjamin Price, J.P.

Pg 153. 7 Dec 1721. Ephraim Clarke, of Elizabeth Town, Essex Co., East NJ, yeoman, and Elizabeth Clark, his wife, sells to John Clawson, of Acquickanunque, Essex Co., East NJ, bricklayer, for £32[?], for several tr. in Elizabeth Town, beg. at a tree and running to William Winman's land wch. he lately bot. of Ephraim Clark, then s.e. with Winman's line to land of Charles Tooker, late of sd. Elizabeth Town, dec'd, and then with his line to a brook called Peach Garden Brook, then up same to the beg., being 32 a.; bnd. n.w. a tr. of land, n.e. by land of Wm. Wininatnz, s.e. by land of sd. Tooker, dec'd, & s.e. by sd. brook. ALSO, a tr. lying betw. the absd. granted tr. and land of Jonathan Woodruff, being 4 a., bnd. n.e. by Richard Barker, s.e. by absd. granted tr., , s.w. by absd. brook, and n.w. by sd. Woodruff. ALSO, a small parcel on the n. side of a highway, running from Thomas Johnson's land n.w. to the Country Road, being .75 a. of land; bnd. n. by land of Ebenezer Spining late of Elizabeth Town, dec'd, and now in possession of John Hendrick, s.e. s. by land of Thos. Johnson, s.s.w. by highway. Wits.: Samuel Whitehead, Jonathan Woodruff. Signed: Ephraim Clarke, Elizabeth Clarke. Ackn.: 19 Dec 1721, Samuel Whitehead apprd. bef. Isaac Whitehead, Judge, Essex Co.

Pg 155. 5 Jul 1720. John Bishop, Junr., of Woodbridge, Middlesex Co., East NJ, has for diverse causes forever quit claimed unto his brother, Moses Bishop, of the afsd. place, all that plantation lying within Woodbridge at a place known as Rahway with the salt meadow there now in possession of my honored father, John Bishop. Wits.: Noah Bishop, John Alston. Signed: John Bishop, Junr. Ackn.: 17 Apr 1721, Noah Bishop apprd. bef. Adam Hude, Judge, Middlesex Co.

Pg 157. 7 Nov 1721. John Bishop, of Woodbridge, Middlesex Co., East NJ, Esqr., for the love and good will and for preventing any difference and contentions that may arise concerning the property hereafter given, do freely grant unto my loving son, Moses Bishop all that farm I now live on within Woodbridge at Rahway, excep. only what I have previously sold or conveyed in other ways, and also my salt marsh that I am now in possession at Rahway Meadows, an also one freehold Right of all divisions in the Commons of Woodbridge; excep. only the uses & present benefit of the granted premises during my natural life and also to look well after and maintains my wife, Mary, his natural mother as directed in my will. Wits.: John Robison, Moses Rolfe. Signed: John Bishop. Ackn.: 3 Apr 1722, Moses Rolfe, Esqr., apprd. bef. John Parker, Majesty's Council.

Pg 159. 11 Apr 1721. Will of: Albert Terhunen, of Flatland, King's Co., Island of Nassau, NY. He bequeaths unto his wife, Aeltie, all of his estate, houses, barn, land and meadows that he now owns in the afsd. place, but if she should remarry she shall have the use of his estate for the brining up of his children so that they can be with the major part of his Exec. His eldest son, John Terhunen shall be of lawful age & as soon as my son shall come of lawful age (and my wife shall be remarried), he shall be immediately possessed of all my above sd. estate in the absd. place and shall be his forever. AND, when my eldest son takes possession of my estate, he shall give rent for sd. estate being so much as he can best agree with the major Exec. for the bringing up of my non-aged children until my youngest child shall come to be of the age of 15 years & no longer, & in 2 years after my youngest child shall come to 15 years, my son, John Terhunen shall pay his mother £100 for her use during her natural life & after her decease the £100 shall evolve to my 5 children: John, Gerritt, Anne, Williamtie, and Sarah Terhunen equally. In further consideration of the absd. estate, my son John Terhunen shall pay to my 4 absd. children, to them & their heirs, £560 with each receiving an equal portion allowing (that is to say that after the remarriage of my wife and my son, John, being possessed of my estate, shall pay to his brother, Gerritt, £100 at the end of 3 years after my youngest child reaches 15 years of age, so he shall pay from sd. payment yearly & every £100 and the last payment £60 until the £560 is duly paid. AND, every child shall receive their portion as they marry or come of lawful age. BUT, if my son, John, has no mind to have of my estate, then my estate shall be sold to the highest bidder and the money from it shall be equally divided amongst my five children. ALSO, the tr. of land lying in Piscataqua Twp., NJ, wch. I bot. of Mr. Walter Thong, merchant, in NY, to be sold to pay my lawful debts, and empower my Exec. or their major part, to dispose of same. It is my will & order that my goods and chattels shall upon the remarriage of my wife to be divided into 2 equal parts with one half for the use of my wife during her natural life and after her death to be equally divided among the 5 children, while the other half shall be equally divided among my 5 children immediately upon my wife's remarriage. AND, I give £5 bef. any division of my estate to my son, John, as his birth right and [?] my son John & to my son, Gerritt my Negro man, Tom, for them to have him at my wife's decease or remarriage. I appoint my wife, Aeltie & my father John Terhunen & my father –in-law, Peter Nevins and my Brother Roeloff Terhunen and my brother in law, Koert Voorhies to be Executors of this my last will & guardians of my children. Signed: Albert Terheunen. Wits.: Pieter Wycoff, John Elberson, S. Gerritson, [one other name that can't be read]. Ackn.: William Burnet, Esqr., Gov. of Province of NY, NJ. Will Proved – NY - the will of Albert Terhunen, 18 Dec inst. [1721]. Administration was granted unto Aeltie Terhunen, John Terhunen, Peter Nevins, Roeloff Terhunen and Koort Voorhies, Exec. Inventory to be completed bef. 18 June next ensuing. Recorded at out Fort in New York – 17 Mar 1721. Signed: Js. Bobin, Dep. Secr.

Pg 162. 27 Dec 1721. Arent Schyler, of Bergen, East NJ, Gent., sells to Joannis Jacobse Vanwinckel, Essex Co.,,, East NJ, yeoman, for £100, for a tr. of land within Newark, beg. at a spring by a highway and then numerous courses to the beg., being 168 a., bnd. w. by Capt. John Morris, wch. sd. land was surveyed to sd. Schuyler in part of 200 a. in Right by deed from Michael Kearny of Perth Amboy, Gent., dated 2? Aug 1721, and wch. sd. Kearny had Right to 400 a. in East NJ. Wits.: Steph. Van Courtland, John King, Casparus Schyler. Essex Co. – 19 Feb 1721/2, Arent Schyler apprd. bef. Isaac Whitehead, Judge, Essex Co.

[Note: Page numbering changes to Page 364 instead of 164 but deed is part of the preceding Page 163.]

Pg 365. 28 [?] 1721. William Harrison, of Somerset Co., NJ, yeoman , sells to John Stevens, of Perth Amboy, Middlesex Co., NJ, for £50, for land in Somerset Co., on e. side of Milston River, beg. at a corner of a tr. of sd. Stevens by a small brook from sd. River, and following the brook to its head, and then several courses to the n.e. corner of sd. Steven's land, and then several courses to the beg. Wits.: Andrew Roleson, Mary Ellison. Signed: Willm. Harrison. Ackn.: 29 Nov 1721, William Harrison apprd. bef. John Parker, Majesty's Council.

Pg 368. 16 Mar 1721. Ganata Harrison, wife, of William Harrison, quit claims unto John Stevens, for a competent sum of money, all her rights to the absd. 50 a. Wits.: Andrew Johnston, Richard Bishop. Signed: Gannatta Harrison. Ackn.: 16 Mar 1721, Gannatta Harrison, wife of William, apprd. bef. John Parker, Majesty's Council.

Pg 369. 6 Apr 1722. Major John Harrison, of Perth Amboy, Middlesex Co., NJ, sells to Thomas Leonard, of Somerset Co., NJ, Esqr., for £30 , for a lot of land in Perth Amboy, beg. at a corner of Market Place on w. side of High Street and then along same to the corner of the house of Mr. Eiers lives in, the several courses to the beg.; bnd. e. by High Street, s. & w. by sd John Harrison and n. by the [?] and part by the Market Place. Wits.: Jacob Doughty, Willm. Yard. Signed: John Harrison. Ackn.: 5 May 1722, John Harrison, Esqr., apprd. bef. John Wills, Majesty's Council.

Pg 371. 12 Sep 1721. John Walls, of Newark, Essex Co., East NJ, joyner, forever quit claims to Joseph Burwell, of the afsd. place, cooper, for a competent sum of money, a tr. of land in Newark now in occupation by sd. Burwell, beg. at the s.e corner of the house lot form. of John Treat now to Jonathan Crane, then several courses to Broad Street and then along same to beg.; bnd. s.e. by sd. street, s.w. by sd. Crane, n.w. by land form. of Joseph Wood, n. e. partly by John Williamson. Wits.: Jno. Cooper, Moses Ball. Signed: John Walls. Ackn.: 27 Oct 1721, John Walls of Newark apprd. bef. Joseph Harrison, Judge, Essex Co.

Pg 372. 1 Aug 1720. John Hamilton and James Alexander, Esqrs., sell to Jacob Arents, of Newark, Essex Co., NJ, doctor, for £82, 4 shillings, for 200 a. , to be taken up and surveyed in the unappropriated lands of East NJ, being part of 1,500 a. they bot. from Isabella Davis, heir of Gawen Lawrie, dec'd, Proprietor. Wits.: Richd. Bishop, John Gilbert. Signed: James Alexander, and John Hamilton by his attorney, sd. Alexander. Ackn.: 27 Apr 1722, James Alexander apprd. bef. Isaac Whitehead, Judge, Essex Co.

Pg 373. 4 Aug 1704. [Hard to read] Joseph Bond & Hanna Bond, of Newark, Essex Co., East NJ, sell to John Linsly, of Newark, for diverse good causes and a competent sum of money, for a tr. of land in Newark being 20 a.; bnd. e. by [?], s. by Kenny Lyon, w. by highway, n. by John Col[?]on, Junr. Wits.: Robt, Hays, Zach. Burwell. Signed: Joseph Bond, Hannah Bond made her mark. Ackn.: 1 Jan 1704[1705?], Joseph Bond apprd. bef. Theophelias Peirson.

Pg 375. 16 Apr 1717. John Baldwin, Junr., of Newark, Essex Co., East NJ, school master, sells to John Lindsley, Senr., of the afsd. p[lace, wheelwright, for £60, for a tr. of upland & meadow, within the bnd. of Newark, lying on Bound

Creek, being 11 a., 20 chains by 10 chains, the w. end fronting highway; bnd. n. w. by highway, s. by sd. John Lindsley, s & e. by sd. crk., and e. by Jonas Wood. Wits.: Joseph Brown, Azubah Thompson. Signed: John Baldwin. Ackn.: 16 Apr 1717, John Baldwin apprd. bef. Joseph Harrison & Jonathan Crane, both Justices, Essex Co.

Pg 376. 31 Oct 1721. Jacob Arents, Newark, Essex Co., East NJ, physician, sells to Tunis Johnson, alias Paer, of the afsd. place, yeoman, for £28, for a tr. of land within Newark near the Passaic River, beg. at the end of sd. Johnson's land and being 20 chains by 15 chains & 2 rods, bnd. e. by sd. Johnson's land bot. of John Gardner, s. by Hance[?] Spear, and being 31 a. Wits.: John Cooper, John Day. Signed: Jacob Arents. Ackn.: 15 Feb 1721, John Cooper apprd. bef. Joseph Harrison, Judge, Essex Co.

Pg 377. 15 Feb 1721. Tunis Johnson Pier, of Essex Co., NJ, for the love and affection wch. he bears toward his son, Abraham Pier, of the afsd. place, does freely grant unto him, a lot of land in Essex Co., beg. on the w. side of of the highway and several courses to the beg., being 2 a.; bnd. e. by the highway, n.w. & s. by Tunis Johnson Pier's land. Wits.: John Cooper, Joseph Harrison. Signed: Tunis Pier made his mark. Ackn.: 15 Feb 1721, Tunis Pier apprd. bef. Joseph Harrison, Judge, Essex Co.

Pg 377. 14 May 1717. Rec'd of my brother William Robinson £150, wch. is in full of my portion left me by my dec'd. father and is in full received by me. Wits,: Jos. Gilman, William Strayhearn. Signed: Mary Hay. Ackn.: 28 Feb. 1717/18, William Strayhearn apprd. bef. Isaac Whitehead, Judge, Essex Co.

Pg 378. 12 Jun 1722. Daniel Hollinshead, Somerset Co., NJ, Gent., releases unto Gunsley John Ayrest, of the afsd. place, for 5 shillings, a tr. of land on Millstone Brook adjoining a tr. of land form. Walter Benthall's now Francis Elrington's land, beg. on the s. side of sd. Millstone where Benthall's brook runs into it, and then several courses to sd. Millstone, and then to the beg., being 800 a.; bnd. n. & e. by land form. Clement Plumstead, w. by sd. Elrington, s. by unsurveyed lands; and wch. tr. is now possessed by sd. Ayrest. Wits.: John Harrison, James Thomason. Signed: Danl. Hollinshead. Ackn.: 13 June 1722, Daniel Hollinshead apprd. bef. John Parker, Majesty's Council.

Pg 379. 13 Jun 1722. Daniel Hollinshead, Somerset Co., NJ, Gent., releases unto Gunsley John Ayrest, of the afsd. place. WHEREAS, sd. Hollinshead released one-fourth of a tr. of land on the Millstone & Cranbury Brook, supposed to contain 3,200 a., whose share was 800 a. by a deed, dated sometime in March 1720 or early 1721, **and whereas sd. Ayrest has been taken by the pirates** and the former deed supposed to be burnt. NOW THIS INDENTURE, sd. Hollinshead for £600 sells unto sd. Ayrest a tr. of land on the Millstone Brook, beg. on the s. side of sd. Millstone where Benthall's brook runs into it, and then several courses to sd. Millstone, and then to the beg., being 800 a.; bnd. n. & e. by land form. Clement Plumstead, w. by sd. Elrington, s. by unsurveyed lands; and wch. tr. is now possessed by sd. Ayrest; wch. land is now in his possession by transferring uses into possession. Wits.: John Harrison, James Thomson. Signed: Danl. Hollinshead. Ackn.: 13 Jun 1722, Daniel Hollinshead, Esqr., apprd. bef. John Parker, Majesty's Council.

Pg 381. 1 Jul 1718. George Willocks, of Perth Amboy, Middlesex Co., NJ, Gent., and Margaret, his wife, release and confirm to Jacobus Beakman, of Flatbush, Kings Co., NY, chirurgan [surgeon], for £134, for a tr. of land in Hunterdon Co., NJ, adjoining to the n. side on wch. Adrian Lane has erected a mill commonly known as Holland's Brooke being part of a larger tr. belonging to sd. Willocks, beg. by the sd. brook at the w. corner of 500 a by them sold to John Vannoice, of Kings Co., NY, in Nov last past and then from sd. brook to Vannoice's land and then several courses, being 300 a.; bnd. s.e. by Vannoice, s.w. by sd. brook, n.w. by 400 a. by him sold by date of these Presents to Margareta Freeman, wife of Bernard Freeman, minister, of Flatbush, King's Co., NY, and n. e. belonging to sd. Willocks. Wits.: Aeneas Mackensie, Pieter Corlelyou. Signed: Geo. Willocks, Margaret Willocks. Ackn.: 18 Jun 1722, Peter Corlelyou apprd. bef. John Parker, Majesty's Council.

Pg 384. 1 Jul 1718. [Hard to read] George Willocks, of Perth Amboy, Middlesex Co., NJ, Gent., and Margaret, his wife, sell to Margareta Freeman, wife of Bernardus Freeman, minister, of Flatbush, Kings Co., NY, for £180, for 400 a., for a tr. of land on the s. side of Holland's Brook in Hunterdon Co., NJ, beg. at the w. corner of a 300 a. tr. sd. Willocks sold to Jacobus Beakman, of Flatbush and several courses; bnd. s.e. by sd. Beakman, s.w. by sd. brook, n.w. & n.e. by land of sd. Willocks. . Wits.: Aeneas Mackensie, Pieter Corlelyou. Signed: Geo. Willocks, Margaret Willocks. Ackn.: 18 Jun 1722, Peter Corlelyou apprd. bef. John Parker, Majesty's Council.

Pg 386. 5 May 1722. [Hard to Read] John Burnet, of NY City, NY, Gent., sells to Josiah Ogden, Middlesex Co., East NJ, for [?], for a tr. of land of 75 a., to be taken up & surveyed in the unappropriated lands in East NJ, wch. descended from Robert Gordon, of Cluney, Esqr., to his grandson, Robt. Gordon, Esqr., of Cluney & conveyed by him to his uncle, Augustus Gordon and from sd. Augustus to John Burnet. Wits.: Michael Kearny, Thomas Jackman. Signed: John Burnet. Ackn.: 14 Jun 1722, Thomas Jackman apprd. bef. Adam Hude, Judge, Middlesex Co.

Pg 387. 10 Sep 1721. Thomas Gordon, Esqr., of Perth Amboy, Middlesex Co., NJ, grants and confirms unto Thomas Gordon, Junr., his son, for the natural love & affection he has for his son, for a tr. of land lying on Assinpink Brook at the upper corner of Doctor Hamilton's land, then to land form. Patented, and several courses to sd. Brook and then down same to the beg. Wits.: Joseph Hall, John

Melvin, both subjects made their marks. Signed: Thomas Gordon. Ackn.: 7 Jul 1722, Joseph Hall apprd. bef. David Lyell, Majesty's Council.

Pg 389. 29 May 1722. John Burnet, sold to Josiah Ogden & James Alexander, for £32, two-third parts with the whole divided into three parts, being a tr. of land in Essex Co., on a brook betw. the mountains that runs w. from Newark and Pasaick River, beg. at a road over sd. mountains by the plantation of John Johnson, Junr. to Whippany where the road crosses the sd. brook, then several courses to the beg., being 100 a. ALSO, two-third parts of a tr. in Essex Co. lying as the mountain adjoining to the bounds of Newark, beg. on the n. part of a steep place of mountain at the rear of the land of John Johnson, Junr., then along sd mountain to the beg., being 23.8 a. Wits.: Par. Parmyter, John Stuckey. Signed.: John Burnet. 29 May 1722, Paroculus Parmyter apprd. bef. David Provoost, Judge, Bergen Co.

Pg 390. 20 Jan 1696/7. John Johnson, of Newark, Essex Co., East NJ, sells to Thomas Davis, of the afsd. place, for a competent sum of money, for a tr. of upland or pine bogs in the afsd. place, being 10 chains by 13 chains; bnd. n. by Thomas Davis, s. by swamp, e. & w. by unsurveyed land, being 12 a. Wits.: John Cooper, Samuel Alling, Robt. Young [?]. Signed: John Johnson, Martha Johnson made her mark. Ackn.: 2 Jan [Feb?] 1698/9, John Johnson apprd. bef. John Curtis.

Pg 391. 16 Jan 1692/3. Memorandum. It is concluded and agree betw. John Davis & Thomas Davis, both of Newark, Essex Co., East NJ. WHEREAS, there being some former difference concerning an Estate left by their father, Stephen Davis, dec'd, and there now being a willingness to put an end to all further differences and that Brotherly love may continue with them, they have concluded the following agreement. The division of lands, and in particular the homestead, is to be as follows as it is now set out & divided by the line that runs betw. them and that part of the homestead wch. belongs to a division line betw. them it is agreed betw. the two brothers-John Davis & Thomas Davis: The sd. John shall have the side of the homestead adjoining upon Samuel Plum's at the front in breath that the highway and at the rear of the river and then as it runs [and there are other terms and conditions set forth as to building, as to the Second Division as dealt with in the Patent regarding 11a. and mentions it being next to John Cockburn, William Braid[?], Mrs. Bonds and Jonathan Sarjant. ALSO, mentions another 7 a. wch. Thomas has 2 a. of it that were given to him by his father. It also mentions 5 a. mentioned in the Patent lying near Morris Creek wch. is to be divided betw. them with Thomas having the part on that side that joins upon Samuel [Rolf/Rose] . The agreement was sealed by both parties binding themselves with £50 that shall be paid by him that does not abide by the terms ratified herein. Wits.: Edward Ball, John Gardner. Signed: John Davis, Thomas Davis. Ackn.: 1 Feb 1692/3 - bef. Thomas Johnson, Justice, John Curtis, Justice.

Pg 392. 15 Mar 1703. Mathew Camfield, of Newark, Essex Co., East NJ, freeholder, sells to Thomas Davis, of the afsd. place, for a competent sum of money, for a certain tr. of upland within Newark, being part of my Second Division, wch. tr. of upland is 20 chains by 6 chains; bnd. n. & e. by Mathew Camfield, w. by land of William Bruin, s. by Thomas Davis. Wits.: Wm. Muir, John Alling. Signed: Mathew Camfeild. Ackn.: 10 May 1704, John Alling apprd. bef. John Curtis and on 24 Apr 1722, John Alling apprd. bef. Joseph Harrison, Judge, Essex Co.

Pg 393. 10 Jan 1708/9. John Davis, of Newark, Essex Co., East NJ, yeoman, sells to Thomas Davis, of the afsd. place, for £45, for a tr. of land in Newark Twp., adjoining sd. Thomas Davis' home lot, being 12 rods by 13 rods at the e. end; bnd. w. by highway, n. by the house lot of Jno. M[?]less, e. by Passyack River, s. by the sd. Thomas Davis. Wits.: Jno. Cooper, Joseph Dock. Signed: John Davies. Ackn.: 25 Apr 1722, John Cooper apprd. bef. Joseph Harrison, Judge, Essex Co.

Pg 394. 21 Nov 1706. [Can't read] John Davis sold ... Wits.: Theophilus Peirson, John Cooper. Ackn.: Nov 1706, John Davis apprd. bef. Theophilus Peirson and on 25 Apr 1722, John Cooper apprd. bef. Joseph Harrison, Judge, Essex Co.

Pg 395. 17 May 1720. Joseph Brain & John Brain, both of Newark, Essex Co, East NJ, yeomen, sell for a competent sum of money, to Thomas Davis, of the afsd. place, yeoman, for a tr. of land within Newark, on the n. side of Second River beg. at the s.w. corner of sd. Thomas Davis's land near the house, s.w. to a swamp, by a small run, s. to sd. River, ; bnd. s. by sd. River, e. by Daniel Dodd or a highway, n. partly by his own land & partly by our own land, w. by swamp land of sd. Thomas Davis, being 9 a. Wits.: Jno. Cooper, John Harrison. Signed: Joseph Bruin, John Bruin. Ackn.: 25 Apr 1722, John Cooper apprd. bef. Joseph Harrison, Judge, Essex Co., NJ.

Pg 396. 6 Aug 1700. Edward Riggs, of Newark, Essex Co., East NJ, sells to Thomas Davis, of the afsd. place, for a competent sum of money, for a piece of fresh meadow within Newark in the pine meadow betw. two rivers, the Second River and Third River, being 12 a., bnd. w.s.w. by John Johnson and unappropriated land. Wits.: John Gardner, Sarah Covington. Signed: Edward Riggs, made his mark. Ackn.: 7 Feb 1705, Edward Riggs apprd. bef. Theophilus Peirson.

Pg 397. 27 Apr 1722. Thomas Gordon, of Perth Amboy, Middlesex Co., NJ, Esqr., made his will and appointed several tr. of land to be divided into five equal parts for a settlement to each of my children: Thomas, John, Margarett, Mary & Euphaim. Also, in consideration of the natural love and affection he had toward his youngest son, John, he sold unto him one-half of his plantation on the Rariton River and Cheesquaks' Creek; bnd. by Thomas [?arns'] land, being the w. half part of the tr. ALSO, one-half of the meadow belonging to the plantation bot. of John Ireland. Wits.: John Barclay, John Stevens, Margaret Thomson. Signed: [No signature] Ackn.: 13 Aug 1722, John Barclay, John Stevens, and Margaret Thomson apprd. bef. John Parker, Majesty's Council.

Pg 398. 17 Jan 1717. John Harrison, of Rocky Hill, Somerset Co., NJ, Gent., sells to William Hudgson, of Perth Amboy, Middlesex Co., NJ, brick layer, for £31, for a lot of land in Perth Amboy on the n. side of the highway towards, the Market Place, beg. by sd. highway by the s.w. corner of William Eirs' lot and then along same to Brigadier Hunter's lot or pasture and along same for several courses to sd. highway and then several courses to the beg., being 7.7 a. Wits.: John Marsh, Thomas Brittain. Signed: John Harrison. Ackn.: 24 Feb 1717, John Harrison apprd. bef. Adam Hude, Judge, Middlesex Co.

Pg 399. 9 Aug 1722. William Hugson, Perth Amboy, Middlesex Co., NJ, brick layer, and Lydia, his wife, leases to William Burnet, Esqr., Gov. of NJ, for 5 shillings, for one year, under transferring uses into possessions [the absd. lot in Perth Amboy – Page 398, currently in his possession]. Wits.: James Smith, Michl. Kearny. Signed: William Hodgson, Lydia Hodgson. Ackn.: 9 Nov 1722, William & Lydia Hodgson apprd. bef John Parker, Majesty's Council.

Pg 400. 10 Aug 1722. William Hugson, Perth Amboy, Middlesex Co., NJ, brick layer, and Lydia, his wife, releases to William Burnet, Esqr., Gov. of NJ, for a competent sum of money, the lot and premises, under transferring uses into possessions [the absd. lot in Perth Amboy – Page 398, currently in his possession]. Signed: William Hodgson, Lydia Hodgson. [can't read rest.]

Pg 402. 20th [Jan/Jun ?] 1722. [Deed hard to read] Jacob Doughty, of Burlington, NJ, yeoman, sells to Edward Burling, of NY City, merchant, for ? , for 105 a. of land in Crosswicks, East NJ, beg. at a tree a corner of land surveyed sold out of a tr. of land form. of Robert Burnet & since conveyed to Thomas Parker, Esqr., ... John Hepborn, then along the line several courses to the beg. as by the Indenture. AND, WHEREAS, by another sale made betw. John Chambers and the afsd. Doughty, dated 24 Jul 1719, and for the sd. consideration sd. Chambers conveyed land to sd. Doughty, a tr. of land in Monmouth Co, East NJ, beg. at a swamp and several courses, bnd. by land form. of Robert Burnet, being 245 a. WHEREAS, BY THIS INDENTURE, Jacob Doughty and his wife, Amy, sold for £280, unto Edward Burling, for two parcels of land now into one plantation for 350 a. Wits.: Charles Doughty, Wm. Huddleston, Rachel Seaman, Grace Cowperthante. Signed: Jacob Doughty, Amie Doughty. Ackn.: 14th of 7th month 1722, Jacob & Amy Doughty apprd. bef. John Wies[?].

Pg 405. 1 Mar 1720. Lancaster Syms, of NY City, Gent., and Catherine, his wife, lease unto Allane Jarrett, of NY City, mariner, for 5 shillings, for one year, for one full and equal half of a tr. of land on Milston River, Somerset Co., East NJ, beg. on the w. side of sd. River below the mouth of Aertsen brook, then courses to the rear of Thomas Hart's line and then to Hart's lower corner by sd. River and then up same to the beg.; bnd. n. by Thomas Barker's land, s. by John Aertsen's lot and e. by sd. River, being 708 a., wch. tr. contains one-sixth part of a greater tr. form. granted to Gerradus Beekman, Adrian Beekman, William Creed, John Aertsen, Thos. Cardale, & the sd. Lancaster Symns by Thomas Hart, of London, merchant, and one of the Proprietors of East NJ, wch. afterwards by deed of partition betw. the absd. persons, on 9 Jan 1702, was divided betw. them, and was assigned to sd. Syms the sd. tr. being sold. Wits.: Ebenezer Wilson, Antho. Ham. Signed: Lancaster Symes. Ackn.: 28 Jul 1721, Anthony Ham of NY City, Gent., apprd. bef. David Jamison, Esqr., Chief Justice, NJ.

Pg 407. 2 Mar 1720. Lancaster Syms, of NY City, Gent., and Catherine, his wife, release unto Allane Jarrett, of NY City, mariner, for 5 shillings, for one year, for £100, land now in his possession under transferring uses into possessions, wch. is the land described below [and also in the absd. deed – Page 405]. WHEREAS, Thomas Hart, of London, merchant, one of the Proprietors of East NJ, by Rip Vandam, of NY, merchant and lawful attorney, authorized for sd. Hart and instrument dated 14 Dec 6th Year of Wm. & Mary, by an instrument signed by Rip Van Dam but the name Thomas Hart, bearing date 23 Jul, 1702, and did release and confirm unto the Gerrardus Beekman, Andrian Beekman, William Creed, John Aertson, Thomas Cardale and Lancaster Symes, that one certain part of his Proprietary granted unto him by Patent from other Proprietors, dated 5 Jun 1688, wch. sd. tr. of land on Milston River, Somerset Co., beg. where a small run comes into the sd. River where the land of Thomas Barker also beg., and then several courses to Nepoick brook and then as it runs to the beg.; bnd. e. by sd. River, n. by Thomas Barker's land, s. by Walter Benthall's land and w. by land unappropriated, being 4,000a. AND, WHEREAS, a certain deed of partition , dated 9 Jan 1702, under the names of William Beekman, of Flatbush, King's Co., NY, Gent.; Adrian Beekman of the afsd. place, yeoman, of the first part, and William Creed, of Jamaica, Queen's CO., NY, yeoman, of the second part; John Aertson, of Brencklin, King's Co., NY, yeoman, of the third part; & Lancaster Symes, of NY Gent., of the fourth part, divided it into equal parts among themselves. AND, the absd. persons released & granted unto sd. Symes the one-sixth part being 708a. AND, WHEREAS the indenture dated 11 Jan 1702 made betw. sd. Symes unto Rip Van Dam, of NY City, merchant, and sd. Symes gave unto sd. Van Dam one-half of the sixth part. Wits.: Ebenezer Wilson, Antho. Ham. Signed: Lancaster Symes. Ackn.: 28 Jul 1721, Anthony Ham apprd. bef. David Jamison, Esqr., Chief Justice, NJ.

Pg 416. 4 Oct 1722. John Harrison, of Amboy, Middlesex Co., NJ, Gent., sells to Henry Davis, of the afsd. place, yeoman, for £206, for a tr. of land in afsd. county, beg. on the e. side of Milston River at the upper corner of Benjamin Pridmore's land on sd. River and then along his line several courses to the sd. River and then down same to the beg., being 206 a. Wits.: Benjamin Randolph, Richd. Bishop, Benj. Harrison. Signed: John Harrison. Ackn.: 4 Oct 1722, John Harrison apprd. bef. John Parker, Majesty's Council.

Pg 418. 2 Dec 1721. David Lyell, of Monmouth Co., NJ, Esqr., and a Proprietor of East NJ, sells to Samuel Leonard, of Middlesex Co., East NJ, Gent., for £32, 5 shillings, for 100 a. of land to be taken up & surveyed in the unappropriated lands of East NJ. Wits.: Robert Mitchel, Nickolas Hollen made her mark. Signed: David Lyell. Ackn.: 19 March 1721/2, David Lyell, Esqr., apprd. bef. Thos. Gordon, Esqr., Majesty's Council.

Pg 419. 18 Apr 1722. William Ladd, of Woodbridge, appoints in his place his loving and trusty brother in law, Joseph Leigh, of the afsd. place, boatman, along with Ladd's loving wife, Susanna, as his lawful attorney to recover & receive any sums of money and do whatever needs to be done, as if he himself was personally present and in his name. Wits.: Thankfull Leigh, John Place. Signed: Wm. Ladd. Ackn.: 30 Oct 1722. Thankfull Leigh appeard bef. Adam Hude, Judge, Middlesex Co.

Pg 420. 3 Mar 1717/18. Steven Kent & David Kent, both of Woodbridge, Middlesex Co., NJ, yeoman, sell to Obadiah Ayers, of the afsd. place, planter, for £31, for a tr. of land being a half part of the First Division lot in Woodbridge Commons, # 59, drawn in right of sd. Steven Kent, and being the n.[?] most part of the lot, beg. at the n.w. corner of John Ileslee's land on a place called Horse Neck, and then several courses to John Taylor's First Division lot and then along his line to his s.e. corner and then several courses to sd. Ileslee's lot; bnd. n. by common land, w. by sd. Taylor, s. by common land, e. part by the other half part and part by Ileslee. Wits.: Jno. Smith, John Ayers. Signed: Stephen Kent, David Kent made his mark. Ackn.: 21 May 1722, John Ayers apprd. bef. Adam Hude, Judge, Middlesex Co.

Pg 421. 26 Jan 1721. John Ayers, of Woodbridge, Middlesex Co., NJ, for the love & affection he has to his loving son, Obadiah Ayers, of the afsd. place, gives and confirms unto his son, a parcel of land of 35 a., in Woodbridge at Horse Neck and is part of a lot that was drawn in right of John Taylor's First Division lot in Woodbridge Commons and part of the Third Lot Division, beg. at the corner of the 60 a. lot in the Third Division, and then several courses to the n.e. corner of the 60 a. lot and then to land form. of Steven Kent's, to the beg. Wits.: Samuel Ayers, James Wilkison. Signed: John Ayers. Ackn.: 8 Feb 1721/1722, John Ayers apprd. bef. John Parker, Majesty's Council.

Pg 421 [Page mis-numbered, should be 422. Written sideways on this page states: :This deed is assigned to Joshua Smally Lib. K-:77]. 27 May 1722. James Alexander, of NY City, NY, sells to John Burnet, of the afsd. place, merchant, for £24, for 61.9 a. to be taken up & surveyed in the unappropriated lands of East NJ, being part of 500 a. bot. of James & Charles Dockminique, Edward Rickerds & other Proprietors of East NJ. Wit.: Isaac Stuckey, Par. Parmyter. Signed: Ja. Alexander. Ackn.: 29 May 1722, James Alexander apprd. bef. Josiah Ogden, Esqr., Judge, Essex Co.

Pg. 422. 11 Nov 1721. Samuel Royse, of Piscataway, Middlesex Co., NJ, Gent., sells to John Van Horne, of NY City, NY, merchant, for £112, for a tenement tr. & premise on the n. side of Raritan River within Piscataway, being 120 a. and is now in the occupation of Daniel Nuwes [?], merchant, and by a certain lease & release of mortgage for the same premises made from Sd. Royse to sd. Van Horne, dated 4th & 5th Aug 1719, provided the sale is on the condition if sd. Royse shall truly pay unto sd. Van Horne £112, by 11 Nov 1723, then sd. Royse shall be able to reenter the sd. premises and possess same. Wits.: J. Stevens, George Johnston. Signed: Samuel Royse. Ackn.: 4 Feb 1722/3, Samuel Royse apprd. bef. John Parker, Esqr., Majesty's Council.

Pg 424. 13 Mar 1719. Samuel Oliver, of Elizabeth Town, Essex Co, NJ, yeoman, sells to by Elijah Davis, for the afsd. place, cordwainer, for £14, for a small tr. of upland in Elizabeth Town, being part of the pietle or house lot of John Haindes, late of Elizabeth Town, dec'd, beg. at the corner of John Reides fence by the highway, next the River and then by the highway 3.5 rods, and then several courses to the fence of John Rose[Ross?] and then several courses to the beg., being 14 rods of ground; bnd. n.e. by the sd. highway, n.w. by the land of John Rose[Ross?], s.w. & s.e. by land of John Ninds, dec'd, being in possession of Capt. Mathias Dehart. Wits.: Samuel Whitehead, Gershom Higgins. Signed: Samuel Olliver, Mary Olliver. Ackn.: 31 Jan 1722/23, Gearshum Higgins apprd. bef. Joseph Bonnel, Judge, Essex Co.

Pg 426. 18 Jan 1722. Jameke Brocke, of NY City, NY, widow of Abraham Bocke, late of the afsd. place, yeoman, dec'd, & Isaac Bockee, of the afsd. place, cooper; Abraham Bockee, of the afsd. place, cooper; Sampson Benson, of the afsd. place, inn holder, & Maritie, his wife; Jarol Hassing, of the afsd. place, yeoman & Jaromine, his wife; Dirk Bonson, of the afsd. place, yeoman, and Catalina; Hendrick Barre[?]. of the afsd. place, turner, and [?]anneke, his wife; & Sarah Bockee, of the afsd. place, spinster, all co-heirs of Abraham Bockee, dec'd, sell to Abraham Van Horne, of the afsd. place, merchant, for £450, for a piece of land, now in possession of [can't be read] on 13 Apr 1706 and conveyed to sd. Abraham Bockee, dec'd by Octavo Coanraats, as attorney empowered by Jacob Osterland and John Heyser and the same was conveyed with others by Peter Sonmans, Esqr., by deed, dated 28 Oct 1703, wch. was granted to sd. Sonmans by deed from East NJ, beg. at Lawrence's Creek by

Honey Brook and then to a bridge on the road from the farm to a slip of John Inion's toward the house of George Rescarrick, then along sd. road and then several courses to the beg.; bnd. n. by land of Osterland and Keyser, w. by road, e. & s. by Lawrence's Creek, being 392 a. Wits.: Abrah. Governeir, John Everson. Signed: [By all – names difficult to separate & read.] Ackn.: NY – 30 Nov 1722, bef. Abraham Governier apprd. bef. David Jamison, Esqr., Chief Justice, of NJ.

Pg 429. 20 Feb 1723. [Deed difficult to read.] Adrian Beekman, of Flatbush, King's Co., NY ... for a competent sum of money sells to Capt. Gerardus Beekman, the one-sixth part of 670 a. [This deed is in reference to the land divided into one-sixth parts in deed on Page 407 in divided 9 Jan 1702/3.] And, the one-sixth part of Adrian Beekman's beg. at Thomas Cardale's lower corner, than by meadow, and along the line of Gerardus Beekman, and then the line of sd. Cardale; bnd. n. by Gerardus Beekman's lots. By sd. Cardale's lot, and e. by Milstone River., being 670 a. Wits.: Jan Anderson, Johannis Jansen. Signed: Adrian Beeckman. Ackn.: 24 Feb 1702/3, Adrian Beekman apprd. bef. Henry Filkin, Justice of Peace, King's Co., Nassau Island, NY and on 23 July 1722, Johannos Jansen apprd. bef. David Jamison, Esqr., Chief Justice, NJ.

Pg 431. 18 Apr 1722. Gerardus Beekman, City of NY, Esqr., am seized of a tr. of land in NJ fronting on the Milstone River, wch. was afterwards divided into 4 lots named Lot 1-4. Lot 4, I gave to my son, Gerardus Beekman wch. I have already given to him.; Lot 3 to my son Christopher Beekman wch. I have already given him. And, being willing any other sons - Henry Beekman should have lot 2 and my son William Beekman to have Lot 1. Now, I Gerardus Beekman and Magdelena, my wife as wed, for the natural love and paternal affection and £400, give unto my son, Henry Beekman, Lot 2; fronting e. on Millstone River, s. by Christopher Beekman, n. by William Beekman, and w. by Peter Sonmans. Wits.: Lomons Willemes, Chrest. Beekman. Signed: Jerard Beekman, Mag. Beekman. Ackn.: 23 Jan 1722, Gerardus Beekman and wife apprd. bef. David Jamison, Esqr., Chief Justice, NJ.

Pg 432. 18 Apr 1722. 18 Apr 1722. Gerardus Beekman, City of NY, Esqr., am seized of a tr. of land in NJ fronting on the Milstone River, wch. was afterwards divided into 4 lots named Lot 1-4. Lot 4, I gave to my son, Gerardus Beekman wch. I have already given to him.; Lot 3 to my son Christopher Beekman wch. I have already given him. And, being willing any other sons - Henry Beekman should have Lot 2 and my son William Beekman to have Lot 1. Now, I Gerardus Beekman and Magdelena, my wife as wed, for the natural love and paternal affection and £400, give unto my son, William Beekman, Lot 1, ; bnd. e. by Milstone River, s. by Henry Beekman, n. by Peter Stryker, w. by Peter Sonmans. Wits.: Wits.: Lomons Willemes, Chrest. Beekman. Signed: Jerard Beekman, Mag. Beekman. Ackn.: 23 Jan 1722, Gerardus Beekman and wife apprd. bef. David Jamison, Esqr., Chief Justice, NJ.

Pg 434. 25 Apr 1723. John & Thomas Whitlock, of Freehold, Monmouth Co., East NJ, yeomen, sell to Nathaniel Morgan, of the afsd. place, for a competent sum on money, one-fourth part of a third part, fo a seventh part of a forty eighth part of the undivided lands in East NJ, wch. were conveyed by deed from John Wall, son of Garret Wall, dated 1 Aug 1715. Wits.: Joseph Morgan, Katherin Lyell, Mary Whitlock made her mark. Signed: John Whitelock, Thomas Whitlock. 23 Apr 1723, John Whitlock apprd. bef. David Lyell, Esqr., Majesties Council.

Pg 435. 17 Apr 1722. Thomas Leonard, of Perth Amboy, Middlesex Co., NJ, Gent., sells to John Vanhorn, of NY City, NY, merchant, a tr. of land beg. at Millston River at the corner of Walter Benthall, and then several courses to William Penn's land, and along his line to land late of Henry Greenland and along his line to the sd. River and then down same to the beg., where the sd. Vanhorn lately by deeds of lease and release, dated the 21st & 22nd days of Dec 1719, bot. from John Johnston & Geo. Willocks 630 a. on the w.n.w. AND, WHEREAS, by this indenture, John Vanhorn & Thomas Leonard for £900 have bot. the residue of the same tr.; excep. 40 a. beg. by land form. sd. Benthall's and now belonging to Francis Elrington, where the brook unites with sd. River above John Harrison's Mill, and then along sd. Elrington's land and then from Elrington's land to the sd. River at right angles in order to make 40 a. AND, the sd. residue of the tr. is divided betw. sd. Leonard and sd. Vanhorn. AND, NOW, sd. Leonard has granted & quit claimed unto the sd. Vanhorn all that part of the residue, beg. on the w. side of sd. River at the mouth of a small run opposite to Rocky hill and then several courses back to the beg., being 629 a. ; excep. the absd. 40 a. Wits.: Wm. Trent, John Stevens. Signed: Thos. Leonard. Ackn.: 17 Apr 1722, Thos. Leonard apprd. bef. John Parker, Majesty's Council.

Pg 437. 9 Nov 1722. Sarah Couzens, of Newark, Essex Co., NJ, seamstress, do by these Presents appoint my friend & beloved Brother, John Dennis, of the afsd. place, weaver, to be my trus and lawful attorney for me and in my name to do whatever his necessary on my behalf. Wits.: Johannes Dow, D. Rouset. Signed: Sarah Cosens. Ackn.: 13 May 1723, David Rouset apprd. bef. Josiah Ogden, Judge, Essex Co.

Pg 438. 5 Apr 1723. Andrew Gordon, eldest son & heir at law to Thomas Gordon, Esqr., late of Majesty's Council, NJ, dec'd, for quieting and settling and preventing jealousies wch. have or may arise due to mistakes, etc. in my dec'd father's Will, do declare that I will confirm & ratify my father's Will, dated 21 Jul 1721, under his hand, made in favor of my youngest brother, John, dated the 27 Apr 1722, as well in Right of my loving Mother as of my other Brothers & Sisters and do by these Presents for me, release & forever quit claim unto my Loving Mother, Jannet, Exec. of my father's Will, all action & actions, etc. whatsoever in Law & Equity, wch. I now have or may have; excep. only the legacy left to me by sd. Will, and I rest well contented with the provision has made for me in his lifetime. AND, by these Presents, grant & agree to and with my said mother, brothers & sisters: Thomas, John, Margarett, Mary & Eupem Gordon as in the manner following: my sd. Mother Jannet Gordon and my brothers Thomas & John and my sisters Margarett, Mary & Euphem shall stand seized of the several lands & tenement as devised by my father until division be made according to the directions of sd. Will, and whatsoever they shall draw of my father's estate hereafter be disposed of by my mother, his Exec., by the will, and I will execute in writing for releasing of the same to the purchasers from my mother and to each of my brothers & sisters. Wits.: Saml. Leonard, Jno. Barclay. Signed: Andrew Gordon. Ackn.: 5 Apr 1723, Andrew Gordon apprd. bef. John Parker, Majesty's Council.

Pg 440. 27 Apr 1722. James Alexander, of NY City, sells to John Wells, of Newark, Essex Co., NJ, joiner, for £40, for 100 a. of land to be taken up & surveyed in the unappropriated lands of East NJ, being part of the 1,500 acres bot. by John Hamilton & sd. Alexander from Isabella Davis, grand-daughter of Gawen Lawrie, Proprietor, and in part of 365.25 a. of the remainder of sd. Hamilton's share, wch. sd. Alexander bot. from him. Wits.: Evan Drummond, Tho. Jackman. Signed: Ja. Alexander. Ackn.: 17 May 1723, Thomas Jackman apprd. bef. John Parker, Majesty's Council.

Pg 441. 20 Mar 1705. Sir Thomas Lane, Paul Dockininique, Edward Richeir, Esqrs., and the rest of the West NJ Society, by Lewis Morris, their attorney sell to Thomas Gordon, Gent., for a competent sum of money sell and confirm to sd. Gordon a tr. of land in Piscataqua, Middlesex Co., East NJ, beg. at the s.w. corner of a tr. now or late belonging to Robert Burnet, of Lathantie, then along his line and along Daniel Mackdaniel's line to Thos. Fitzrandolph's corner, then along his line several courses to the beg.; bnd. n. by sd. Burnet's land, e. & w. by unappropriated land, s. by part by sd. Mackdaniel & part by Fitzrandolph. Wits.: Alexander Innes, John Barclay. Signed: Lewis Morris for the East NJ Society. Ackn.: 16 Jun1707, John Barclay apprd. bef. Rich. Townly, Esqr., Majesty's Council.

Pg 443. 1 Jun 1722. Adam Hude, of Woodbridge, Middlesex Co., NJ, Esqr., for the friendly affection and love I have for Samuel Lockheart, of the afsd. place, merchant, gave & grant and quit claim unto him several tr. of land & meadow within Woodbridge, sold to Hude by James Lockheart, dec'd, dated 19 Dec 1718, beg. at a corner of Stephen Kent now Mathew Moor's house lot & addition; bnd. e. by sd. Moor's land, s. by highway, w. by land then in Commons, being 10 a. ALSO, 6 a. of land beg. at the of J. Lockheart's 12 a., part of his Second Division lying in the fork of Kent's Brook, then numerous courses to the beg., being part of the Third Division lot. ALSO, 4 a. of slat meadow in the Raritan Meadows, beg. at the house lot pond; bnd. n. by meadow of Henry Allwood, dec'd, then from sd. pond to the Neat Creek, then s. as the crk. runs to the meadow of John [LNU], & part by Thornall's meadow now David Dunham's. Wits.: James Thomson, Mathew Moros. Signed: Adam Hude. Ackn.: 21 Jun 1721, Adam Hude apprd. bef. Ro. Gillchrist & Tho. Pike, Judges, Middlesex Co.

Pg 444. 4 May 1721. Able Smith, of Hempstead, Queens Co., NY, yeoman, and his wife, Deborah; Timothy Halstead, and Caleb Halstead, the son of sd. Timothy; all of the afsd. place, yeomen, for £1,500, for a certain farm within Elizabeth Town, NJ, commonly known by the name of Thomson's or Watson's Point or Willson's farm, beg. by a gate at the beg. of the road that leads to Elizabeth Town, then along a fence and then numerous courses to Samuel Weynank, then to the fence of Benjamin Price, and then by a fence of Andrew Joline and then to the beg. ALSO, 40 a. of upland adjoining the farm at a square piece on the n.w. side of the farm, beg. at Thompson's Creek, all wch. premises and land and meadow lay in Elizabeth Town, being 503 a. Wits.: Jos. Hicks, Rem. Remser, Wm. Symonds. Signed: Abel Smith made his mark, Deborah Smith. Ackn.: 4 May 1721, Abel Smith and wife apprd. bef. Jos. Hicks, Judge, Queen's Co., NY. Essex Co, NJ – Elizabeth Town – 7 June 1722, Abel Smith apprd. bef. Joseph Bonnel, Judge, Essex Co.

Pg 447. 9 May 1702. William Dockwra, of London, merchant, by his attorney Richard Saltar, of Freehold, Monmouth, East NJ, by a letter of attorney, dated 25 Mar 1701, by and with the consent of Capt. Andrew Bown, of Middletown, Monmouth Co., sell to John Couerson & Bragoon Braghar, of Somerset Co., planters, for £440, for a tr. of land commonly called Milston River, beg. by the mouth of a small gully on the sd. River and then to Raritan River and then several courses to the beg., being 2,000 a.; bnd. n.n.w. by sd. Raritan River & Milston River, s. by lands of sd. Dockwra, s.e. by land of Evert Vanwickland. Wits.: Andrew Bowne, Wm. Bowne, George Summer[?]. Signed: Wm. Dockwra by Richd. Saltar, attorney. Ackn.: Perth Amboy, 18 Mar 1723, Richard Saltar apprd. bef. David Lyell, Majesty's Council.

Pg 449. 25 May 1722. Absalom Ladner, of Elizabeth Town, Essex Co., East NJ, sadler, and Elizabeth, his wife, sell to James Banks, for £105, for a lot in Elizabeth Town, being 1.5 a., ; bnd. e. by a large of Thos. Woodruff, s. by Elizabeth Town Creek, w. by the house lot of Benjamin Ogden, n. by a street or highway. Wits.: John Cooper, [FNU] Zenger [?], John Cook, John Ward. Signed: Absalom Ladner, Eliza. Ladner. Ackn.: 21 Jul 1722, John Cooper apprd. bef. David Lyell, Majesty's Council.

Pg 451. [Can't read ink faded] 1720. Mary Morin, of NY City, NY, by a power of attorney unto me by my well beloved husband, Samuel Morin, dated 23 Aug 1717, by these presents constitute my trusty & loving friend, Peter Gandy, of the afsd. place, mariner, to be my lawful attorney for me in my name, to do whatever is necessary. Wits.: [FNU] La Cante, Elias Pelle Frazier.

Pg 452. 21 Mar 1717[?]. Mary Tappen, of Woodbridge, Middlesex Co., NJ, widow of Isaac Tappen, dec'd, for the love I bear toward my two sons, Abraham & Benjamin Tappen, both of Woodbridge, for their encouragement that they may live on and keep the house & land in repair for their own benefit, wch. was left them in their father's Will, do give and grant unto them my Right and Claim for my lifetime of all the house & lands, meadows & orchards in the bounds of Woodbridge, being 20 a. of upland & 12 a. of meadow, whereon I, Mary Tappen do live, including my dec'd husband's home accommodations and 22 a. in the Second Division lot. Wits.: David Tappen, John Campyon. Signed: Mary Tappen made her mark. Ackn.: See Memoradum – Page 453.

Pg 453. 21 Mar 1717/1718. Memorandum - Abraham Tappen & Benjamin Tappen, two brothers, both of Woodbridge, Middlesex Co., NJ, Whereas, the within home & land shall be in common betw. them, for their peace, shall be in equal and share & share alike & when they shall see cause to part, he who has the buildings shall give so much towards the building as shall be adjudged by two men by them mutually chosen as one half of the buildings shall be esteemed worth towards helping the other to build that has not buildings & in all improvements on the sd. place, they both agree by these Presents that these items as left by to them by their Father's will shall be equally shared, each a like part share and proportion. Wits.: David Tappen, John Campyon. Signed Abraham Tappen, Benja. Tappen. Ackn.: Taken 21 ~~April~~ Mar 1717/1718, Mary Tappen apprd. bef. Adam Hude, Judge, Middlesex Co.

Pg 454. 29 Nov 1722. Philip Cazier, of Staten Island, Richmond Co., Gent., have quit claimed & by the Presents release unto Peter Gandy, of Perth Amboy, mariner, all manner of actions, bills, bonds, debts due, account sums and sums of money, etc. against sd. Gandy and also Bonds of sd. Gandy and Samuel Morrine, mariner, of NY, for the sloop "*White,*" delivered unto the sd. Morrin's wife, wch. heirs, etc for or by reason of any matter cause or things from the beginning of the world unto the day of the absd. date. Wits.: John Pettinger, Richd. Menwell. Signed: Phillip Cazie. Ackn.: None.

Pg 455. 2 Apr 1721. Daniel Hollinshead, of Rocky Hill, Somerset Co., NJ, merchant, leased to John Parker, of Woodbridge, Middlesex Co., NJ, merchant, for 5 shillings, 400 a., to be taken up & surveyed in the unappropriated lands of East NJ, in the being one-half of an undivided one forty eighth part wch. Hollinshead had Right. Wits.: George Willocks, Edward Vaughan. Signed: Daniel Hollinshead. Ackn.: 27 May 1721, Daniel Hollinshead apprd. bef. John Hamilton, Esqr., Majesty's Council.

Pg 456. 4 Apr 1721. Daniel Hollinshead, of Rocky Hill, Somerset Co., NJ, merchant, released to John Parker, of Woodbridge, Middlesex Co., NJ, merchant, for £115, [for the property in the absd. deed – Page 455] re:

transferring uses into possessions. Wits.: Geo. Willocks, Edwd. Vaughan. Signed: Daniel Hollinshead. Ackn.: 4 Apr 1721, Daniel Hollinshead apprd. bef. John Hamilton, Esqr., Majesty's Council.

Pg 458. 20 Mar 1723. Rodrigo Peecheco, of NY City, NY, merchant, by power of attorney of Daniel ~~Hollinshead~~ Nunez, of Piscataque, Middlesex Co., East NJ, appointed his trusty friend Hendrick Vroome & Mary Nunez, of Piscataque, his true and lawful attorneys to act on his behalf in all matters in his name. Wits.: John Borrow, Thomas Long. Ackn.: 25 Mar 1723. Rodrigo Peeheco apprd. bef. John Parker, Majesty's Council.

Pg 459. 6 Nov 1722. Daniel Nunes, of Piscataway, Middlesex Co., NJ, appointed his trusty friend Rodrigo Pacheo, of NJ City, NY, merchant, and to act in his place as his attorney in all matters necessary. Wits.: Hendrick Vroome. Signed: Daniel Nunes. 25 Mar 1723, Hendrick Vroome apprd. bef. John Parker, Majesty's Council.

Pg 460. 17 May 1723. George Hickle, yeoman, of Amboy, Middlesex Co., appointed in his place as his attorney, his trusty friend and brother, Obadiah Higbee, to act in his place & name in all necessary matters. Wits.: John Blake, John Blake, Junr. Signed: George Hickle, made his mark. [Name is HICKLE in all places but names his brother as HIGBEE.] Ackn.: 20 Sep 1723, John Blake apprd. bef. David Jamison, Esqr., Chief Justice, NJ.

Pg 460. 30 Apr 1719. Samuel Des Marest, of Hackensack, NJ, yeoman, & Mary, his wife, sell to Cornelius Herring, of Orange Town, Orange Co., Esqr., for £100, for a tr. of land in Bergen Co, East NJ; bnd. e. by road from Tapan to Hackensack, w. by Hackensack Kills or Creek, n. by Cornelius Vanhorn's land, then s. till it amounts to 224 a., to sd. Samuel De Marree, and wife Mary. Wits.: Heynyss [Dutch name], Wm. Hudleston. Signed: Samuel Des Marest, Mary Des Marest made her mark. Ackn.: Orange Co. – 30 Apr, 1719, "Acknowledgesd bef. me By the Conveyors – Witness my hand." Daniel Dehlerich.

Pg 462. 4 Aug 1718. Benjamin Borden, of Anchocoss[?], Burlington Co., West NJ, yeoman, for the natural love and affection I bear unto my son, Safety Borden, of Freehold, Monmouth Co., East NJ., and for a competent sum of money, grant & confirm unto him, a tr. of land in Freehold, being 450 a., being part of a tr. I bot. of Job Throckmorton on 13 Mar 1699, beg. in the rear line of the whole tr., being the n. corner of 100 a. I form. granted unto my son, Benjamin Borden, and then several courses to the line of the Patent being the Pines, then along same to the beg.; bnd. s.w. by the afsd. 100 a., s.e. by my own land, n.e. by the Pines as per original Patent, n.w. by unsurveyed land. Wits.: Anne Foster, Josias Foster. Signed: Benjm. Borden. Ackn.: 9 May 1723, Benjamin Borden apprd. bef. Peter Bard, Esqr., Majesty's Council.

Pg 463. 30 Jan 1721/2. [Deed hard to read] Benjamin Borden, of Anchocoss[?], Burlington Co., West NJ, yeoman, for the natural love and affection I bear unto my son, Safety Borden, of Freehold, Monmouth Co., East NJ., and for 10 shillings, confirm unto him, a tr. of land in Crosswicks in Freehold, beg. by the Burlington Path to the n.e corner of land in the possession of Richard Borden And then several courses, being part of the whole tr. bot of Job Throckmorton, 30 Mar 1699. Wits.: Richard Borden, Mary Borden made her mark. Signed: Benjm. Borden. Ackn.: 9 May 1723, Benjamin Borden apprd. bef. Peter Bard, Esqr., Majesty's Council.

Pg 464. 12 Nov 1718. Richard Dockwra, of Epsom, Surrey Co., England, Gent., eldest son & heir of William Dockwra, late of London, merchant, dec'd; William Dockwra, of Christ Church College, in Oxford, clerk, another son and Admin. of his father's Will; Mary Freeman, of London, widow; Margaret Bowells, of Parish of Lambeth, Surrey Co., widow; Thos. Warburton, of Turnershall, Hertford Co., Gent., and Anne, his wife; and Andrew Nickolls, of Province of NJ, in America, Gent., & Rebecca, his wife (wch. sd. Mary Freeman, Anne Warburton, Margaret Bowels, & Rebcecca Nickolls, are the daus. of the sd. William Dockwra, dec'd). WHEREAS, William Dockwra, dec'd in his Will, dated 26 Oct 1712, did bequeath unto his wife, Rebecca Dockwra two proprieties or four twenty-fourth of East NJ remaining unsold and to be sold to pay any debts, and all the rest of his estate bequeathed a half part to his wife, Rebecca, and the other one half divided amongst his absd. children and made his wife his sole Exec. AND, WHEREAS, his sd. wife, Rebecca, died during his lifetime and Letters of Admin where issued 2 Nov 171[?], [deed is very difficult to read due to faded ink but this appears to be a power of attorney given by Dockwra's descendants unto Thos. Humphry to recover and do whatever is necessary in their names regarding the lands in NJ wch. were owned by Dockwra at the time of his death and also involves the admin. & assigns of Phineas Bowles, late of London, merchant & mortgage of part of sd. premises and others lawfully claiming under sd. Dockwra's will. Some other surnames that can be made out are: Grooms, Peter Sonmans, heir of Arent Sonmans, late of London, dec'd.] Wits.: Robt. Burgess, Scrib, Richd. Fearne. Signed: Thos. & Ann Warburton, Rebecca Niccolls, Mary Freeman, Margt. Bowles, Rich. Dockwra, Willm. Dockwra. Ackn.: 4 Dec 1718, Richard Fearne, of Lombard Street, London, Gent., apprd. bef. Sir John Ward, Knight Lord Mayor & Alderman of London, and stated that he was present and observed those absd. persons sign, seal and as their several acts & deeds deliver & execute to Thomas Humphreys, of London, Gent., the original deed or Letter of Attorney now produced to him the sd. sd. Richard Fearne fair & un-cancelled, dated 12 Nov 1718, and Fearne stated that he was a witness to the sealing & delivery of the same on the back side of the sd. deed or Letter of Attorney together to Robert Burgess & Grantham Bird the two other witnesses and set & subscribed his name as here doth appear. [It was noted that Andrew Nicholls, of NJ, Gent., was now back in England.]

Pg 470. 22 mar 1722/3. Samuel Royce, of Piscataqua, Middlesex Co., NJ, Gent., sells to John Vanhorne, of NY City, NY, merchant, for 25, for two tr. of land in Somerset Co. ONE, adjoining the rear of land of William Post on the w. side of Millstone River, beg. at the s.w. corner of land form. of Cataline Brockaw on sd. River and then along the line and along the rear line of land form. John Cobus, and then to the beg., being 70.8 a. ALSO, a tr. of land in Somerset Co., adjoining the e. side of Royce Brook beg at the s.w. corner of Dirick Folker's land on sd. Millstone and along the line John Spreed, and then to sd. Brook and down same to corner of sd. Folker's land and then to the beg., being 8.5 a.; bnd. n.w. by Clement Elsworth, e. part by sd. Folker & part by Speed's land, s. by John Speed's land. Wits.: John Harrison, Alexander Mackdowall. Signed: Samuel Royce. Ackn.: 22 Mar 1722/3, Samuel Royce apprd. bef. William Eier, Esqr., Judge, Middlesex Co.

Pg 472. 6 Feb 1703/4. Isaac Tappen, of Woodbridge, Middlesex Co., NJ, cooper, for the natural love and affection her has toward his son, David Tappen, of the afsd. place, granted & confirmed unto him, 60 a. of upland within Woodbridge at the place called Metuchen, on the w. side of his son, Jacob Tappen, form. his dec'd son, Isaac Tappen, being the other half of his own accommodations, e. by a swamp and land of William Isley, s. by land [?], n. by land of Elisha Parker. ALSO, 10 a. of salt meadow in the Raritan Meadows, being one half of 20 a. of meadow wch. he bot. of Benjamin Hull, of Piscataway, in the afsd. place, by a deed dated 29 Mar 1692. Wits.: Benjamin Cromwelle, Adam Hude. Signed: Isaac Tappen. Ackn.: Isaac Tappen apprd. bef. Richard Townley, Esqr., Judge, Supreme Court.

Pg 473. 18 Dec 1718. James Clarkson, of Woodbridge, Middlesex Co., NJ, yeoman, sells to David Tappen, of the afsd. place, for £9, for a tr. of land being a Fourth Division lot in Woodbridge, being 8 a., beg. at the s.e. corner of William Stone[?] addition, then to a road or highway to Richard Sopper[?] plantation, then along same to Lot 33, then several courses to s. corner of Joseph Iseslee, dec'd his Second Division Lot then along sd. line to s.e. corner of sd. lot, and then back to the beg. ALSO, an addition to his land on the s. side of sd. 8 a. Wits.: Edwd. Crowell, Robt. Hude. Signed: Ja. Clarkson. Ackn.: 19 Dec 1718, James Clarkson apprd. bef. Adam Hude Judge, Middlesex Co.

Pg 475. 23 Mar 1717. Richard Mount, of Cranberry, in the City of Perth Amboy, Middlesex Co., East NJ, yeoman, and Rebekah, his wife, sell to Joseph Dennis, of Middletown, Monmouth Co., East NJ, cooper, for £200, for a tr. of land in Cranberry, being 200 a., beg. at the s.w. corner of a tr. belonging to John & Thomas Morford, the two sons of Thomas Morford, dec'd, wch. is also the s.e. corner of Richard Mount, Junr.'s land, and then runs several courses to the

w. line of Richard Mount, then several courses to the corner of George Mount's land, then to the beg.; bnd. n. by Richard & George Mount, e. by John Morford's land, s. by sd. Richard Mount & w. by the bnd. line if the tr, of land being part of the land granted to sd. Richard Mount by deed from John Harrison, dated 4 July 1710. Wits.: John Morford, made his mark , Joseph Applegate, Willm. Laurence, Junr. Signed: Richard Mount, Rebekah Mount, both made their marks. Ackn.: 27 Feb 1722[?], William Lawrence, Junr. apprd. bef. David Lyell.

Pg 478. 1 Feb 1717. John Harrison, of Somerset Co., NJ, Esqr., sells to David Lee, of Middlesex Co., NJ, yeoman, for £150, for a parcel of land in Middlesex Co., beg. on the e. side of Millstone River at the upper corner of Benjamin Maples' land on sd. River, then along his line for several courses to Daniel Bayly's land and then along his line to sd. River and then down same to the beg.; bnd. n. by sd. Maple's land, e. by the land of sd. Harrison, and s. by sd. Bayly's land, and w. by Millstone River, being 200 a. Wits.: Charles Beekman, Tho. Yates. Signed: John Harrison. Ackn.: 14 Feb 1723, John Harrison apprd. bef. John Parker, Majesty's Council.

Pg 479. 5 Apr 1723. Samuel Leonard, Esqr., of Perth Amboy, Middlesex Co., NJ, sells to Andrew Gordon, Gent., of Freehold, Monmouth Co., NJ., for £100, for a tr. of land on Deep Brook near the Division Line betw. Middlesex Co. and Monmouth Co., East NJ, to be divided equally, beg. where sd. Brook divides itself and then up the brook on the part called Whitlock's Brook, then numerous courses back to the beg., and sd. Leonard is possessed of the absd. & sold half-part of the absd. tr. , the whole being divided into two parts. Wits.: John Gordon, Daniel Ketcham. Signed: Samuel Leonard. Ackn. 14 Jan 1723, Daniel Ketcham apprd. bef. David Lyell, Esqr., Majesty's Council. Also, on 10 Mar 1723, Samuel Leonard apprd. bef. David Lyell, where a mistake in the deed was corrected.

Pg 17 Feb 170[?]. Jediah Higgins, of Piscataway, Middlesex Co., East NJ, cordwainer, and Mary, his wife, sell to Henry Crosley, late of NY and now of Piscataway afsd. for £90, for all the tr, of land and meadow in Piscataway being 57 a., being land against John Gilman's land of Cohansey River in West NJ and against Nicholas Harris, late of Piscataway, afsd. WHEREAS, the sd. Higgins by a Patent from the Proprietors of East NJ, dated 30 Sep 1686 was seized of a tr. of land fronting the meadow at Raritan River, beg. by a highway and then running several courses to the beg., bnd. e. by a highways, by the meadow, w. by John Long, and n. by unsurveyed land, wch. land is 22 a. ALSO, the sd. Higgins by a deed from John Gillman, of Cohansey River in West NJ, planter, dated 23 Feb 1688/9, beg. by a small brook and then up the line that parts Edward Slater's land and the sd. land, then upon the Division Line, and then several courses; bnd. w. by sd. Slater, s. by meadow, e. by Hopewell Hull, and n. by Thomas Higgins, being 33.5 a. ALSO, a piece of meadow betw. the meadow of sd. Hull and Hugh Dunn, being 1.5 a. Wits.: Saml. Walker, John Royse, Thomas Fitz Randolph. Signed: Jediah Higgines, Mary Higgines, made her mark. Ackn.: 23 Dec 1723, Thomas Fitzrandolph apprd. bef. John Parker, Majesty's Council.

Pg 484. 18 Sep 1714. William Rogers, of Woodbridge, Middlesex Co., NJ, school master, sells to David Dunham, of the afsd. place, blacksmith, for £50, for a tr of land in Woodbridge, being a tr. of land the major part of the Freeholders, gave to George Ewbanks, school master in sd. town, and the form. husband of my wife, Elizabeth Rogers, by deed dated 5 Apr 1711, being 10 a. at a place called Red Brook, beg. by a tree by the sd. brook and then several courses to and area by the highway that leads to Rahawack, and then to the beg. Wits.: John Martyne, John [LNU]. Signed: William Rogers, Elizabeth Rogers made her mark. Ackn.: 30 Sep 1714, William Rogers apprd. bef. Elisha Parker, Majesty's Council.

Pg 486. 19 Dec 1721. John Johnston, Esqr., sells to Robert Barclay, of Piscataway, Middlesex Co., NJ, yeoman, for £170, 12 shillings, for a tr. of land in Piscataway, beg. at the s. corner of John Hutton's land, and then numerous courses to the beg., being 179 a.[in another place in the deed it says 167 a. of the absd. 179 a.], wch. sd. Johnston granted to sd. Barclay by deed dated 4 May 1718. Wits.: John Irleand, Thomas Gordon, Junr. Signed: John Johnston. Ackn.: 20 Dec 1721, John Johnston apprd. bef. Thomas Gordon, Majesty's Council.

Pg 487. 20 Dec 1721. John Johnston, Esqr., sells to John Ireland, of Piscataway, Middlesex Co., NJ, yeoman, for £150, for a tr. of land in Piscataway, beg. at the s. corner of land of Robert Barclay and then several courses to the beg., being 160 a. Wits.: Thomas Gordon, Junr., Amico Grandens[?]. Signed John Johnston. Ackn.: 20 Dec 1721, Thomas Gordon, Esqr. apprd. bef. Thomas Gordon, Esqr., Majesty's Council.

Pg 489. 14 Feb 1703/4. Zebulon Pike, of Woodbridge, Middlesex Co., NJ, yeoman, in consideration that David Herriot, Junr., of the afsd. place, cooper, conveyed to him all right & title for land in Woodbridge Twp., that form. belonged to John Foreman, late of Woodbridge, dec'd, that by deeds of division and quit claim, dated 30 Feb in the 10th year of the Reign of his Majesty, was granted to sd. Herriot by the absd. Pike & James Brown, being one Third Division lot in Woodbridge being 10 a. with allowance for land on the e. side of the road to Amboy. Then a lot of 8 a. with allowance for bad land on the road from Woodbridge to Piscataway being a Fourth Division lot in Commons. Then one Fifth Division lot in Papiack Neck and a £10 Right. ALSO, all the Right to land in the Commons of Woodbridge, not yet divided. AND, for diverse causes, sd. Pike has confirmed and conveyed a tr. of land in Woodbridge Twp. , being 30 a., beg. at a small swamp on the w. side of sd. swamp, bnd. by Margaret

Stone[?] land, wch. she bot. of John Pike, form. of Woodbridge, dec'd, then e. on the highway to the place where Abraham Tappen built a house & Cellar, then to appoint of land in the fork of a brook and then to the line of Margaret Stones'[?], then to the beg.; bnd. e. by Joseph Pike's land, s. by a small brook, w. by Margaret Stone's land , n. by sd. highway. ALSO, a tr. of land of 16 a and 26 rods, betw. branches of the absd. brook, beg. a the fork in the sd. brook, then up the n. branch of brook to land form. of Margaret Stone, then to the line of the sd. land and then several courses to Pike's Farm, and then to the division line of Zebulon Pike & Joseph Pike and then to the beg. Wits.: Samuel Lockhart, Nathall. Pike. Signed: Zebulon Pike, Jeannet Pike. Ackn.: 13 Mar 1723/4, Zebulon Pike apprd. bef. Adam Hude, Judge, Middlesex Co.

Pg 491. 11 Dec 1718. Jeremiah Reader, of Woodbridge, Middlesex Co., NJ, planter, and Elizabeth, his wife, for £35, sells to Elisha Frazee, of Elizabeth Town, Essex Co., NJ, house carpenter, conveyed a tr. of land in Woodbridge Twp. of 13 a., bot. from John Pike, late of Woodbridge, dec'd, by deed dated 4 Dec 1707; bnd. e. by a highway at the rear of Obadiah Ayers & John Foreman's house lot, s. by a highway that parts the farm John Pike had by a deed of gift from his father, Captain John Pike, dec'd, w. by John Job's land and n. by a house lot of John Islee. Wits.: Thomas Pike, Jno. Pike, Thomas Collier[?]. Signed: Jeremiah Reder, Eliz. Reader, both made their marks. Ackn.: Elizabeth Reader, wife of Jeremiah Reader gives & resigns up all her Rights to the land above. And, on 2 Apr 1719, Thomas Pike apprd. bef. Adam Hude, Judge, Middlesex Co.

Pg 493. 17 Aug 1722. [Hard to read due to ink] Miles Bunn, of Woodbridge, Middlesex Co, NJ, and Mary, his wife, sell to John Dove, of the afsd. place, for £120 for 115 a. of upland and 32.5 a. of meadow; bnd. w. by the division line betw. Woodbridge and Piscataway, n. by land in Common, e. by Coll. Parker's land & s. by meadows form. of Captain Francis Drake. WHEREAS, the Proprietors by a Patent, for a lot within Woodbridge, dated in Dec 1670 conveyed unto Richard Powell of the afsd. place 115 a. of upland and 35.5. a. of meadow and was conveyed by Powell to [?] Potter of Staten island by deed dated Dec 1686, and by the will of sd. potter dated 19 Mar 1694 as given to his son, Henry Potter...and wch. sd. patent...dated 27 Jun 1705 was by Henry Potter conveyed unto Mile Bunn of these Presents. Wits.: David Tappen, Robt. Hude. Signed: Miles Bunn, Mary Bunn. Memo – It is agree that Miles Bunn & wife and John Dove named in the Indenture shall only clear and pay Quit Rents on lands & meadows named in the deed only until it was in possession of sd. Dove, wch. was 16 Aug 1720. and is agreed to bef. sealing of these presents. John Dove, Miles Bunn. Ackn.: 14 Mar 1723/24, Mile Bunn, and wife Mary, apprd. bef. Adam Hude, Judge, Middlesex Co.,

Pg 495. 23 May 1720. [Very difficult to read] William Ladd, of Woodbridge, Middlesex Co., NJ, shipwright, sells to John Gosney, of the afsd. place, planter, for £100, for a tr. of land in Woodbridge, being 41a., beg. near the w. corner of Bald Hill .... Wits.: Joseph Leigh, Thankful Leigh. Signed: William Ladd. Ackn.: 6 Oct 1720, William Ladd apprd. bef. Adam Hude, Judge, Middlesex Co.

Pg 496. 7 May 1716. George Willocks & John Harrison, both of Perth Amboy, Middlesex Co., NJ, Gent., sells to Andrew Robeson, late of Woodbridge, now of Perth Amboy, blacksmith, for £76, for land in Perth Amboy, beg. by Smith Street on the n. side by a lane that parts the lot lately sold by sd. Willocks & Harrison to Philip Cazie, of Richmond Co., NY, then along Smith Street numerous courses to the afsd. lane, and then along same, to the beg. Wits.: John Stevens, Josiah Ogden. Signed: George Willock, John Harrison. Ackn.: 3 Jul 1716, both Harrison & Willocks apprd. bef. Elisha Parker.

Pg 497. 18 Mar 1723/4. Joseph Bloomfield, of Woodbridge, Middlesex Co., East NJ, weaver, sells to Benjamin Bloomfield, of the afsd. place, cordwainer, for £38, for a tr. of land in Woodbridge form. belonging to John Bloomfield, being 9 a., beg. by the brook that runs though the home lot and then to the road to Piscataway. Wits.: John Heard, John Gosney. Signed: Joseph Bloomfield. Ackn.: 18 Mar 1723/4, Joseph Bloomfield apprd. bef. Adam Hude, Judge, Middlesex Co.

Pg 499. 24 Feb 1717. Robert Drummond, of Elizabeth Town, Essex Co., NJ, vintner, sells to William Looker, of the afsd. place, yeoman, for £400, for his horse cart, cart house, and all other houses and chattel of all kinds, and his money plate, corn and household goods of what sort and generally all of his moveable estate, and in whose hands or possession so ever the same is or maybe found that belongs to sd. Drummond, and any where within Elizabeth Town or elsewhere in NJ. AND, sd. Drummond delivered to sd. Looker at the signing of these presents one silver salt dish or salt celler being a part of the premises. Wits. And. Niccolls, Samuel Whitehead. Signed: Robert Drummond. Ackn.: 5 May 1720, Samuel Whitehead apprd. bef. Isaac Whitehead, Judge, Essex Co.

Pg 501. 24 Feb 1723. [difficult to read] James Martin & William Patterson, both of Elizabeth Town, Essex Co., East NJ, Gent., are bound unto William Looker and Joshua Clark, of the afsd. place, yeomen, for £400, to be paid, dated 24 Feb 1723. The Condition of the obligation is that as the absd. Looker & Clark after several requests of Robert Drummond, dec'd, and Anne Drummond and for their only duty after and cause did come together with the sd. Robert Drummond and Anne Drummond unto Robert Hunter, Esqr., Capt. & Gov. of NJ, etc. by an obligation on 9 Nov 1716 in the amount of £1,200 conditioned for the true and full Administration of the goods & chattels of [FNU] Nowell, late of the NY City, dec'd, now is therefore the above bounden James Martin and William Patterson shall and do at all times ... kept harmless...the absd. Looker & Clark...Exec....Wits.: Andrew Jopline, Thomas Jackman. Signed: James

Martin, William Patterson. Ackn.: [?] 1723/4. Thomas Jackman apprd. bef. James Alexander, Majesty's Council.

Pg 502. 10 Sep 1708. Walter Newman of Middletown, Monmouth Co., East NJ, planter, sells to Thomas Elison, of Hempstead, Queens Co., Nassau Island, NY, for £200, for a tr. of land called Neverscuncks Side, near to Chesquakes, being 164 a., beg. at a tree and then on William Dockwra's line and to the beg.; bnd. e. by sd. Dockwra, s. by Thomas Warne, w. by Thomas Warne, and n. by land of the Scot's Proprietors. AND, Mary Newman, the wife of Walter Newman, willingly gives up her Right of Dowry and power of thirds to the above premises. Wits.: Thomas Warne, Mary Warne, Wm. Watson. Signed: Mary Newman, Walter Newman made his mark. Ackn.: 14 Sep 1708, Walter Newman apprd. bef. Peter Sonmans, Majesty's Council, and stated that he saw Mary Newman sign same.

Pg. 504. 20 Mar 1723. Thomas Ellison, of Perth Amboy, Middlesex Co., East NJ, husbandman, sells to Seth Ellison, of the afsd. place, for a competent sum of money, for a tr. of land within Perth Amboy, beg. at the n.e. corner of William Carhart's land, and then numerous courses to sd. Carhart's land and then to the beg., being 84 a. Wits.: Sten. Warne, Jonathan Quimby[?]. Signed: Thomas Ellison. Ackn.: Mar? 1723/4, Thomas Ellison apprd. bef. David Lyell.

Pg 505. 16 May 1714. John Johnston, of Freehold, Monmouth Co., NJ, Esqr., sells to John Hutton, of Piscataway, Middlesex Co., NJ, cooper, for £80, for land in Piscataway near the Great Ponds n. of the road from Amboy to Burlington, beg. at the s.e. corner of Robert Barclay, then numerous courses to the beg., wch. land was granted to sd. Johnston by Patent, dated 27 June 1701. Wits.: John Barclay, Lewis Johnston. Signed: John Johnston. Ackn.: 23 May 1723/4, John Johnston apprd. bef. James Alexander, Esqr., Majesty's Council.

Pg 506. 27 Sep 1715. John Barclay, of Perth Amboy, Middlesex Co., NJ, Gent., sells to William Hodgson, of the afsd. place, brick layer, for £17, for a lot in Perth Amboy, beg. on High Street at the n.w. corner of Wm. Dockwra's land, then along High Street; bnd. w. by sd. street, s. by sd. Dockwra's lot, e. by John Barclay's lot, & n. by unappropriated land. Wits.: J. Stevens, Zachariah Weeks. Signed: John Barclay. Wits.: 28 Sep 1715, John Barclay apprd. bef. Thos. Farmer.

Pg 507. 5 Oct 1721. George Willocks, of Perth Amboy, Middlesex Co., NJ, Gent., sells to Reice Williams, of the afsd. place, for £30, for a lot on w. side of High Street in Perth Amboy, , being 128 feet by 45 feet; bnd. e. by High Street, s. by William Eier's lot, w. by Margaret Latut's[?] lot (both being sold to them by sd. Willocks), n. by lot late possessed by Peter Sonmans. Wits.: Geo. Leslie, Michael Henry. Signed: Geo. Willocks. Ackn.: 1 Mar 1723/4, George Leslie apprd. bef. James Alexander, Esqr., Majesty's Council.

Pg 508. 22 Jan1719. George Willocks, of Perth Amboy, NJ, Gent., and his wife, Margaret, sell to John Lufburrow, Junr., of the afsd. place, cooper, for £23, 10 shillings, for a lot and tenement in Perth Amboy, on the w. side of the land from the n. side of Smith Street to Willock's Lane, wch. lot beg. by the lane and then 172 feet from Smith Street and by the n.e. corner of the other lot belonging to sd. Willocks now in the tenure of William Harrison and then several courses and then along sd. lane and then sever courses; bnd. e. by sd. Lane and on the other sides land owned by sd. Willocks. Wits.: Edward Vaughan, May Angele made her mark. Signed. : Geo. Willocks, Margaret Willocks. Ackn.: 25 Mar 1724, Edward Vaughan apprd. bef. John Parker, Majesty's Council.

Pg 510. 19 Mar 1723. Thomas Ellison, of Amboy, Middlesex Co., East NJ, yeoman, sells to William Carhart, of the afsd. place, for a competent sum of money, for a tr. of land in Amboy Twp., being 90 a. and being part of a tr. of 164 a. conveyed to sd. Ellison by deed from Walter Newman and to the sd. Newman by deed from John Hampton and to the sd. Hampton by Patent from the Proprietors, dated 8 Jan 1685, bnd. e. by land of William Dockwra, s. by land of Thos. Warne, n. by Scots Proprietor's land. Wits.: Sten. Warne, Jonathan Quimby[?]. Signed: Thomas Ellison. Ackn.: 21 Mar 1723/4, Thomas Ellison apprd. bef. David Lyell, Esqr., Majesty's Council.

Pg 512. 21 May 1723. Jonathan Hunter, of Edgemont, Chester Co., PA, tanner, and his wife, Margery, sell to William Cheesman , of Middletown, Monmouth Co., East NJ, cordwainer, for £470, for a tr. of land in Middlesex Co., East NJ, at the rear of lots on the w. side of South River, beg. near a small run of water, then numerous courses back to the beg. ALSO, a tr. adjoining the above mentioned tr., beg. by Thomas Fullerton's s.w. corner of his lot on South River, then several courses to the beg.; with both tr. being 500 a, and are the tr. wch. were granted and conveyed unto John Johnston, Esqr., to George Norton, of NY, butcher, by a deed, dated 28 Jan 1709. Wits.: William Lawrence, Junr., Johannes Smock made his mark. Signed: Jonathan Hunter, Margery Hunter signed in the presence of Mary Taylor, Ann Worrilaw, Jno. Taylor. Ackn.: 21 May 1723, Margery Hunter brought the conveyance, with her signature, bef. Isaac Taylor, Esqr., Justice of the Peace, Chester Co., PA. Also, on 29 May 1723, Jonathan Hunter apprd. bef. John Johnston, Junr., Majesty's Council, NJ.

Pg 514. 10 Mar 1723/4. Robert Barclay, of Piscataway Twp., Middlesex Co., East NJ, yeoman, sells to Daniel Baker, of the afsd. place, yeoman, for £110, for one half of a tr. of land that sd. Barclay bot. of John Johnston, in Middlesex Co., beg. at the n. corner of John Hutton's line, then to another corner of Hutton's, then to Hutton's line and back to the beg., being 89.5 a. Wits.: William Cheesman, Samll. Royse. Signed: Robert Barclay made his mark. Ackn.: 31 Mar 1724, Robert Barclay apprd. bef. John Parker, Majesty's Council.

Pg 516. ___ Jul 1710. John Harrison, of Somerset Co., NJ, Gent., son and heir of John Harrison, of the afsd. place, late dec'd, sells to Richard Mount, late of Middletown Twp., Monmouth Co., and now of Middlesex Co, yeoman, for £225, land in the bounds of Middlesex, being 500 a., beg. at the s.w. corner of John Morford on the Millstone, below the mouth of Benthall's Brook and then down same, to sd. Millstone and then to Cranberry Brook, and then up same to the line of John Morford's land and then along his line to where it beg.; bnd. n. by Cranberry Brook, s. by sd. Millstone, e. by Morford's land. ALSO, a tr, near the absd, tr. on the s. side of Millstone, being 40 a., beg. at the meeting of Benthall's Brook and the sd. Millstone, then to the w. corner of sd.. Morford's land on the s. side of sd. Millstone, then along his line to sd. Millstone and down same to the beg.; bnd. n. by sd. Millstone, n.e. by sd. Morford's land. Wits.: Benjamin Fitz Randolph, Tho. Leonard, Tho. Broderwuk. Ackn.: 19 Feb 1719/20, John Harrison, grantor, apprd. bef. James Alexander, Recorder, City of Perth Amboy. 19 Feb 1719, Richard Mount for 5 shillings paid by Joseph Dennis has sold and assigned over to sd. Dennis all the lands contained in the within Deed to make 200 a. Wits.: John Harrison, Ja. Alexander. Signed: Richard Mount made his mark.

Pg 519. 14 Mar 1710/11. John Jaques, of Woodbridge, Middlesex Co., East NJ, yeoman, sells to Daniel Stillwell, of the afsd. place, for £60, for a tr. of land within Woodbridge, beg. by a country road were William Robeson's Saw Mill at the entrance of the highway along w. by the mill pond, and then numerous courses back to the country road and then to the beg., being 60 a. Wits.: John Alston, John Bishop. Signed: John Jaquias. Ackn.: 14 Mar 1710/11, John Jaquish, apprd. bef. John Bishop, Justice, Middlesex Co. Also, on 28 May 1719, John Alston apprd. bef. John Parker, Majesty's Council.

Pg 521. 31 Dec 1707. [Deed hard to read] John Godden, of Newark, Essex Co., NJ, carpenter, sells to Edward Hancock, of the afsd, place, for a competent sum of money, several pieces of landing Newark, being 13.5 a. of upland adjacent to house wch. Godden bot. of William Brant, as it is already surveyed & set over, being part of the house lot; bnd. e. by Passayage River, n.& w. by the union[?] highway, s. by Godden's land. ALSO, 27.5 a. of other upland wch. sd. Godden bot. of William Brant within Newark and on Long Hill betw. the path that leads unto Watceston and the Second River and part of ye sd. lot and adjacent to Widow Crane's line; beg. at the sd. path the s. bounds , then to sd. Crane's line, bnd. by sd. Brant, e. from [?] corner by sd. River, and then s. until it meets with sd. highway or path wch. leads to Watceston. ALSO, part of [?] lot of meadow at Morres's Creek, being 5 rods of meadow on the e. side of sd. crk. ; bnd. n. by Thomas Davis, w. by Elnathan Baldwin. ALSO, a full quarter of a whole purchase wch. sd. Godden made of William Brant, in Newark. Wits.: John Prudden, Senr., Gerrardus Beekman, Jonathan Pierson. Signed: John Godin, Mary Goddin. Ackn.: 20 Jan 1707[8?], John & Mary Godin apprd. bef.

Theophilus Pierson. Also, 20 Apr 1724, John Prudden apprd. bef. Josiah Ogden, Judge, Essex Co.

Pg 523. 19 Feb 1723. Mary Chapman, alias Eire, wife of John Chapman, of Porsmouth, Southton, merchant, and sole Exec. of the last will of William Eire, late of Porsmouth, and also John Chapman, do appoint, John Haskile, of NY in America, Gent. and John Wetson[?], of the same place, our true & lawful attorney to act in our name and to do whatever is necessary in our stead relating to that wch. William Eier, dec'd, was seized of at the time of his death. Wits.: Tho. Fitch, Abrahm. Wynkoop. Signed: Mary Chapman, John Chapman. Ackn.: 17 Apr 1724, Thomas Fitch & Abraham Wynkoop apprd. bef. James Alexander, Majesty's Council and stated that they saw Mary & John Chapman sign the absd. Power of Attorney.

Pg 525. 10 Jan1722. John Harrison, of Perth Amboy, Middlesex Co., Gent., and Elizabeth, his wife, sell to David Jamison, Esqr., of NY City, for £191, 18 shillings, 3 pence, 3 farthings for one half of a tr. of land in Perth Amboy, betw. the 4 old houses and Thomas Warne's 19 a. lot, being 36 a., wch. form. belonged to Andrew Hamilton, Esqr., and by him by his will was devised to his wife, Agnes Hamilton, who disposed of it by Indenture to absd. Harrison, on 11 Dec 1708. ALSO, a tr. of land in Perth Amboy of 18 a., beg. one chain from Raritan River and s. by the highway on the bank of sd. River, east by Thomas Rudyard's land, w. by William Dockwra's land & n. by the highway from the market place. ALSO, his estate Right to the lands and those as in the Patent to Thomas Warne, dated 10 May1688 that was lately bot. by sd. Harrison from sd. Warne. Now, upon the condition that if John Harrison shall pay unto sd. Jamison at or in the dwelling house of sd. Jamison in NY City, the sum of £191, 18 shillings, 3 pence, 3 farthings, on or bef. 1 May next, the sale shall be voided. AND, John Harrison toward the payments for former debts due by him to sd. Jamison, sd. Harrison did assign over to sd. Jamison two bonds under the hand of John Vanhorne, NY City, merchant, executed by Henry Harrison, both dated on 22 Sep 1721 be paid to sd. Jamison the sum of £200, payable to Henry Harrison, or attorney, for the payment of £100 bef. 1 May 1723, the other is in the penalty of £200 payable to Henry Harrison bef. 1 Mat 1724; wch. bonds had been assigned from Henry Harrison to sd. John Harrison for their full value [and the various payment arrangements continue]. Wits.: John Johnston, John Johnston, Junr. Signed: John Harrison, Elisa Harrison. Ackn.: 16 Apr 1724, John Harrison & Elizabeth, his wife, apprd. bef. John Parker, Esqr., Majesty's Council.

Pg 529. 27 Jun 1724. John Harrison, of Perth Amboy, Middlesex Co., East NJ, Esqr., is firmly bound unto David Jamison, of NY City, NY, Esqr., in the sum of £216. The condition of the above obligation is that the absd. Harrison shall pay unto sd. Jamison £108 on or bef. 1 July 1725, the absd. obligation to be void.

Wits.: Lewis Johnston, John Barclay, Signed: John Harrison. Ackn.: 3 Jul 1724, John Barclay apprd. bef. John Parker, Majesty's Council.

Pg 529. 18 Jan 1720. Phillip Picke, of Elizabeth Town, Essex Co., NJ, tailor, and Mary, his wife, sell to William Clark, of the afsd. place, tailor, for £120, for several tr. of land at the n.w. corner of the land of John Warren, late of sd. Elizabeth Town, dec'd, now in possession of Benjamin Ogden, and then several courses to the s.e. corner of land form. Benjamin Ogden's now is possession of Thomas Ogden, of afsd. town, then to the s.e. corner of lot form. belonging to Joseph Whitehead, late of Elizabeth Town, dec'd, then along sd. Whitehead's land now is possession of Richard Herriman to a highway, being 6 a. ; bnd. n. by Joseph Whitehead, of Durham, New England, dec'd, s. by land of Benjamin Ogden, w. by highway. ALSO, a small tr. at Great Neck, beg. by a small swamp and then several courses to beg., being 6 a.; bnd. w. by unsurveyed land, s. by Thomas Price, e. by unsurveyed land, n. by Richard Herriman and land of Stephen Herriman. ALSO, all of the good & Chattels of sd. Phillip Pike as mentioned and specified in a certain list attached. Wits.: Samuel Whitehead, Samuel Kenney. Signed: Phillip Picke, Mary Picke made her mark.

Attached **SCHEDULE**: One cow, 2 round tables, 13 chairs, 2 chest, 2 feather beds, 2 bedsteds, 2 sets of curtains, 5 coverlets, 2 blankets, 9 sheets, 5 pillows, 2 bolsters, 2 iron kettles, 1brass kettle, 1 iron pot, 7 platters pewter, 6 pewter plates, 2 basons pewter, 3 porringers pewter, 12 spoons, 3 pewter pots, 2 tin pans, 12 earthen cups, 3 wooden bowls, 4 table cloths, 2 empty barrels, one half anker, 1 runlet, 1 pr. Tongs, 1 iron peal:, 1 box iron, 2 heaters, 1 pr. money scale, & 2 Bibles, 2 looking glasses, 1 Brish. 2 stands, 1 [?] pot, 4 men's coats, 3 vests, 8 pillow cases, 3 pr. breeches, 3 men's shirts, 4 pr. men's stockins and 2 men's hats, 4 wooden bowels, 1 stone jug, 4 glass bottles, 2 pr men's shoes, 1 pr. small bellows, 1 frying pan, 2 trammells, 1 brass candlestick and 2 iron candlesticks, 1 pressing iron, 1 pr. Taylor shears, 2 trunks, 3 napkins, 2 water pails. Ackn.: Essex Co., NJ - 14 Jan 1723, Samuel Whitehead apprd. bef. Joseph Bonnell, Judge, Essex Co.

Pg 533. 14 Sep 1716. Asa Gildersleeve, late of Long Island, now resident of Elizabeth Town, Essex Co., NJ, yeoman, sells to Sarah Simons, Hamptsed, Queens Co., Nassau Island, widow, for £70, for a tr. of land within Elizabeth Town, beg. at a tree and then running several courses to the beg., being 100 a.; bnd. n.e. & s.w. by land for a highway , s.e. by land of Joseph Woodruff, n.w. by land...151[?]. ALSO, a tr. by a crk. that then several courses to the beg., bnd. by a meadow form. of Capt. John Baker, dec'd, s. by Joseph Williams, of Elizabeth Town, w. by Benjamin Williams' meadow wch. was form. White's meadow, & n. by the crk that runs by the fence, being 4 a. Wits.: Will. Bradford, Senr., John Hyatt. Signed: Asa Gildersleeve. Ackn.: 1 Mar 1722/23, Asa Gildersleeve apprd. bef. Joseph Bonnell, Judge, Essex Co.

Pg 536. 23 Jul 1705. Robert Gordon, of Cluny, Scotland, Esqr., leases to Augustus Gordon, of London, Surgeon, for 5 shillings, for a half part of a full twenty-fourth part of land in America, in NJ, under transferring uses into possessions. Wits.: Richard Strachant Rutherford, Alex. Home, Gilbert Kurltowne[?]. Signed: Robert Gordon. Ackn.: 11 Aug 1705, Pat. Johnston, Wm. Hutchesone, bailie, Rob. Blackwood.

Pg 537. 24 Jul 1705. Robert Gordon, of Cluny, Scotland, Esqr., releases unto Augustus Gordon, of London, Surgeon, for a competent sum of money, now in his possession, the one-twenty-fourth part of land in East NJ. WHEREAS, Robert Gordon, late of Cluny, dec'd, grandfather of the sd. Robert Gordon, and father of the sd. Augustine Gordon, was at the time of his death seized of a one-twenty-fourth part of land in East NJ, wch. land at the time of the death of the sd. Robert Gordon, the grandfather, dec'd to Robert Gordon, his eldest son & heir and father of the sd. Robert Gordon, party to these Presents, and at the death of the sd. Robert Gordon, the father, descended to the sd. Robert Gordon of these Presents, as Eldest son & heir. Wits.: Richard Strachant Rutherford, Alex. Home, Gilbert Kurltowne[?]. Signed: Robert Gordon. Ackn.: 11 Aug 1705, Pat. Johnston, Wm. Hutchesone, bailie, Rob. Blackwood.

Pg 540. 2 Oct 1705. Augustine Gordon, of London, Surgeon, leases to John Burnet, citizen & grocer, of London, for 5 shillings, for a half part of a full twenty-fourth part of land in America, in NJ, under transferring uses into possessions. Wits.: J.B. Peters, attorney, J. Parsett, clerk. Signed: Augustin Gordon.

Pg 541. 3 Oct 1705. Augustine Gordon, of London, Surgeon, releases to John Burnet, citizen & grocer, of London, for a competent sum of money, for a half part of a full twenty-fourth part of land in America, in NJ, now in his possession, under transferring uses into possessions, land that descended from Robert Gordon, late of Cluny, dec'd, father of sd. Augustine, and at his father's death, descended unto Robert Gordon, his eldest son and elder brother, of sd. Augustine Gordon, and at the death of Robert, the eldest son, descended to his Eldest son, Robert Gordon, now of Cluny, Esqr., nephew of sd. Augustine Gordon, and the land is free & clear whatsoever by sd. Augustine Gordon, of Robert Gordon his father, Robert Gordon his eldest brother, and Robert Gordon, his nephew. AND, further, it is agreed that John Burnet shall have for his own use 500 a. of the absd. land and the sd. Augustine Gordon shall have liberty to any unchosen tr. for 500 a. and the rest of the land to be divided up into equal lots and drawn by a disinterested person to be named from time to time by sd. Burnet and sd Augustine, and the first lot drawn to be for sd. Burnet an the next lot for sd. Gordon until the whole residue of the one half of a Propriety to be used up. Wits.: J.B. Peters, attorney, J. Parsett, clerk. Signed: Augustin Gordon. Ackn.: 3 Oct 1705, [rest cannot be read] 23 Jan 1722 bef. [FNU] Jackson.

Pg 546. 6 Jun 1706. Augustine Gordon, of London, Surgeon, leases to John Burnett, citizen & grocer, of London, for 5 shillings, for one half of a one forty-eighth part land of East NJ, including that is now or at anytime heretofore the last day of June 1685 that is growing on or belonging to the sd. premises, by transferring uses into possessions. Wits.: J.B. Peters, J. Parsett. Signed: Augustine Gordon.

Pg 547. 7 Jun 1706. Augustine Gordon, of London, Surgeon, releases to John Burnett, citizen & grocer, of London, for a competent sum of money, for one half of a one forty-eighth part land of East NJ, and assigns the aforementioned property over to John Burnet. Wits.: J.B. Peters, J. Parsett. Signed: Augustine Gordon. Ackn.: 7 Jun 1706, John Burnet paid the consideration money to afsd. Gordon. And, on 23 Jan 1722, Aaron Pritchard, citizen and turner, of London, and Martha Peters, of London, widow, apprd. bef. the Mayor of London, and both testified that Aaron Pritchard was acquainted with John Baptest Peters & John Parsett, the two absd. witnesses.

Pg 551. 20 Sep 1711. Robert Gordon, of Cluny, in Scotland, Esqr., son & heir of Robert Gordon, late of Cluny, dec'd, leases to John Burnet, of London, citizen & grocer, for 5 shillings, one half of a one forty-eighth part land of East NJ, for transferring uses into possessions. Wits.: Pat. Grant, Ja. Cheyne, Alexander Forbes, Wm. Black. Signed: Robert Gordon.

Pg 552. 21 Sep 1711. Robert Gordon, of Cluny, of Scotland, Esqr., son of Robert Gordon, late of Cluny, dec'd, leases and releases unto John Burnet, citizen and grocer, of London, a one forty-eighth part land of East NJ, to all the lands set-out, dated 23 & 24 Jul 1705, granted unto Augustine Gordon, of London, surgeon, and sd. Augustine did by lease & release of 2 Oct 1705, released unto John Burnet one half of the moiety. ALSO, by a lease & release of 6 & 7 of June 1706 confirmed unto sd. Burnet the other half of the moiety. AND, when this was done, by sd. Augustine, the sd. Robert Gordon of these Presents was under the "age of one and twenty years," wch. means the lease & release by sd. Robert Gordon to sd. Augustine Gordon was invalid and sd. Augustine's had no such Right. AND, WHEREAS, Kenneth Gordon at the request of sd. Robert Gordon did agree to with sd. Augustine Gordon that the sd. Robert Gordon should as soon as he attained the age of 21, make & execute a legal conveyance to sd. Augustine Gordon, and is doing so by this deed directly to sd. Burnet. Wits.: Pat. Grant, Ja. Cheyne, Alexander Forbes, Wm. Black. Signed: Robert Gordon. Edinburgh, Scotland – 20 Sep 1711, Robert Gordon apprd. and signed a lease and a release of 21 Sep 1711 to John Burnet bef: Tho. Houton, Tho. Dick, Wm. Carmuchull, Justices. Wits: Ja. Cheyne.

Pg 555. 2 Jul 1723. William Vilant, of Philadelphia, PA, goldsmith, son and heir of David Vilant, late of East NJ, merchant, dec'd, leases to Andrew

Hamilton, of Philadelphia, PA, Gent., and George Willocks, late of Perth Amboy, NJ, but now of Philadelphia, Gent., for 5 shillings, for a one-tenth part of a one-forty-eighth part of NJ; excep. one half lot at South River sold by sd. David Vilant to Mary Lowrie and one other half lot reserved unto sd. William Vilant, wch. were David Vilant's first Division of 10,000 a. to be laid out for each Propriety. Wits.: Thos. Hukells, Peter Feurt. Signed: William Vilant. Ackn.: 7 Oct 1723, William Vilant apprd. bef. John Hamilton, Esqr., Majesty's Council.

Pg 557. 3 Jul 1723. William Vilant, of Philadelphia, PA, goldsmith, son and heir of David Vilant, late of East NJ, merchant, dec'd, sells to Andrew Hamilton, of Philadelphia, PA, Gent., and George Willocks, late of Perth Amboy, NJ, but now of Philadelphia, Gent., for a competent sum all the one-tenth part of a one forty-eighth of East NJ; excep. those items below. WITNESSETH, David Mudie, dec'd, merchant, of Perth Amboy, East NJ in America, for £65, sold to David Vilant a one-tenth part of a one forty-eighth of East NJ. ALSO, for the half part of sd. Mudie's lot in Wickatunck granted to him in two Patents, dated 13 Aug 1686 and 1 Sep 1686 and was signed over to sd. Vilant on 19 Sep 1686. AND, sd. Vilant sold the half lot at South River to Mary Lowrie, dec'd, widow, of Gawen Lawrie, form. Gov. of East NJ, by deed dated 25 Oct 1688. Wits.: Thos. Hukells, Peter Feurt. Signed: William Vilant. Ackn.: 7 Oct 1723, William Vilant apprd. bef. John Hamilton, Esqr., Majesty's Council.

Pg 560. 5 Feb 1715/16. [Can't read faded in spots] John Bowne, of Middletown, Monmouth Co., NJ, is bound to Mr. Richard Hartshorne and William Lawrence, Senr., for £5,260, to be paid to the sd. William Lawrence, Senr., and Richard Hartshorne but to the only use of sd. John Bowne's wife, Francis & John Bowne, Anne Bowne, & Lydia Bowne, son and daughters of Obadiah Bowne and Richard Saltar, William Saltar, Ebenezer Saltar, Deborah Saltar, James Saltar and Oliver Saltar, the children of Captain Richard Saltar and Margaret Hartshorne, Richard Hartshorne and William Hartshorne, the children of William Hartshorne. AND, Thomas Taylor, James Bowne, Samuel Willet, their heirs, Exec., Admin., or assigns to the amount I do bind myself by these Presents. Signed & sealed this 5 Feb 1715/16.

The Condition of the obligation of the bound John Bowne is to be used and truly paid to Francis Bowne the full sum of £45 a year and every year during her natural life at the dwelling house of Richard Hartshorne or William Lawrence, Senr. and pay or cause to be paid to John Bowne, son of Obadiah Bowne, the full sum of £400 when he shall be 21 and a half, and to Anne and Lydia Bowne £200 to each when 18, and to Richard Saltar, William Saltar, Ebenezer Saltar, Deborah Saltar, James Saltar and Oliver Salter £125 to each of them when 21 for the boys and the girls when they are 18. ALSO, to pay to Richard Hartshorne and William Lawrence, Senr., the sum of £60 a year for 3 years to

commence at such time as the sd. Hartshorne and Lawrence shall think fit to be
employed in schooling & education for the afsd. Anne & Lydia Bowne,
Margaret Hartshorne, and Deborah Saltar. ALSO, to pay discharge to absd.
Richard Hartshorne, Margaret Hartshorne and William Hartshorne, the children
of afsd. William Hartshorne £150 to each of them and to the boys when they
shall first be at age 21 and to the girls at age 18. AND, that my Negro Jack
serve his mistress the afsd. Frances Bowne for the space of 2 years to
commence at such time that sd. Hartshorne & Lawrence shall think fit and she
does not require his servitude and sd. Thomas Taylor, James Bowne and Samuel
Willet to have their debts & obligations discharged and given them wherein they
stand bound to me at the signing of this bond all wch. sums I grant and dispose
in manner afsd. for and in consideration as well as services of same as of the
natural love and affection I beare to others of the persons above named and upon
the performance of every of the above articles in the above condition then the
above obligation to be null and void but in case of failure or negligence in all,
any or any one of the afsd payments or aquittances then the whole obligation
absd. to stand and remain in full force.& virtue. Wits.: Joseph Dennis, John
Saltar. Signed: John Bowne. Ackn.: 3 May 1716, Obadiah Bowne & Richard
Saltar apprd. bef. John Reid., Judge, Monmouth Co.

Pg 562. 30 Mar 1704. Martin Beekman, of Palea Haywarin [?[, Middlesex Co.,
NJ, blacksmith, and Heecke[?], his wife, sell to Gabriel LeBoytoulx, for £71, for
a tr. of land of 55 a.; bnd. e. by land form. of Benjamin Hull, s. by Raritan River,
w. by La Flore alias [???]pial's land, and n. by Common land. Wits.: John
Royse, Thomas Grubb, Robert Woogsa[?]. Signed: Martin Beakman, Noocka
Beekman. Ackn.: 7 Sep 1724, John Barclay and Samuel Royse, Gent., both of
Perth Amboy, Middlesex CO., apprd. bef. John Parker, Majesty's Council, and
declared that they were well acquainted with the handwriting of John Royse and
believe it is his handwriting on the above document.

Pg 564. NY City – October 1708. Josias Morlet, of NJ, yeoman, gives,
confirms and grants unto William Waldren, of NY City, NY, for the "love &
affection he beareth unto his present wife Rebecca" has given afsd. Waldren all
those tr. of land, etc. as mentioned below to and for the sole & proper use &
behoof of the sd. Rebecca Merlot and her heirs forever. WHEREAS, Stephen
Kent by a deed, dated 21 Aug 1696, sold unto Josias Morlett and Abraham
Lentine sundry parcels of land and meadow and swamp divided and to be
divided in Woodbridge Twp, Middlesex Co., NJ, of wch. they were seized and
possessed and wch. sd. Lentine died whereby the Right in the property & the
premises lawfully devolved unto afsd. Josias Morlet, the survivor. Wits.: Joseph
Waldron, Gerredt Degraw, Wappein Van De Water. Signed: Josyas Morlet.
Ackn.: 1 Jul 1724, Gerret Degraw & William Van De Water apprd. bef. James
Alexander, Majesty's Council.

END OF BOOK C-2

Book D-2 – East New Jersey Land Records 1722-1727

Earliest Dated Deed – 1685
Also, contains birth dates and circumcision record of two brothers, a full detailed deed map in 1722 showing adjoining lands, roads and homes & names of the land owners; a 1691 pre-nuptial agreement; and a West NJ deed.

Pg 1. 8 May 1706. Thomas Codrington, of NY City, NY, Gent., and Margaret, his wife, sell to Phillip French, of the afsd. place, Gent., for 1,600, for all the contiguous tracts mentioned below amounting to 2,754 a. WHEREAS, the Proprietors of East NJ, by a deed dated 28 Feb 1683 sold unto sd. Codrington, then a merchant in NY, for the a competent sum, 877 a. at a place called Raritan on the n. side of the Raritan River, Middlesex Co., East NJ, lately surveyed unto him by Warrant, beg. at a tree by sd. River and the corner of John Royse, and then along sd. River to a bank of upland , and then into the woods by a line of marked trees that divide it from Captain John Palmer's land, and then to the line of sd. Royse and by the sd. River; bnd. s. by the commons or hills, e. by sd. Royse, being 877 a. but with allowance of 41a. for highways. AND, WHEREAS, by another Indenture dated on the same date as above unto John Royse, then known as John Royse of NY, merchant, and for the same amount of land at Raritan, beg. to the w. of the middle brook and then several courses to the beg; bnd. s. by sd. River, w. by land of Thomas Codrington, n. by hills, and e. by land laid out for the Proprietors being meadow and upland of 877 a. and Royse to have 836 a. AND, WHEREAS, sd. Royse on 13 Aug 1685, by an Indenture and an Indenture dated the day bef., for £420, from Captain Thomas Codrington, of Raritan, on Raritan River, in Middlesex Co., East NJ, Esqr., sold all the land or plantation of the deed dated 28 Feb 1683 unto sd. Royse. AND, WHEREAS, the Proprietors by an Indenture, dated 14 May 1688 sold to Captain Codrington, of Raritan, Middlesex Co., East NJ, another part of the land at the rear of his other land on the Raritan, being 1,000 a., by the foot of the Blue Hills at the n.e. corner of the land sd. Codrington bot. from sd. Royse
And over the hills one mile, and the several courses to the n.w. corner of sd. Codrington land bot. of Captain Palmer and the long the rear to the beg.; bnd. s. by his own land and all other sides by unappropriated land. Wits.: Welford

Webbster made his mark, Lydia Leventhorp, George Homes made his mark.
Signed: Thomas Codrington, Margaret Codrington. Ackn.: 15 May 1706,
Thomas Codrington gave to the within sd. Philip French by the personal
ceremony of "Turf and Twigg" in the name of the whole. Wits.: John Viett,
John Field, made his mark. Signed: Peter Dumont. AND, on 4 Mar 1722,
Lydia Vernon, late Lydia Leventhorp, apprd. bef. Cornelius Van Horne, Esqr.,
Judge, Somerset Co., and stated that she saw Thomas Codrington and his wife,
Margaret, sign & seal the document.

Pg 6. 13 Feb 1721. Barbadoes. William Foster [Forster], of St. Michael, on the
Island of Barbadoes, appointed Mary Forster, in Perth Amboy, Middlesex Co.,
East NJ, spinster, his true and lawful attorney in his name and to do whatever is
necessary in his name. Wits.: Samll. Bourdet, Junr. Signed: Wm. Forster.
Ackn.: 31 May 1722. Samuel Bourdet, Junr. apprd. bef. John Parker, Majesty's
Council.

Pg 7. 20 Nov 1722. Cornelius Van Horne, of NY City, NY, merchant, and
Elizabeth, his wife, of one part & Joseph Reade, of the afsd. place, merchant,
and Anne, his wife, of the other part are involved with [the three tr. of land as
found in the absd. deed – Page 1, from Thomas Codrington to Philip French.]
wherein sd. Codrington sold to sd. French all three tr. of land amounting to
2,754 a. in Raritan, Middlesex Co., East NJ. AND, WHEREAS, sd. French by
his will, dated 29 May 1706, bequeathed unto his three daughters, Elizabeth,
Anne & Margaret all his sd. lands and estate at Rariton lately bot. from sd.
Codrington, and in case any of his sd. dau. should die bef. 18 years old or to be
married, then the legacy of sd. child shall belong to the surviving child or
children in equal shares. AND, WHEREAS, Margaret, the youngest dau. of sd.
French died bef. reaching 18 years of age and bef. she was married, and
Elizabeth, the eldest dau. of sd. French married the afsd. Cornelius Van Horne,
and Anne, the second dau. of sd. French married the afsd. Joseph Reade, the
afsd. sd. Van Horne and Reade have Rights of their sd. wives and they became
jointly seized each of one half of all the three tr. of land being 2,754 a. AND,
Whereas, the parties think it convenient to partition all of the absd. land between
them, had the tr. surveyed by Alexander Mackdowell and Michael Van Vegten
and John Brokar in the presence of Adolph Philips and Philip French, men
elected and mutually chosen for the purpose to lay out in four lots in a survey
annexed, and each of the parties of these Presents may hold and enjoy each of
their half parts of the three absd. tr. of land. AND, sd. Joseph Reade & wife,
Anne, to have all the e. lot of land bot. by sd. Codrington from sd. Royse, beg.
at the mouth of middle crk. and then along the Raritan River and to include that
gore of land bot. by Madame French in her lifetime of Major Rudgers; bnd. by
middle crk., with Mr. French remitting on the condition that the sd. Brokar shall
enjoy for 10 or 12 years the meadow land wch. Madame French gave him leave
to fence in being 4 a. by the sd. River, and then several courses to a large stone
by sd. River for the boundary & partition betw. Joseph Reade and Cornelius Van

Horne afsd. and then several other courses. And, also a lot adjoining and behind the last mentioned lot. AND, sd. Reade and wife, Anne, his wife agree that sd. Van Horne and his wife, Elizabeth, shall have and enjoy the other half of the three tr. of land beg. at a large stone by the Raritan River and the partition stone to another stone in the orchard in the old division line betw. sd. Reade & Van Horne and then several courses to the n.e. corner of Mr. Van Vegten's land and along his line to sd. River and then to the beg. stone. ALSO, the lot adjoining and behind the last mentioned lot & part behind Michael Van Veghten's lot, being the w. half of the tr, of land. Wits.: Susanna French, Lringna Rasortsalin, Phillip French. Signed: Cor. Van Horne, Senr., Elizabeth Van Horne, Jos. Reade, Anne Reade. Ackn.: 8 Jan. 1722/3, Cornelius Van Horne , and Elizabeth, his wife, and Joseph Reade, and Anne, his wife, apprd. bef. Thomas Farmer, Judge, Somerset Co. [The map of the property division is drawn in the deed book showing the boundaries and the homes of Routa Van Horne, Michael Van Veghteen, and Thos. Church.]

Pg 15. 22 Feb 1721. Samuel Royse, of Perth Amboy, Middlesex Co., NJ, Gent., sells to John Van Horne, of NY City, NY, merchant, for a competent sum of money and all of the quit rents and unpaid quit rents to John Royse, as found due on the below mentioned tr. of land mentioned below, being in Somerset CO., NJ and sold by John Royse to several persons, and including those due on 330 a. sold by Samuel Royse to Annanias Allen. WHEREAS, the Proprietors conveyed by Patent, dated 16 Nov 1685, to John Royse, dec'd, by the name of John Royse of NY, merchant, father of the sd. Samuel Royse, a tr. of land on the s. side of Raritan River and n. on Millstone River, to be called Royse Field, beg. at a place called Hunter's Wigwam on Millstone River, then to a small brook called Manam Laqua , then to the sd. River and then to a spot at the w. end of an Island form. Robert Van Quillan's, then running as the Millstone runs to the beg., and minus two parcels of meadow supposed to be 250 a. being excepted, being 3,000 a. ALSO, the Proprietors confirmed unto sd. John Royse, dec'd, by the name of John Royse of East NJ, Gent., a tr. of land in East NJ, beg. at the w. end of a small island of meadow in the Raritan River heretofore laid out for Thomas Couper[?], merchant, one of the Proprietors, s. & w. in a line of three miles and 240 chains long from sd. island to the head of a brook in the n. of sd. tr. laid out for Clement Plumstead, merchant, and also a Proprietor, and then to Peack Brook as it runs into the sd. Millstone 3.5 miles and then down same into the Raritan River and then up sd. Raritan abt. 6.5 miles and it runs to the w. end of sd. Island. AND, ALSO, excep. two pieces of meadow on the s. Side of sd. Raritan form. granted to James Graham, John White, Samuel Winder and Cornelius Carsen, Gentlemen, dated 23 Sep 1690. AND, WHEREAS, John Royse, dec'd, in his lifetime granted several tr. reserving payments of rents unto his heirs; being John Robeson, dec'd, of NY City, merchant, by a deed, dated 17 Dec 1685, sd. John Royse, dec'd and also sell unto sd. Robeson a piece of land at Roysefield, beg. at a tree on the e. side of an Island of meadow in the Raritan River belonging unto sd. Robeson and then several courses, being 300 a. AND,

ALSO, John Royse, dec'd, sold on 14 Aug 1701, being John Royse, of Piscataqua, Middlesex Co., East NJ, Gent., to Derick Volkerse of Norman's Hills, Kings Co., NY on Nassau Island, NY, yeoman, a tr. of land in Somerset Co., East NJ, on the Millstone River, beg. at sd. River at the trees of Annanies Allen and then along his line to Royse Brook and then down same to the sd. Millstone and then to the beg., with sd. Volkerse to allow a road out of same next to sd. Allen down the river. AND, WHEREAS, John Royse by another deed dated14 Aug 1701, of Middlesex Co., sold to John Vortman, of the afsd. place, yeoman, a tr. of land beg. at a small brook by Millstone River and the several courses to the beg.; bnd. s. & w. by land of John Royse, n. by John Covert, e. by Covert's meadow and Vortman's meadow. ALSO, a piece of meadow and upland near the Millstone River; bnd. w. by his land, n. by Covert's meadow, and with both the upland & meadow being 1, 020 a. AND, WHEREAS, John Royse, of Piscataqua, Middlesex Co., Gent., sold to John Coverts, of the afsd. place, yeoman, for a tr. of land beg. near the edge of a meadow by the Millstone River and several courses to the beg.; n. by Bragoon Bragard's land, s. by John Vortman, w. by sd. Royse. ALSO, a piece of meadow by the sd. Millstone and up same to the edge of upland, and then along same to the beg., ; bnd. n. by sd. Bragard, e. by sd. Millstone, s. by Vortman's meadow, w. by Vortman, being all together upland & meadow, 512 a. AND, WHEREAS, John Royse sold to Clement Ellsworth, of NY City, shipwright, for a tr. of land in Somerset Co., East NJ, on 29 Jun 1702, beg. by Royse Brook and then several courses, being 200 a., bnd. s. by afsd. Bragard, n. by afsd. Allen, w. by John Royse's land, e. by Royse Brook. AND, WHEREAS, John Royse on 3 Mar 172, sold to Ketlyeu Broeckaer, the relict of Bargoon Broeckaer, of Somerset Co., a tr. of land in Somerset Co., beg. by the Millstone River and near a great hallow and then to the edge of a meadow and to the beg.; bnd. n. by Derick Volkerse and John Royse, w. by land of Royse, s. by land of John Coverts. ALSO, a piece of meadow adjoining the tr., bnd. e. by sd. Millstone, n. by meadow of Volkerse, w. by absd. land, and John Coverts, s. by meadow of Coverts, in all being 612 a. AND, WHEREAS, John Royse, on 9 Nov 1701, sold to Edward Drinkwater, of Somerset Co,., East NJ (since dec'd), a tr. of land in Somerset Co., being 200 a., beg. by the w. bank of Peter's Brook and then along the hillside to a gully, and then back to the sd. brook and then over it to the beg. AND, WHEREAS, John Royse sold to Annanias Allen, of Somerset Co., East NJ, by deed dated 30 Sep 1704, land in Somerset Co., being 100 a., beg. near the gully on the Millstone River being a corner of Derick Volkerse, then to the sd. River and then down same to the beg. AND, WHEREAS, Samuel Royse, by a deed, dated 7 Jun 1718, sold to Annanias Allen, of Somerset Co., for 10 shillings, for a tr. of land at Royse Field, Somerset Co., beg. on the w. side of Royse's Brook at the lower corner of Clemem Elsworth's land on sd. Brook and then along his line to Van Veghten's line to the sd. Brook and along same to the beg., being 330 a. Wits.: Geo. Leslie, Benja. Harrison, Elisa Harrison. Signed: Samll. Royse. Ackn.: 21 Mar 1723, Samuel Royse apprd. bef. William Eier, Mayor, Perth Amboy.

Pg 24. 12 Apr 1722. Robert Combs, of Woodbridge, Middlesex Co., NJ, planter sells to John Van Horn, of NY City, merchant, for £64, for a tr. of land in Woodbridge, being 120 a., being one half of land granted by the Proprietors to Thomas Blomfield, Senr., late of Woodbridge, dec'd, by a Patent, wch. land is on the w. side, beg. at the s. corner of the sd. farm, being half way on the line of the whole farm, and then several courses to a stake in the s. line in the middle betw. the first corner and the s. corner, then to the west line of the farm to the beg.; bnd. w. by Thomas Pursell and George Morris farms, n. by land lately laid out in Fourth Division lots., e. by the remaining part of the farm, and s. by the land in common. Wits.: Martha Thomson, Moses Rolfe. Signed: Robert Combs made his mark. Ackn.: 12 Apr 1722, Robert Combs apprd. bef. John Parker, Majesty's Council and acknowledged that the contents of the within mortgage was his voluntary act.

Pg 25. 30 Jul 1716. Sir Evan, alias Eugenius Cameron, of Lochiel, Scotland, Knight, gives and confirms unto sd. Donald Cameron, younger, of Lochiel, grandson of sd. Sir Evan Cameron, for the love and affection he bears unto sd. Donald Cameron, a parcel of land being thirteen-fortieths of a twenty-fourth part bot. from Thomas Cox, of London, Gent., on 2 & 3 Apr 1685, with Patent from the Proprietors of East NJ, dated 24 May 1690. Wits.: Major Donald Cameron, of Lieutenant Gen'l & Murray, his Regiment, Robert Mackey, vintner, of Carondale, John Cameron, Sewiter[?] to Sir Evan, and Alexander Cuming, notary in Lochaber, Dunblain – 24 Oct 1721, Alexander Cuming apprd. bef. John Finlayson, of Dunblain. Ackn.: 17 Nov 1721, Alexander Home & John Din, Notaries of Edinburgh, apprd. bef. Jo. Drummond, Jo. Drummond, M.D., Ed. Drummond. It was also signed by Jo: Wightman, Provost, Arch. Mc Stantony, baylie, Js. Drummond, baylie, O. Rindesay, bailie.

Pg 27. 17 Nov 1721. Donald Cameron, of Lochiel, Scotland releases and confirms unto Evan Drummond, of Glasgow, merchant, for a competent sum of money, thirteen-fortieths of a twenty-fourth of a tr. of land in America in East NJ, wch. sd. Cameron had Right by a deed, dated 2 & 3 Apr 1685 from Thomas Cox, of London, and by a Patent, dated 24 May 1690. Wits.: John Din, Alexa. Home. Signed: Donald Cameron. Ackn.: 17 Nov 1721, Donald Cameron apprd. bef. Jo: Wightman, Provost, Arch. Mc Stantony, baylie, Js. Drummond, baylie, O. Rindesay, bailie.

Pg 29. 2 Apr 1685. Thomas Cox, of London, Gent., leases to Sir Eugenius Cameron, of Lochiel, Scotland, Knight, for 5 shillings, for thirteen-fortieths of a twenty-fourth, [being the land in the absd. deed – Page 25]. Wits.: Dally Thomas, Charles Cox, Mathew Forrest, Henry Mills signed at Garway's Coffee House. 30 Nov 1719 – Edinburgh, Scotland - Wm. Wilson & George Aedie, Notaries, signed same bef. Ja. Taylor, Evan Drummond, John Taylor, John

Cameron, John Watt. 1 Dec 1719, Jo. Campbell, Robert Wightman, James Laing, James Newland signed same.

Pg 30. 3 Apr 1685. Thomas Cox, of London, Gent., releases and confirms unto Sir Eugenius Cameron, of Lochiel, Scotland, Knight, land already in his possession, by transferring uses into possessions, thirteen-fortieths of a twenty-fourth, [being the land in the absd. deed – Page 25] in East New Jersey, in America. 1719 – Edinburgh, Scotland - Wm. Wilson & George Aedie, Notaries, signed same bef. Ja. Taylor, Evan Drummond, John Taylor, John Cameron, John Watt. 1 Dec 1719, Jo. Campbell, Robert Wightman, James Laing, James Newland signed same.

Pg 33. 17 Jul 1722. Evan Drummond, of Glasgow, merchant, leases to James Alexander, of NY, Gent., for 5 shillings, for one-fourth of all lands heretofore at any time Patented & one-half of all the lands remaining & hereafter to be taken up & surveyed pertaining to the thirteen-fortieths of a twenty-fourth part of land [in the absd. deeds] in East NJ for one year, under transferring uses into possessions. Wits.: Thos. Jackman, Isaac Stucky. Signed: Evan Drummond. Ackn.: 26 Jun 1723, Evan Drummond apprd. bef. David Lyell, Esqr.

Pg 34. 18 Jul 1722. Evan Drummond, of Glasgow, merchant, releases to James Alexander, of NY, Gent., for a competent sum of money, for one-fourth of all lands heretofore at any time Patented & one-half of all the lands remaining & hereafter to be taken up & surveyed pertaining to the thirteen-fortieths of a twenty-fourth part of land [in the absd. deeds and repeats the prior deeds as it came down to sd. Drummond] in East NJ for one year, under transferring uses into possessions. Wits.: Thos. Jackman, Isaac Stucky. Signed: Evan Drummond. Ackn.: 26 Jun 1723, Evan Drummond apprd. bef. David Lyell, Esqr.

Pg 35. 5 Apr 1723. Evan Drummond, of Glasgow, merchant, leases to James Alexander, of NY, Gent., for 5 shillings, for the remaining one-half (one-half being heretofore sold by sd. Drummond to sd. Alexander by deeds of the 17th & 18th of July last of all the remaining lands to be taken up & surveyed pertaining to the thirteen-fortieths of a twenty-fourth part of land. AND, Drummond assigns unto sd. Alexander three-fourths (the other one-fourth already belonging to the sd. James Alexander by deeds from sd. Drummond, for a lot lying in Perth Amboy on the n. side of the Church there lately built; bnd. e. by Water Street, s. by the lot form. of David Mudie, w. by High Street, n. by the lot form. of Andrew Galloway. AND, to have the other remaining one-half together with the lot in Perth Amboy for one year. Wits.: Thos. Jackman, Isaac Stucky. Signed: Evan Drummond. Ackn.: 26 Jun 1723, Evan Drummond apprd. bef. David Lyell, Esqr.

Pg 36. 6 Apr 1723. Evan Drummond, of Glasgow, merchant, releases to James Alexander, of NY, Gent., for a competent sum of money, for the land [in the absd. deeds and repeats the prior deeds as it came down to sd. Drummond] in East NJ for one year, under transferring uses into possessions. Wits.: Thos. Jackman, Isaac Stucky. Signed: Evan Drummond. Ackn.: 26 Jun 1723, Evan Drummond apprd. bef. David Lyell, Esqr.

Pg. 39. 10 May 1705. William Dockwra, of London, merchant, by his attorney Richard Saltar, of Freehold, Monmouth Co., NJ, and with the consent of Capt. Andrew Bowne and Mr. Richard Hartshorne, of the afsd. place, sells to Richard Davis and Thomas Pursell, both of Monmouth Co., NJ, yeomen, for 400 a. of land being one of the Raritan lots form. called Mathews lot called # 11; bnd. n. by Raritan River, n.w. by a lot form. called Richard Jones' lot, # 12 and on the rear by land since Patented to sd. Dockwra, and on s.e. side of sd. Dockwra's Patented lot, for all that tr. of land in Somerset Co., being abt. 900 a., beg. at the mouth of Login Brook, and several courses to the rear of Raritan lots and the land already sold by my attorney, Richard Saltar, till it comes to the Millstone River and then up same to the beg., being part of sd. Dockwra's 2,000 a. lot laid out on the sd. Millstone; bnd. n.w. by sd. Millstone, s.w. by land form. called Langford land, s.e. by Captain Harrison's land, & n.e. by Raritan lots and land sold by my attorney. Wits.: Andrew Bowne, John Stout. Signed: William Dockwra, by his attorney, Richard Saltar. Ackn.: [Can't read date.] Richard Saltar, form. attorney for William Dockwra, of London, merchant, apprd. bef. David Lyell, Esqr.

Pg 41. 20 Aug 1723. Daniel Hollinshead, of Somerset Co., NJ, merchant, sells to Major James Brown, of Rhode Island, for £, for a lot of land in Perth Amboy, being 1 chain by 10 chains; bnd. e. by Water Street, n. form. by George Willocks' lot, w. by High Street and S. by lot of Miles Forster, dec'd, wch. land was Patented to Thomas Barker. Wits.: Michll. Kearny, Thos. Jackman. Signed: Daniel Hollinshead. Ackn.: 21 Aug 1723, Daniel Hollinshead apprd. bef. John Parker, Majesty's Council.

Pg 42. 25 Feb 1722. James Alexander and Evan Drummond, both of NY, Gent., lease to Michael Kearny, of Perth Amboy, Middlesex Co., NJ, for 5 shillings, a lot of land in Perth Amboy on the s. side of the road to Piscataway, beg. at Robert Burnet's n. corner on the county road, and then numerous courses back to the beg.; bnd. e. by the road, s. by sd. Burnet, s.w. by Peter Sonmans, n.w. by John Johnston's land, n. by unappropriated land, being 8.33 a. Wits.: J. Kinsey, Alexr. Mackdowall. Signed: Ja. Alexander, Evan Drummond. Ackn.: 2 [ink blot] 1724, Evan Drummond apprd. bef. William Trent, Esqr., Chief Justice, NJ, and on 28 Apr 1724, James Alexander, Esqr., apprd. bef. William Trent, Esqr., Chief Justice, NJ.

Pg 43. 26 Feb 1722. James Alexander and Evan Drummond, both of NY, Gent., release to Michael Kearny, of Perth Amboy, Middlesex Co., NJ, for £32, 12 shillings, 6 pence, for land in his actual possession, under transferring uses into possessions, [for the land in the absd. deed – Page 42]. Wits.: J. Kinsey, Alexr. Mackdowall. Signed: Ja. Alexander, Evan Drummond. Ackn.: 2 May 1724, Evan Drummond apprd. bef. William Trent, Esqr., Chief Justice, NJ, and on 28 Apr 1724, James Alexander, Esqr., apprd. bef. William Trent, Esqr., Chief Justice, NJ.

Pg 45. 28 Mar 1724. John Barclay, of Perth Amboy, Middlesex Co., NJ, Gent., sells to Michael Kearny, for £10, for a lot of land in Perth Amboy, lately in the possession of Thomas Turnbuck, dec'd, being 9 chains by 1 chain; bnd. s. & n. by two streets, e. by a lot form. Patented to Patrick Murdock, and w. by a lot form. Patented to John Collens and in wch. Gilbert the bu[t]cher now lives. Wits.: Samuel Stone, William Thomson. Signed: John Barclay. Ackn.: 22 Apr 1724, John Barclay apprd. bef. William Trent, Esqr., Chief Justice, NJ.

Pg 47. 29 Apr 1723. Sir Gerrard Conyers, Knight, etc. of London, England, stated that Joseph Hewit, of London, Gent., came bef. them and under oath and testified that he had examined two copies of a Lease & Release made from Samuel Groome, Senr. to James Brain, Senr., and sd. Hewit stated that he was present and saw, James Brain, Senr. [Junr?], one of the sons of the James Brain, Senr., sign & seal the deed to James Brain, Junr., who also signed a Declaration of Trust for whose use & whith whose money he bot. the premises in the Lease & Release, and to and for the use of his father, Benjamin Brain. Signed: Jackson.

Pg 47. 21 Sep 1682. Samuel Groome, Senr., of the Parish of Stepney, County of Middlesex , [England], mariner, leases to James Brain, Senr., of the afsd. place, merchant, for 5 shillings, for one-half of a one-twelfth part of East NJ, in the possession of sd. Brain under transferring uses into possessions. WHEREAS, sd. Groome was seized of one-twelfth of East NJ in America, extending e. & n. along the coast and the Hudson River from the e. side of a harbor called Little Egg Harbor as shown on a map of the tr., and then several other courses of the tr. Wits.: Robt. West, Samuel Groom, Junr., Edmund Banister, Ben. Wetton. Signed: Samuel Groom, Senr.

Pg 48. 22 Sep 1682. Samuel Groom, Senr., of the Parish of Stepney, County of Middlesex , [England], mariner, releases to James Brain, Senr., of the afsd. place, merchant, for £350, for one-half of a one-twelfth part of East NJ, in the possession of sd. Brain under transferring uses into possessions. [Deed goes for 5 pages into the history the land from & with James, Duke of York beginning in 1664 lease & release dealing with John, Lord Berkley & Sir George Carteret, & William Penn, of Rickmansworth in County of Hertford, Esqr.; Gawen Lawery of London, merchant; Nicholas Lucas, of Hertford, County of Hertford; and

Edward Billing, of Westminster in County of Middlesex, Gent.; Edward, Earl of Sandwich; John Earl, of Bath; Thomas, Lord Crew, Bernard Greenwich, Esr.; Sir Robt. Atkins and Sir Edward Atkins, Thomas Cremer. Thomas Peacock, Elizabeth Carteret; William Penn of Warringhurst, County of Sussex, Esqr.; Thomas Rudyard, of London, Gent.; Thomas Hart, of Enfield, County of Middlesex, merchant; Richard Mew, of Stepney, merchant; Thomas Wilcox, of London, Goldsmith; Ambrose Rigg, of Gatton Place, of County of Surrey, Gent.; John Heywood, Citizen & skinner, of London; Hugh Hartshorne, Citizen & skinner, of London; Clement Plumstead, Citizen & skinner; until several of those named above became seized of the undivided one-twelfth part of the tr.] Wits.: Robt. West, Samuel Groom, Junr., Edmund Banister, Ben. Wetton. Signed: Samuel Groom, Senr.

Pg 53. 20 Mar 1713. James Brain, Senr., of Stepney Causey, in the Parish of Stepney at Stebunheath, County of Middlesex, [England], leases to James Brain, Junr., of Parish of St. John's Hackney, in sd. county, Gent., nephew of James Brain, Senr., for 5 shillings, for a one-third of one-half of the one-twelfth of East NJ, in America, being the part of land from Hudson River in a straight line over to the Delaware River and the to the n. point of the tr. now called the North Partition Point and then s. in a straight line to a point on the dividing line betw. East NJ and West NJ, now in his possession by transferring uses into possessions. Wits.: W. Martyn, [can't read]. Signed: James Brain.

Pg 54. 21 Mar 1718. James Brain, Senr., of Stepney Causey, in the Parish of Stepney at Stebunheath, County of Middlesex, [England], releases to James Brain, Junr., of Parish of St. John's Hackney, in sd. county, Gent., nephew of James Brain, Senr., for 33, 6 shillings, 8 pence, the land now in his possession all of the one-third part of the one-half of the one-twelfth of East NJ, in America. [This deed reviewed the entire history of the land from 1682 to the present as in the absd. deed – Page 48]. AND, WHEREAS, James Brain's indentures of Lease & Release by his last will, dated 1 Nov 1690, did devise unto his three sons, James Brain, Sr., a partly to this deed, John Brain and Benjamin Brain with each have one-third of the land. In East Jersey, in America. Wits.: W. Martyn, Jos. Hewit. Signed: James Brain.

Pg 60. 28 Jan 1722. James Brain, [Junr.]of Parish of _____, County of Essex, Gent., son and heir apparent of Benjamin Brain, of London, merchant, sells to Benjamin Brain. James Brain, Junr., part of the lease & release, by appointment by his father, the sd. Benjamin Brain and in Trust for him and the sd. £33, 6 shillings, 8 pence, paid unto James Brain, Senr., for the purchase, was the proper monies of the sd. father, Benjamin Brain, and therefore the sd. James Brain, Junr., in the Trust in him by his father and in consideration of 5 shillings confirms unto sd. Benjamin Brain the one-half of the one-twelfth of East NJ, in America. [WHEREAS, by the lease & release dated 20 & 21 Mar 1718 [the lease is dated by the writer 1713] as reported in the previous deeds.] Wits.: W. Martyn, Jos. Hewit. Signed: James Brain.

Pg 62. 1 Nov 1690. James Brain, of Parish of Stebbinheath alias Stepney, County of Middlesex, [England], merchant, being weak of body but of sound mind do make my will and give unto Elizabeth, my wife, those two house in Whitehart Court, in Grace Church Street, London, now in occupation of John Rust & John Hill, and also the house I now live in for the term of her natural life if my lease so long continue and the house in my own occupation to her and to her Exec. during the term of the lease by wch. I hold clear of ground rent during her life. I give unto my sd. (sic) all my household stuff, linen, woolen, brass, pewter, bedding, plate, and other of household stuff. I give unto Elizabeth my wife £100 to be paid by my Exec. in three months next after my decease. I give to my dau., Elizabeth Trigona, wife of Henry Trigona, mariner, the house she now lives in paying there out yearly to my son, Benjamin Brains, 20 shillings for ground rent, and also to her my house in Wapping now in occupation of Thomas Lawrence on the condition that yearly pay unto my son, John Brains, one moiety of ground rent of my estate in Wapping & upon further condition that in case she shall die bef. the expiration of several leases by wch. the house she now lives in on Brook Street and the house of the sd. Lawrence and all the houses shall accrue to all the children of sd. Elizabeth during the lease's terms. To my grandchildren – Henry, Trigona, Elizabeth Trigona, Mary Trigona, & Brains Trigona, the children of my dau. Elizabeth Trigona, £250 apiece to be paid to the sd. Henry & Brains at their respective ages of 21 years and unto sd. Elizabeth & Mary at their respective ages of 21 years or days of their marriages. I appoint my three sons – James Brains, John Brains, and Benjamin Brains as Exec. and the survivor of them as Trustee. To my niece Elizabeth Johnson and to her children the house she now lives in Brooks Street during the lease and she & they pay to my son, Benjamin, 20 shillings a year for ground rent. Unto my son, James, all my estate in Poplar Marshes during his life and after his decease unto the male heir of his body. I give one moiety unto to be equally divided among my daus. and one-quarter part to my grandson, Thomas Brains, son of my son, John and the other quarter to my grandson, James Brains, son of my son Benjamin Brains. Unto my son John Brains the house he lives in and to his Execs. to pay one moiety of his ground rent. To Benjamin, my son, my other fours houses in Brook Street now in occupation of John Harris, Mary Johnson, Samuel Bradley & Edward Payne. Unto my two friends, John Sellwood & William Saunders, £50. Unto my three sons – James, John & Benjamin each one-third of my houses, lands, etc wch. I have bot. in East NJ in America, and all the other goods, chattels, credits, shipping merchandise after funeral expenses are paid. [He then signed 3 sheets of paper of the will.] Wits.: Cuthbert Drew, Rowland Raine, Jos. Pidgeon. [There is a long paragraph in Latin.] Signed: Thos. Welham Reg. Dep.

Pg 64. 8 Aug 1722. James Dunnidge, notary, London, swore in the presence of witnesses that Benjamin Brains, of London, merchant appointed as his attorney, John Hamilton, of NJ, in America, and granting unto sd. Hamilton to take two-third parts of a twenty-fourth part of East NJ in America, and for him to act in his place to do all that is necessary to sell the sd. land. Wits.: Tho. Smith, Tho. Fitch. Signed: Benjamin Brain. Ackn.: Attested bef. Jabus Dunnidge, Notary Public. Ackn.: 28 Nov 1722, Thomas Smith apprd. bef. David Jamison, Esqr., Chief Justice, NJ, that he saw Benjamin Brain sign & seal same.

Pg 66. 22 Mar 1692. Robert Burnet, of Lethmtie, Scotland, Gent., leases to Robert Sandiland, son of dec'd James Sandiland, town clerk, of Aberdeen, Scotland, Gent., the below mentioned tr. of land for £56, 5 shillings. WHEREAS, Robert Burnet is seized of one-twenty-fourth of East NJ, in America, being the part of land from Hudson River to the Little Egg Harbour, and then to the Delaware River and the to the n. point of the tr. now called the North Partition Point and then s. in a straight line to a point on the dividing line betw. East NJ and West NJ and then s. to the sd. partition line. Wits.: Alexr. Gordon, Robert Burnet, George Black. Signed: Robert Burnet. Ackn.: None

Pg 67. 23 Mar 1692. Robert Burnet, of Lethmtie, Scotland, Gent., releases to Robert Sandiland, son of dec'd James Sandiland, town clerk, of Aberdeen, Scotland, Gent., for £56, 5 shillings, for a one –sixteenth of the one-twenty-fourth part of the tr. of land mentioned below, now in his possession by transferring uses into possessions. WHEREAS, John Haywood, citizen and skinner, of London, by deed dated _____ for a competent sum of money, release & confirmed one-twenty-fourth part of East NJ, unto sd. Robert Burnet. Wits.: Alexr. Gordon, Robert Burnet, George Black. Signed: Robert Burnet. Ackn.: London - 18 Mar 1723, admitted and sworn to bef. Thos. Ruck, Notary Public, dwelling in London., and sd. Ruck apprd. bef. Jabus & Isaac Delpeet. AND, on 18 Mar 1723, testimony to the absd. transaction was bef the Lord Mayor of London, Jackson.

Pg 71. 5 Jul 1712. Thomas Childs, of NY, inn-holder, and Elizabeth, his wife, sell to Elizabeth Jouet, of Elizabeth Town, Essex Co., NJ, shop keeper, for a competent sum of money for a lot of land & premises in Elizabeth Town, being 1.5 a. ; bnd. e. by Jonathan Clement, dec'd, s. by Elizabeth Town Creek of river, w. by Benjamin Ogden, Senr., and n. by a street or highway. Wits.: Joshua Hunlock, John Hendrick, Wm. Dixon. Signed: Tho. Child, Elizabeth Child made her mark. Ackn.: 22 May 1724, John Hendrick & William Dixon apprd. bef. Isaac Whitehead, Judge, Essex Co.

Pg 73. 25 Feb 1716. Elisha Parker, of Perth Amboy, Middlesex Co., NJ, merchant, sells to Jacob Buisas, of Piscataway, of the afsd. place, yeoman, for £300, for a tr. of land in Piscataway Twp., beg. at Samuel Dotie's n. corner, and then near to Ambrose Brook and then along same and several courses to the beg.; bnd. s. by William Clawson & John Cuthans lot on Raritan River, n.w. by John Smally, lot & part by unappropriated lands, n. by Amborse Brook, s. by Widow Grubb's and Art Arrison. Wits.: John French made his mark, [can't read the rest]. Signed: Elisa Parker. Ackn.: 27 Feb 1723/4. John Parker, eldest son of Elisha Parker, of Perth Amboy, Esqr., dec'd, Exec. of his last will, personally came bef. Adam Hude, Esqr., Judge, Middlesex Co., and stated that sometime bef. his father's death, he has understood and has heard that the within granted land & premises was sold by his sd. father, Elisha Parker, to Jacob Buisas and he very well knew his father's handwriting and believes his father signed same. AND, John Barclay, Gent., and Moses Rolph, Esqrs. also knew Elisha Parker's handwriting and swore it was his bef. Adam Hude. AND, further, John French apprd. and stated that at the signing through some omission did not sign the same but did sign his mark on the above as evidence it was signed by Elisha Parker, on 2 Mar 1723/4.

Pg 75. 25 Feb 1716. I, Elisha Parker, of Perth Amboy, Middlesex Co., NJ, merchant, am bound unto Jacob Buise, of Piscataway, Somerset Co., NJ, yeoman, for £20, on the Condition that Elisha Parker signed an instrument to convey a certain tr. of land in Piscataway Twp. AND, WHEREAS, Elizabeth, sd. Parker's wife doth refuse to sign and seal the conveyance now sd. Elisha Parker do indemnify and hold harmless the sd. Buise for any reason that may arise for the reason of the sd. Elizabeth, his wife, her not signing & sealing the afsd. instrument, then his present obligation to be void. Wits.: John Freench, Jno. Brown. Signed: Elisha Parker. Ackn.: 2 Mar 1723/4, John French apprd. bef. Adam Hude, Judge, Middlesex Co.

Pg 75. 20 Nov 1718. Henry Taylor, of Woodbridge, Middlesex Co., East NJ, turner, made his trusty friend William Elstone, of the afsd. place, turner, to be his attorney and to act in his place, and to do whatever is necessary to recover debts & sums of money from Benjamin Force, Abraham Everet, Peter Elstone Junr., Samuel Stone, Joseph Tharpe, all of Woodbridge. AND, also William Robeson & Jeffere, free Negro, of Elizabeth Town, Essex Co., NJ. ALSO, Samuel Smith Junr., of Woodbridge. Wits.: Moses Collins, John Bishop. Signed: Henry Taylor made his mark. Ackn.: 24 [G.hen?] 1718. Henry Taylor apprd. bef. John Bishop, Esqr., Majesty's Council.

Pg 76. 5 Nov 1717. Elias Abenaker, of London, merchant, aged 68 years or thereabouts and David De Morrais, of London, lapidary, aged 56 or thereabouts, jointly make Oath on the Holy Bible as follows: Aaron De Lozada & Moses De Lozada are the reputed sons of Jacob De Lozada, of London, merchant, and Rachel, his wife, and were both of them born in the Parish of St. James Duke place London on the several days following. That is to say, Aaron De Lozada was born on 17 May 1695 and the sd. Moses De Lozada was born on 5 Feb 1701. AND, further that these Deponents very well know the matters aforesaid because they were well acquainted with the family and were conversant with

Jacob De Lozada several years bef. the birth of the absd. subjects and were both present at the circumcision of the two sd. subjects. Signed: Elias Abenaker, David de Morray. Ackn.: 5 Nov 1717, Thomas Bockin, Notary, residing in London, certify and attest that the above in is in the proper handwriting of the Right Worshipful, Sir William Withers, Knight, Mayor of London, who placed them under Oath in my presence. Signed: Thos. Bocking, Notary Public. AND, on same date, Guil. Scorey and Edwd. Johnson, both Notaries, certified that absd. Bocking was a Notary. Same was registered on 28 Nov 1717 by Rob. Shaw. Entered in Custom House, London, [?] Dec 1717 by Nathaniel Fourter, clerk.

Pg 77. 15 Apr 1721. Roger Kennyon, of Precinct of Beaufort, Bath Co., NC, Gent., have appointed my good friend John Borrowes, of Piscatua, Middlesex Co., East NJ, merchant, to be my true and lawful attorney, to act in my name, to sell and set over all the lot or lots in Perth Amboy, East NJ, form. bot. from George Willocks and John Harrison, Esqr.. Wits.: Thos. Hier, James Savage. Signed: Roger Kenyon. Ackn.: 18 Dec 1724, James Savage apprd. bef. John Parker, Majesty's Council.

Pg 78. 17 Dec 1724. Josiah Ogden, of Newark, Essex Co., East NJ, am satisfied by & with Benjamin Shipman & John Ball, of the afsd. place, yeomen, for £2,15 shillings, and do release and confirm and by the Presents for me by a deed of conveyance, dated 20 Apr 1724, from James Alexander, Esqr., of NY, wch. granted me the Right of property in the unappropriated lands of East NJ & do now grant unto sd. Shipman & Ball, a certain Proprietary Right to 45 a. to be taken up & surveyed in the unappropriated lands of East NJ. Wits.: Wm. North, Robert Young. Signed: Jos. Ogden. Ackn.: 23 Dec 1724, Josiah Ogden apprd. bef. Samuel Alling, Judge, Essex Co., NJ. 29 Dec 1724, Returned 43.25 a on the within property – James Alexander, Surveyor General.

Pg 79. 11 Jun 1717. John Wall, of Middletown Twp., Monmouth Co., East NJ, yeoman, with the consent of his wife, Mary, sell to Elizabeth Stillwell, the now wife of Gershom Stillwell, of Moreland Maner, Philadelphia Co., PA, form. known by the name Elizabeth Grover, dau. of Joseph Grover, of Middletown afsd., for £300, for a tr. of land and meadow being the plantation on wch. the sd. John Wall now dwells being in Middletown, beg. on the brow of a small hill in the line that parts it from Jarat Wall's land and 20 rods from the brook that parts Daniel Hendrick's land and the tr., and then to Cornelius Dorues land, then along his line to the s.e. corner of sd. Dorues land and then to a small run of water from Dorues fresh meadow and down sd. run to sd. Hendrick's land and then to the beg. at the brook and bnd. of Daniel Hendrick and along his line; bnd. w. by Jarat Wall, n. by sd. Dorues and a small brook, e. by Thomas Smith and s. by sd. Hendricks' land, being 150 a., being part of land given 7 conveyed to sd. John Wall by deed from his father, Jarat Wall, dated 18 Jan 1709/10. AND, the other part was granted and sold to John Wall by his brother, Jarat

Wall, by deed dated 23 Mar 1715. Wits.: Walter Wall, Thos. Stillwell, Willm. Lawrence. Signed: John Wall, Mary Wall made her mark. Ackn.: 21 Jun 1718, John Wall apprd. bef. John Reid.

Pg 81. 28 Mar 1721. Richard Hartshorne and his wife, Margaret, of Middletown, Monmouth Co., East NJ, sell to John Mott, of the afsd. place, cooper, for £70, for a tr. of land in Middletown Twp., beg. at the n. corner of Richard Standly's land, dec'd, and then several courses to the e. corner of Standly's land and then along same to the beg; bnd. n.w. and n.e. by sd. John Mott, s.e. by John Brittain, s.w. by Richard Standly, being 35 a. , and wch. land was granted to sd. Hartshorne by deed from Modecay Gibbons and Rebecca, his wife, dated 4 Dec 1706 and granted by Patent dated 10 Feb 1676. Wits.: Daniel Tilton, John Morris, Saml. Leonard. Signed: Richard Hartshorne, Margaret Hartshorne. Ackn.: 15 Feb 1721/2, Daniel Tilton apprd. bef. James Hubbard, Judge, Monmouth Co.

Pg 82. 4 Dec 1706. Mordicay Gibbons and Rebecca, his wife, , of Middletown, Monmouth Co., East NJ, sell to Richard Hartshorne, of the afsd. place, for £24, for a tr. of land [in the absd. deed – Page 81] being in Middletown on both sides of Posisse Run, beg. in a swamp at the foot of a hill and then several courses back to the beg.; bnd. round by land of Mordicai Gibbons, John Vanhorn, land unsurveyed, Richard Hartshorne, William Jobes[?], and John Cox, being 120 a., wch. land was granted by Patent 10 Feb 1676. Wits.: John Cox, Elias Hamell. Signed: Mordciai Gibbins, Rebecca Gibbins made her mark. Ackn.: 15 Feb 1722, Mordicai Gibbons apprd. bef. James Hubbard, Judge, Monmouth Co.

Pg 84. 17 Aug 1724. John Johnstone, of Perth Amboy, Middlesex Co., East NJ, Esqr., sells to William Lawrence, Junr., of Middletown, Monmouth Co., East NJ, trader, for £40, for a lot of land in Perth Amboy being in length betw. Water Street and low water mark by 66 feet; bnd. e. by low water mark, s. by David Lyell's lot, w. by Water Street, n. by George Willocks, wch. trader lot of land was granted to sd. Johnstone by deed from sd. Willocks, dated 12 Aug 1702. Wits.: John Johnston, Junr., Lewis Johnston. Signed: John Johnston. Ackn.: 17 Aug 1724, John Johnston apprd. bef. John Johnston, Junr., Majesty's Council.

Pg 85. 13 Sep 1722. Elisha Lawrence of Freehold Twp., Monmouth Co., East NJ, yeoman, sells to James Lawrence, of the afsd. place, yeoman, for £17, 10 shillings, for a Right of 120 a. to be taken up and surveyed in the unappropriated lands of East NJ, being in the Right of the Second Dividend land of John Bowne, cordwainer, to Joseph Smith, by deed dated 4 Sep 1713 & was conveyed by sd. Smith to Nicholas Wineright by deed dated 14 Aug 1714, and was conveyed by sd. Wineright to Joseph Lawrence, of Manasquan, in the afsd. place,, and was then conveyed to Elisha Lawrence. AND, sd. the Right for 120 a. of unappropriated land to be taken up in the Right of the Second Dividend of land to John Bowne's share, cordwainer, of Robert Turner's Propriety. John

Saltar, William Saltar, Deborah Saltar. Signed: Elisha Lawrence. 13 Sep 1722, Elisha Lawrence apprd. bef. Richard Saltar, Judge, Monmouth Co.

Pg 86. 1 Apr 1719. Joseph Lawrence, of Manasquan, in Shrewsbury Twp., Monmouth Co., East NJ, yeoman, sells to Elisha Lawrence, of Freehold, of the afsd. place, for £17, 10 shillings, for for a Right to 120 a. to be taken up & surveyed in the unappropriated lands of East NJ, in the Right of the Second Dividend land of John Bowne, cordwainer, and was conveyed by John Bowne to Joseph Smith, by deed dated 4 Sep 1713, and was conveyed by sd. Smith to Nicholas Wainwright by deed dated 14 Aug 1714 and then by him to Joseph Lawrence, by deed, dated 11 Mar 1718. Wits.: Elisha Lawrence, Alexander Ross, Thomas Cu[?]inggame, who made his mark. Signed: Joseph Lawrence. Ackn.: 17 Nov 1724, Thomas Cu[?]inggame and Elias Lawrence apprd. bef. Richard Saltar, Justice. Land was surveyed by Ja. Alexander, Surveyor General.

Pg 88. 19 Sep 1724. Josiah Ogden, of Essex Co., East NJ, sells to Hugh Roberts, of the afsd. place, for a sum of money, for 100 a. of land to be taken up & surveyed in the unappropriated lands of East NJ, being part of land of James Alexander, Esqr., of 500 a. by deed dated10 Apr last. Wits.: Saml. Alling, David Ogden. Signed: Jos. Ogden. Ackn.: 26 Oct 1724, Josiah Ogden apprd. bef. Samuel Alling, Judge, Essex Co. 4 Dec 1724, Returned 94.4 a. & 4.75 a. to Hugh Roberts, Ja,. Alexander, Surveyor General.

Pg 89. 22 Feb 1724. James Alexander, of NY City leases to Evan Drummond, late of Glasgow, North Brittain, merchant, for 5 shillings, 383 a. of land, being part of the Second Addition to the Second Dividend of the unappropriated lands of East NJ, and being thirteen-fourtieths parts of a Propriety form. of Sir Eugenius Cameron, of Lothiel. Wits.: David Lyell, [FNU] Kearny, John Barclay, William Thomson. Ackn.: 25 Feb 1724/5, James Alexander apprd. bef. David Lyell, Majesty's Council.

Pg 90. 23 Feb 1724. James Alexander, of NY City releases unto Evan Drummond, late of Glasgow, North Brittain, merchant, [regarding the land described in the absd. deed – Page 89], for £134[?] , for 383 a. under transferring uses into possessions. Wits.: David Lyell, [FNU] Kearny, John Barclay, William Thomson. Ackn.: 25 Feb 1724/5., James Alexander apprd. bef. David Lyell, Majesty's Council.

Pg 91. 4 Mar 1719. Isaac Ashley, of London, merchant, for him and all the other creditors of Joseph Ormston, of London, merchant. WHEREAS, Joseph Ormston, merchant, by trading, bartering, etc. and also for ready money to be lent and indebted, unto sd. Ashley for £400, and since did become bank and several statutes against bank to the intent to defraud and hinder sd. Ashley and other of his creditors of their just debts [goes into the dates of laws regarding the

68

above. Names – Charles Bere, Benjamin Whiten, Esqrs, Robt. Allen, John Penny & Francis Nott, Gent.]

Pg 93. 10 Aug 1720. Charles Bere, Esqr., Robert Allen & Francis Nott, Gent. leases to Isaac Ashley, of London, merchant, have granted for 5 shillings, and set over to him as much as possible, all properties and or shares of properties at the time of sd. Ormston becoming bankrupt, whether ins East or West NJ in America or Great Britain, [and goes into other details of their decision] pertaining to the issue below. Whereas the Commission of Bankrupt, dated 4 Mar last past hath been awarded against Joseph Ormston, late of London, merchant, and late dec'd, directed to sd. Bere, Allen and Nott with Benjamin Whiten, Esqr., and Robert Allen, Gent, as Commissioners, through testimony appears to them that sd. Ormston for several years as a merchant sold wines and other merchandise as making a living and became indebted to sd. Isaac Ashley for £400 and upwards and to diverse others in other great sums and became bankrupt, and the Commissioners have discovered that being bankrupt the sd. Ormston. Possessed diverse lands and tenements in NJ in America and was also possessed of goods and persons owing him. Signed: By the persons above. Dated in London – 9 Jul 2724 bef. Jabus. Pickle, Notary Public. [This issue continues on to Page 100.]

Pg 101. 6 Aug 1724. Articles of Agreement. Isaac Ashley, of London, merchant, assignee of the state & effects of Joseph Ormston, late of London, merchant, dec'd, was bankrupt and indebted to sd. Ashley for £1,500 and to Charles Dunstar for £1,500. AND, WHEREAS, sd. Ashley by a letter of attorney, dated 9 July last past authorized his attorney sd. Dunstar to sell the lands etc. in NJ as he sees fit, and sd. Ashley for 5 shillings paid by Dunstar as soon as he disposes of the sd. lands shall allow Dunstar after all payments made to Ashley and after £53, 3 shillings and all interest due and to become one on a Bond, dated 25 Jul 1719, wherein sd. Ormston and Charles Dunstar are Bound to John Boughton, of New Inn, County of Middlesex, Gent., in the penal sum of £107 conditioned upon payment of the £53, 3 shillings and interest by 5 Jan next, and to deduct and take to him and themselves as much of sd. debt of £1,500 as sd. Ashley shall receive out of the purchase money for sd. lands toward sd. Ashley's debt. AND, sd. Dunstar for 5 shillings paid by sd. Ashley agrees to sell & dispose of the lands and pay Ashley, after deductions, the performance of same by the sum of £2,000. Wits.: Oliver Withrington at the Rising Sun in Clare Market, Jo. Boughton, [can't read], Robt. Arking. Signed: Isaac Ashley. Ackn.: 21 Dec 1724, Robt. Arking apprd. bef. James Alexander, Majesty's Council, NJ.

Pg 102. 18 Feb 1708/9. Archibald Campbell, dec'd, and James Blackwood, of City of Edinburgh, merchant, and son and heir of Master Robert Blackwood, late of the afsd. city, merchant, dec'd, release unto Charles Dunstar, of the Parish of St. Martin in the fields in the County of Middlesex, merchant, for a competent sum of money, under transferring uses into possessions, a tr. of land being in 24 parts or proprieties to be divided in East NJ in the Right of James, Earl of Perth and was granted to Sir George Mc Kenzie, of Tarvett, Knight and Barronet, and since conveyed to Lord Neil Campbell and then conveyed to sd. Robert Blackwood a moiety of such forth part at his death descended to his son, James Blackwood, and the other moiety of Lord Neil Campbell's descended to his son, sd. Archibald Campbell, and to either of them in America. Wits.: Wm. Penn, Junr., Ro. Davis, Maurie Lisle, Jos. Hammerton, James Thomas, Robt. West, John Mac Cullody, John Scott, John Hamilton. Signed: Archd. Campbell, Jas. Blackwood.

Pg 105. 14 Mar 1723. Memo. It was intended that Archibald Campbell for 5 shillings to release unto Charles Dunstar the bargained premises in New Jersey in America. Wits.: Ralph Aston, John Richmond, Isaac Ashley, Robt. Arking, John Boughton. Signed: Archd. Campbell. 21 Dec 1724, Robert Arking apprd. bef. James Alexander, Majesty's Council, NJ and on the 25 Feb 1724/5, John Hamilton, a witness to the deed apprd. bef. James Alexander, Majesty's Council.

Pg 106. 14 Apr 1724. James Armour, late of Amboy, Middlesex Co., East NJ, in America, and now of the Parish of St. Margaret, Westminster, County of Middlesex, Great Brittain, Gent., leases to Charles Dunstar, of the Parish of St. Martins, in the fields in the Liberty of Westminster, County of Middlesex, Great Brittain, Gent., for one year the land mentioned below. WHEREAS, James Armour is seized of a tr. of land by a deed made to him by Peter Sonmans, Gent., being in the town of Amboy Perth, Middlesex Co., East NJ, being 8.5 chains in length, bnd. n. by William Dockwra's house lot, e. by Water Street, s. by Market Street, w. by Moreat Place. Wits.: Patrick Grame, Colin Mc Cullock, Robt. Arking, Isaac Ashley, Will. Sinclair, John Richmond, Ja. Cutchinsone, Sr., Signed: James Armour. Ackn.: 21 Dec 1724, Robt. Arking apprd. bef. James Alexander, Majesty's Council, NJ.

Pg 107. 15 Apr 1724. James Armour, late of Amboy, Middlesex Co., East NJ, in America, and now of the Parish of St. Margaret, Westminster, County of Middlesex, Great Brittain, Gent., releases to Charles Dunstar, of the Parish of St. Martins, in the fields in the Liberty of Westminster, County of Middlesex, Great Brittain, Gent., for £20, by transferring uses into possessions. WHEREAS, Peter Sonmans, of Amboy Perth, Middlesex Co., East NJ, in America, Gent., by deed poll, dated 5 Dec 1687, sold land in Amboy Perth [as mentioned in the absd. deed – Page 106]. Wits.: Patrick Grame, Colin Mc Cullock, Robt. Arking, Isaac Ashley, Will. Sinclair, John Richmond, Ja. Cutchinsone, Sr., Signed: James Armour. London – 15 Apr 1724, payment made for the property by Charles Dunstar. Ackn.: 21 Dec 1724, Robt. Arking apprd. bef. James Alexander, Majesty's Council, NJ.

Pg 110. 14 Apr 1724. James Armour, late of Amboy, Middlesex Co., East NJ, in America, and now of the Parish of St. Margaret, Westminster, County of Middlesex, Great Brittain, Gent., leases to Charles Dunstar, of the Parish of St. Martins, in the fields in the Liberty of Westminster, County of Middlesex, Great Brittain, Gent., for 5 shillings, the land mentioned below. WHEREAS, James Armour stands seized of land from Samuel More, of Woodbridge, Middlesex Co., East NJ, being both upland & meadow on s. side of Raritan River being 640 a. Wits.: Patrick Grame, Colin Mc Cullock, Robt. Arking, Isaac Ashley, Will. Sinclair, John Richmond, Ja. Cutchinsone, Sr., Signed: James Armour. London – 15 Apr 1724, payment made for the property by Charles Dunstar. Ackn.: 21 Dec 1724, Robt. Arking apprd. bef. James Alexander, Majesty's Council, NJ.

Pg 111. 15 Apr 1724. James Armour, late of Amboy, Middlesex Co., East NJ, in America, and now of the Parish of St. Margaret, Westminster, County of Middlesex, Great Brittain, Gent., releases to Charles Dunstar, of the Parish of St. Martins, in the fields in the Liberty of Westminster, County of Middlesex, Great Brittain, Gent., under transferring uses into possessions, for £5 [land mentioned below and in the absd. deed – Page 110]. WHEREAS, Samuel Moore, of Woodbridge, Middlesex Co., East NJ, America by a deed poll or disposition dated 26 Oct 1687 sold to James Amour both upland & meadow on s. side of Raritan River being 640 a. Wits.: Patrick Grame, Colin Mc Cullock, Robt. Arking, Isaac Ashley, Will. Sinclair, John Richmond, Ja. Cutchinsone, Sr., Signed: James Armour. London – 15 Apr 1724, payment made for the property by Charles Dunstar. Ackn.: 21 Dec 1724, Robt. Arking apprd. bef. James Alexander, Majesty's Council, NJ.

Pg 114. 4 Feb 1724. John Clark, of Elizabeth Town, Essex Co., NJ, yeoman, (son of Richard Clark, of afsd. place, shipwright), and his wife, Phebe, sell to John Hendricks, of the afsd. place, Gent., for £150, for land in Elizabeth Town, beg. by a street or highway at the n.w. corner of John Hendrick's land, and then several courses back to the beg., being 18 a., bnd. e. by sd. Hendricks, s. by Richard Clark, w. part by Daniel Ross and part George Ross, late of Elizabeth Town, dec'd, n. by sd. street or highway. Wits.: Thomas Jackman, John Winance, Junr., Joseph Jackson. Signed: John Clark, Phebe Clark made her mark. Ackn.: 18 Mar 1724, John Winance, Junr. apprd. bef. Joseph Bonnel, Judge, Essex Co.

Pg 117. 16[?] Jul 1720. Mathew Force, of Woodbridge, Middlesex Co., East NJ, planter, sells to his brother, Thomas Force, of the afsd. place, cordwainer, for £70, for a tenement in Woodbridge, being 25 a. [and in another place it says 20 a], beg. on the n. side of a highway 4 rods from Daniel Brittain, then along sd. highway, to Thomas Gage's line and then several courses and along the sd. highway to the beg. Wits.: Thomas Force, John Bishop. Signed: Mathew Force made his mark. Ackn.: 24 Feb 1724/5, Thomas Force apprd. bef. Adam Hude, Judge, Middlesex Co.

Pg 118. 3 Aug 1724. Peter Sonmans, of London, Esqr., leases to Christopher Gildermeester, of London, merchant, for 5 shillings, for 3 month, 2,000 a. in Middlesex Co., East NJ, in America, being part of a tr. of 15,600 a., on both side of the Lawrence Brook in sd. county granted to sd. Sonmans by the Proprietors of East NJ, on 20 Oct 1693, beg. on the line of a 3,000 a. tr. form. sold by Sonmans to Jacob Osterland and John Keyser and s.w. along their line. Wits.: Thos. Smith, Jos. Hatfield Signed: Peter Sonmans. Ackn.: 18 May 1725, Peter Sonmans apprd. bef. John Hamilton, Esqr., Majesty's Council.

Pg 119. 4 Aug 1724. Peter Sonmans, of London, Esqr., releases to Christopher Gildermeester, of London, merchant, for £320, for 2,000 a. in Middlesex Co., East NJ, in America, under transferring uses into possessions, being part of a tr. of 15,600 a., on both side of the Lawrence Brook in sd. county granted to sd. Sonmans by the Proprietors of East NJ, on 20 Oct 1693, beg. on the line of a 3,000 a. tr. form. sold by Sonmans to Jacob Osterland and John Keyser and s.w. along their line. . Wits.: Thos. Smith, Jos. Hatfield Signed: Peter Sonmans. Ackn.: 18 May 1725, Peter Sonmans apprd. bef. John Hamilton, Esqr., Majesty's Council.

Pg 123. 28 Jul 1716. John Drummey, of Middletown, Monmouth Co., NJ, shopkeeper, sells to Mary Drummey, alias Nichols, of the afsd. place, for a competent sum of money all five-thirtieth parts of the sd. 2 a. on Matawan Creek and the twenty-fourth part of the landing & highway on Whingsunk Neck, ess the excep.; and that twenty-fourth part of the 100 a. of land adjoining the land of John Bown now Ambrose Still. ALSO, the 100 a adjoining the sd. Watson's old tr.; all of wch. is mentioned below. WHEREAS, John Drummey owns five-thirtieths of 2 a. of land on the Matawan Creek beg. at a point near the creek at the lower corner of the store house built by Peter Watson, Junr., then several courses to the creek and then down same to the beg., wch. land came to Drummey by deed from Peter Watson, dated16 May 1715. AND, WHEREAS, sd. Drummey owns a twenty-fourth part of the landing highway on Whingsunk Neck, beg. at an old oyster bank landing then known as John Ried's Landing, and then from Matawan Creek to Whingsunk Neck, being 100 feet by 1000 feet; excep. 40 feet wide for the creek from the upper point of the oyster bank e. and 100 feet back from the creek s. ALSO, the twenty-fourth part of 100 a. of land adjoining the land late of John Bowne & now Ambrose Still [?]; bnd. e. by land late of Thomas Hart, dec'd, s. by land of Joseph Soyes sold to John Johnston, Esqr., for the use of him and others to the number of twenty four. AND, WHEREAS, the sd. John Drummey owns 100 a. of land among other tr. beg. 9 chains s. of the n.w. corner of Peter Watson's old tr. where he lives wch. also is a corner of Joseph Soyes land and then to the corner of sd. Joseph Sooy's land and then to the line of the sd. old Watson tr. and to the beg., wch. was conveyed to sd. Drummey by the absd. deed of sd. Watson, dated 16 May 1715. Wits.: David Watson, Abraham Petterson made his mark, Thos. Loving. Signed: John

Drummey. Ackn.: 3 Jun 1725, David Watson apprd. bef. David Lyell, Majesty's Council.

Pg 124. 15 Nov 1708. John Pope, of Elizabeth Town, Essex Co., NJ, yeoman, quit claims unto John Blanchard, of the afsd. place, merchant, for £12, 10 shillings, for the land & meadow claimed by sd. Pope in Elizabeth Town by the Right excep. what he has at Rahway Neck, being all his lands and meadow adjoining & being on the e. side of the highway from Elizabeth Town to Woodbridge. Wits.: Samuel Carter made his mark, Anne Blanchard. Signed: John Pope made his mark. Ackn.: 26 Feb 1724, Samuel Carter apprd. bef. Joseph Bonnel, Judge, Essex Co.

Pg 125. 15 Jul 1701. William Lawrence, Senr., of Middletown, Monmouth Co., East NJ, for the love and natural affection he bears to his son, James Lawrence, but also for a competent sum of money, quit claims unto him a tr. of land within Shrewsbury on the s. side of Manasquan River, being 20 a., beg. below the point of Hartshorne's land & then down same; bnd. by the sd. River; wch. land he claims with other lands granted to him by a Patent from the Proprietors of East NJ, dated 22 Dec 1700. Wits.: Thos. Leeds, Thomas Taylor, Wm. Lawrence, Junr. Signed: William Lawrence. Ackn.: 7 Aug 1704, Thomas Taylor and Thomas Leeds apprd. bef. Lewis Morris, Esqr., Majesty's Council.

Pg 127. 25 Mar 1681. Philip Carteret , Esqr., Gov. of East NJ, and Lady Elizabeth Carteret, Baroness, have grant by these Presents, to James Gyles, of [?]haway, yeoman, a tr. of land on the Rariton River within Elizabeth Town, being 180 a. in breadth 30 chains along sd. River w.n.w. & e.s.e. and 60 chains in length along Bound Creek and bnd. e. & s. by sd. River, and with allowances is 150 a. Wits.: Robert Vanquellin, Henry Green, Robert [LNU]. James Bollen entered it into the record. Signed: Ph. Carteret.

Pg 127. 17 June 1725. [Very hard to read] This is to certify...cause to be surveyed... to Derick [LNU] all that tr. of land whereon he now lives, beg. at the...Bound Brook where it falls into the Raritan River and as the river runs to the line of Benjamin [LNU] and along the line of sd. Benjamin Clark and several courses to...Brook opposite the bounds corner of the three tr. of land of Derick Cononis[?], William Oldin and Peter Boleines, and then to ...Brook and then to the beg., being 180 a., to sd. Derick; wch. land came to him by deed from James Alexander, dated 17 day of instant June. In part of these thirteen-fortieth of a Proprietary from. of Sir Evan Cameron and now vested in the sd. James by conveyances. Signed: James Alexander, Surveyor General.

Pg 128. 20 Aug 1713. [Faded ink - hard to read] Derick Benson, of NY City, Gent., sells to Derick [LNU] of Bergen Co., East NJ, yeoman, for £200 paid by Derick Conynafores[?], for a tr. of land on Raritan River, in Piscataway Twp., Middlesex Co., being 180 a. along the Bound Creek; bnd. e. & s. by land of John

Field, n. by Bound Creek, w. by Raritan River, being 150a. with allowances, as by Patent dated 6 Jan 1681 granted by Lady Elizabeth Carterett as Proprietrix of East NJ to [?], of the sd. place and township, dec'd, wch. said tr. & premises …of the estate of James Giles, dated 12 Apr 1693 grant unto John Petterson, the lot of Perth Amboy, dec'd, who on 28 Feb 1697 by deed of him and his wife, Mary, released the same to Michael Lourier, of NY City, carpenter, who with Susannah, his wife, on 17 June 1701, assigned it over to Johannes Mosserar[?], of Richmond Co [NY], dec'd, after his death, his oldest son & heir, Evert Messlear conveyed the same to Jn. Strumentremd[?] on 2 Aug 1703 unto Derick Benson. AND, ALSO, including one moiety or half of the adjoining Codwises [?]Mill. Wits.: John Michael Sperling, Elias Baily, John Conrad Codwises, Junr. Signed: Direck Benson. Ackn.: 2 ? 1718, Elias Baily apprd. bef. David Jemison, Esqr., Chief Justice.

Pg 130. 28 May 1724. John Harrison, of Amboy, Middlesex Co., East NJ, Gent., sells to John Stevenson, of Borrow Town, West Chester, NY, Gent., for £300, for 545 a. being part of 3 parcels of land wch. John Harrison, dec'd, father to the sd. John Harrison, bot by conveyances from Robert Barclay, of Ury, late Scotland, Esqr., dec'd, being in Middlesex Co., betw. two riverlets known as Manalapan and Matchaponix, being 290 a of upland and meadow and part of a tr. of 608 a. bnd. as 290 a. is in part of the 545 a. absd. wch. land is to be divided beg. at the corner of land called the Great Bog belonging to John ~~Harrison~~ Johnston wch. is the corner also of George Willocks' land or meadow, then along Johnston's land to the Manalapan River and then down same below the mouth of Jassbray Run to sd. Johnston and several courses to the beg. at the bog. ALSO, 185 a. to be divided wch. is part of the 545 a. absd. and is on the w. side of sd. Manalapan by Cranbery Meadows, beg. at the s.w. corner of Robert Barclay's Great Tract, and then several courses to land form. of Thomas Cooper, dec'd, of London, merchant, but now of George Willocks and John Harrison, then to the beg. ALSO, 85 a. of upland and meadow being part of a tr. of 194.5 a. to be divided wch. 85 a. makes up the granted land of 545 a. lying on the e. side of sd. Manalapan; beg. by sd. river below where Mount Brook falls into the same and then near the head of the Great Bog wch. belongs to Cornelius Longfield and then several courses by sd. Longfield's land to land now or late of John Reid and then along his land to sd. Manalapan by Mount Brook and then to the beg. AND, wch. sd. land and meadow by a deed of Release from George Willocks to sd. John Harrison, dated 12 Dec 1724, wch. three tr. of land to be divided equally. Wits.: John Rudyard, Samuel Rouse. Signed: John Harrison. Ackn.: 29 May 1724, John Harrison apprd. bef. John Hamilton, Esqr., Majesty's Council.

Pg 133. 17 May 1725. John Andrews, of Monmouth Co., East NJ, appoints his trusty friend Benjamin Disbrow, of Amboy, Middlesex Co., East NJ, his true and lawful attorney to act in his name to do whatever is necessary on his behalf. Wits.: Josiah Bird made is mark. Signed: John Andrews. Freehold - 16 Aug

1725, Josiah Bird apprd. bef. David Lyell, Majesty's Council that he saw sd. Andrews give his power of attorney to Benjamin Dewsberry.

Pg 134. 18 Feb 1724. Stephen Warne, of Perth Amboy, Middlesex Co., East NJ, Gent., the son & heir of Thomas Warne, of Perth Amboy, afsd. of late dec'd sell to Captain Daniel Hendricks, Middletown, Monmouth Co., East NJ, Gent., for £700, for all that plantation in Perth Amboy afsd. of 360 a., being part his thousand a. tr., form. granted by Patent to absd. Thomas Warne on 30 Nov 1699, beg. at a corner of Dockwra's and Elison's and Scot's Proprietors and then along the land of the Scot's Proprietors to a corner of land lately sold by sd. Stephen Warne to Benjamin Disbrow and along the line of same to the w. line of sd. 1,000 a. , and then 58 chains to the corner of Joshua Warne and along his line to a corner of sd. Disbrow's other tr. and along his line to a small brook and then up same to Seth Elison's land and along his line to the beg.; bnd. n. by part of Scot's Proprietor's land, and part by Disbrow, w. by the 1,000 a. tr., s. by part. of Joshua Warne, and part by sd. Disbrow, and e. part by sd. Disbrow and part by sd. Elison's land. Wits.: Andrew Willson[?], Andrew Gordon, William Lawrence, Junr., Thomas Warne. Signed: Sten. Warne. Ackn.: 18 Feb 1724, Stephen Warne apprd. bef. John Johnston, Junr.

Pg 136. 17 Jun [?]. [Faded ink – hard to read] James Alexander, of NY City, Gent. sells to Derick Conine [?], for £6, 1 shilling, 7 pence, for 15.2 a. of land to be taken up and surveyed in the unappropriated lands of East NJ, wch. previously belonged to Sir Eugenius Cameron in half part and half part by sd. Alexander of Evan Drummond who was vested with the whole thereof by a conveyance from sd. Cameron to his grandson Donald Cameron and then by sd. Donald to the Evan Cameron. Wits.: Alexander Mackdowall, William Oulden. Ackn.: 17 Jun 1725. James Alexander apprd. bef. John Parker, Majesty's Council.

Pg 137. 21 Oct 1724. Stephen Warne, of Perth Amboy, Middlesex Co., East NJ, Gent., sells to William Lawrence, Junr., of Middletown, Monmouth Co., East NJ, trader, for £20, for a tr. of land within Perth Amboy on the w. side of Water Street 33.5 chains long Lyell's lot 157 feet near the eight part of an acre and is part of an acre lot form. granted to Thomas Warne, dec'd by Patent from the Proprietors and by him conveyed to Edward Vaughan and from sd. Vaughan to Stephen Warne by deed, dated 7 Oct 1724. Wits.: John Hooper, [can't read other]. Signed: Sten. Warne. Ackn.: 18 Feb 1725, Stephen Warne apprd. bef. John Johnston, Junr., Majesty's Council.

Pg 138. 25 Aug1725. Richard Dockwra, of Epsom, County of Surray, Great Britain, Gent., eldest son and heir of William Dockwra, late of London, merchant, dec'd; William Dockwra, of Christ Church College in Oxford Clark, another son of sd. William Dockwra, dec'd, and Admin. of the annexed will of sd. Dockwra, dec'd; Mary Freeman, of London, widow; Margaret Bowells, of the Parish of Lambeth, County of Surry, widow; Thomas Warburton, of Turnershall, County of Hartford, Gent., and Anne, his wife, and Andrew Nickolls, of NJ, in America, Gent., and Rebecca, his wife (wch. sd. Mary Freeman, Anne Warburton, Margaret Bowells & Rebecca Nickolls are the daus. of the sd. William Dockwra, dec'd.) by their attorney Thomas Humphreys, late of London, Gent., but now in Perth Amboy, East NJ, of the other part, for £200, sell to Gabriel Stelle, for all the land in Perth Amboy as described below, being 27 a. WHEREAS, Andrew Hamilton, form. Gov. of NJ, by Patent, dated 10 May 1688, granted unto William Dockwra, of London, merchant, and one of their fellow Proprietors, a piece of land within Perth Amboy, Middlesex Co., East NJ being 27 a., beg. a chain from the bank of the Raritan River; bnd. s. by a highway on the bank of sd. Raritan, e. by Thomas Warne's land, n. by the highway from the market place and w. by the Scot's Proprietors land {Lib. B:501-502}. AND, WHEREAS, since granting sd. Patent, sd. William Dockwra, dec'd made his will and divided the lands in NJ among his heirs (as above written), and they became seized of the sd. land and they by their power of attorney, on 12 Nov 1718, empowered sd. Humphreys, Gent. to dispose of the sd. lands of all the two proprieties in East NJ, as in Lib. C-2:464-468. Wits.: Lawr. Smyth, J. Stevens. Signed: Thos. Humphreys, as attorney for the absd. parties. Ackn.: 25 Aug 1725, Thomas Humphreys, Esqr. apprd. bef. David Lyell, Esqr., Majesty's Council.

Pg 141. 30 Sep 1724. Alexander Mackdowall, of Perth Amboy, Middlesex Co., NJ, releases & quit claims unto Michael Van Veghten, of Somerset Co., NJ, for 5 shillings, the below described land, being late land of William Loveridge. WHEREAS, sd. Mackdowall and Michael Van Veghten, of Somerset Co., NJ, Gent., together own a lot of land belonging to William Loveridge, late of Perth Amboy (wch. lot is part of these two lots of land form. of Benjamin Clarke, dec'd, and afterwards sold by Benjamin Clarke, son & heir of Benjamin Clarke, dec'd) to William Loveridge, dec'd, father of the absd. William Loveridge of these Presents, beg. on Water Street 33 feet n. of the s. corner of two lots on sd. street, then along the n. line of sd. lots and several other courses to the beg. AND, WHEREAS, sd. Mackdowall & Van Veghten agreed on a division of sd. lot and by these Presents to be released and become the share to sd. Van Veghten. Wits.: Peter Dumont, John Dumont. Signed: Alexander Mackdowall. Ackn.: Alexander Mackdowall apprd. bef. Robert Lettis Hooper, Esqr., Chief Justice.

Pg 143. 17 Apr 1725. William Hay, Freehold Twp., Monmouth Co., East NJ, and Mary, his wife, sells to Henry Van Kerk, of the afsd. place, for a competent sum of money, on-twelfth of a one-tenth part of a Proprietary in East NJ, being 100 a., in the barrens of Wickatonk, beg. on a branch of Fly Brook and then numerous courses to the Indian Path and then to the place of beg., wch. sd. Hay has by a deed of sale from John Reid, Esqr., dated 19 Feb 1714. Wits.: Adam Croshlie, John Reid, Joseph Morgan, Andrew Morgan. Signed: William Hay,

Mary Hay, made her mark. Ackn.: 17 Apr 1725, William Hay apprd. bef. John Johnston, Junr., Majesty's Council.

Pg 144. Jun 1725. Robert Sandiland, of Speen, County of Berks, at present in London, appointed Coll. John Hamilton, of NY City in America, my true and lawful attorney, with full power to act in his name on his behalf and to do whatever is necessary in his name in NY, East NJ, and PA or elsewhere in America re: lands, etc. Wits.: Antho. Wright, Lloyd Zachary. Signed: Thos. Puck, Notary Public, 1725. Ackn.: 5 June 1725, George Merttins, Mayor of London, swore bef. Jackson , that Robert Sandiland delivered to him his Power of Attorney, and signed same.

Pg 145. 8 Nov 1715. Thomas Leonard, of Somerset Co., NJ, Esqr., and Susannah, his wife, sells to Benjamin Fitz Randolph, of Middlesex Co., NJ, yeoman, for £80, for a tr. of land in Somerset Co., beg. at the s.e. corner of Nathaniel Leonard's land and then n.w. along sd. Nathaniel's line to the land of John & Garret Vanhorn called Peter Sonman's Land, and then an Vanhorn's line runs to the land late in tenure of William Newman, dec'd, and then along sd. Newman's head line and Samuel Allen's head line and then runs to the land of Richard Stockton, then along his line to the n. corner of Thomas Stockton's land and then along his line n.w. as it runs to Benjamin Fitz Randolph and then along his line to Nathaniel Leonard's s.e. corner where it beg.; bnd. w. by sd. Nathaniel's land, n. by sd. Vanhorn's land, w. by land of sd. Newman and sd. Allen, s. by land of Richard Stockton, Thomas Stockton and Benjamin Stockton. Wits.: Nathall Leonard, Robert Stockton, John Stockton. Signed: Thomas Leonard, Susana Leonard. Ackn.: 28 Jan 1720, Thomas Leonard and Susannah Leonard apprd. bef. John Parker, Majesty's Council.

Pg 147. 30 Apr 1720. John Rudyard, of Middlesex Co, East NJ, Esqr., and Deborah, his wife, sells to Rutt Van Horne, of Bergen Co., East NJ, yeoman, for £716, for a tr. of land in Somerset Co., on the n. side of Raritan River, beg. at the mouth of middle brook where it empties into sd. Raritan and runs up the sd. brook on a straight line to a tree on the e. side of a run and then in the n.n.e. line betw. the land of Madame French and sd. Rudyard and then to the foot of the hills. ALSO, another corner betw. French & Rudyard to the n.w. corner of David Couzard's land and then s.s.w. to sd. Raritan and then up same to the beg. ALSO, all that tr. of meadow lying on the w. side of sd. Bound Brook beg. at the n.e. corner of sd. Cozard's land and then several courses to the edge of a bank to a corner of sd. Cozard and then up sd. Brook and then several courses to the beg., with both tr. being in upland and meadow 800 a., being the remaining part of a Patent to Thomas Rudyard, Esqr., dec'd, dated 28 May 1685. Wits.: Thomas Gordon, John Hankins. Signed: John Rudyard, Deborah Rudyard. Ackn.: 18 Sep 1725, John Rudyard, Esqr., apprd. bef. R. L. Hooper

Pg 149. 16 May 1724. George Willocks, of Perth Amboy, Middlesex Co., NJ, now of Philadelphia, PA., Gent., sells to John Barclay, Junr.[?], of Freehold, Monmouth Co., NJ, Gent., for a competent sum of money, for the below mentioned land of John Johnston at the partition line betw. sd. Willocks and John Harrison wch. is the Partition line from Manalapan River and then numerous courses to sd. Johnston's land and then to the land of John Harrison, being [acreage covered by ink blot]. WHEREAS, sd. Willocks is seized of a tr. of land form. belonging to Robert Barclay, Esqr., dec'd, beg. at the corner of land or meadow of John Johnston, Esqr., the Great Bog and then to the line of land form. of Andrew Jaffray[?] now of the sd. Johnston, and then to the land now or late of Cornelius Longfield and then back to the beg. Wits.: Andrw. Johnston, John Stevens. Signed: George Willocks. Ackn.: 12 Aug 1724, John Stevens apprd. bef. James Alexander, Esqr., Majesty's Council.

Pg 151. 22 Apr 1725. Mary Clawson, of Piscataway Town, Middlesex Co., East NJ, Exec. of the will of her late husband, William Clawson, dec'd, dated 10 Mar 1723, sells to Are Boren, of the afsd. place, yeoman, for £320, for a tr. of land in Piscataway Town, beg. by the Raritan River and then to a corner in the middle of a meadow and then to meadow brook and along same to the sd. River and to the beg.; bnd. s. by the land of sd. Borem, n.w. by sd. meadow brook, n.e. by land of John Byse, and s.w. by sd. Raritan River. Wits.: Benjamin Hull, Samuel Convers. Signed: Mary Clawson. Ackn.: 20 Feb 1725, Samuel Convers apprd. bef. Adam Hude, Judge, Middlesex Co.

Pg 152. 1 Sep 1725. Ara Borem, of Piscataway Twp., Middlesex Co., East NJ, yeoman, sells to Aaron Louzada, of Somerset Co., East NJ, yeoman, merchant, and Moses Louzada of the afsd. place, merchant, for £164, for the below mentioned land, beg. at meadow brook and along the middle branch of same and then to sd. Raritan River and then to the beg.; bnd. s.e. by land of Area Borem, n. w. by sd. meadow brook, n.e. by Buyse, s.w. by sd. River, being 35 a. WHEREAS, Phillip Carteret, Esqr., late Gov. in the name of Sir George Carteret, Proprietor, granted unto Edward Slaughter, a tr. of land in Piscataway Twp., on the Raritan River, being 108 a., beg. by the sd. River, and then to a point in a meadow and then as the Patent states, dated 30 Jul 1687. AND, sd. Slaughter by a deed, dated 2 Nov [35 [?] year of reign of Kling Charles II], did sell the absd. land to Capt. John Palmer, Staten island, NY, Esqr., and entered in records on 27 Feb 1683 {Book A:71}. AND, sd. Palmer, Esqr., by deed to sell it to Are Borem by Mary Clawson, relict of William Clawson, by deed, dated 22 Apr 1725. AND, whereas there is one other tr. in Piscataway on the sd. Riaritan adjoining the above sd. tr. is owned by Rohobath Gaunet, who then sold it to William Clawson, dated 6 Mar 1683, and a part of it was sold to Are Borem by absd. Mary Clawson. Wits.: [?]ndert Smack, Robert Richardson. Signed: Are Borem. Ackn.: 21 Sep 1725, Area Borem apprd. bef. John Parker, Majesty's Council.

Pg 155. 1 Dec 1724. James Alexander, of NY City, Gent., sells to Andrew Gordon, of Perth Amboy, NJ, for £14, 16 shillings, for 37 and 15.25 a. to be taken up and surveyed in the unappropriated lands of East NJ, wch. lands are part of thirteen-fortieth parts of a Proprietary form. belonging to Sir Eugenius Cameron, of Lochiel and bot. by sd. James Alexander of Evan Drummond, who was vested with same by a conveyance by sd. Cameron to his grandson, Donald Cameron, and by a conveyance from sd. Donald to sd. Drummond; excep. one-third of the mines and minerals. Wits.: Isaac Stuckey, Ja. Gillchrist. This deed was re-executed by sd. Alexander in the presence of Thos. Sherd, Thos. Redford. Signed: Ja. Alexander. Ackn.: 14 May 1725, Thomas Redford apprd. bef. David Lyell, Majesty's Council. 3 Dec 1724, returned to Andrew Gordon 14.25 a. and on 10 May 1724, returned to Andrew Gordon 38 a. in full of within deed. Signed: Ja. Alexander, Surveyor General.

Pg 157. 25 Nov 1706. Robert Burnet, of Freehold, Monmouth Co., East NJ, a Proprietor of East NJ, Gent. sells to John Ward, of the afsd. place, yeoman, for £48, for 200 a. of land in Freehold Twp, of the afsd. place, being part of a tr. of sd. Burnet's on Doctor's Creek, wch. was surveyed, dated 12 Jun 1705 by William Emley of Nottingham, surveyor, beg. in the Division Line of East NJ at a corner and then several courses to other corners and then to a corner of Alexander Bues, and then to the beg. Wits.: Wm. Emley., [the clerk wrote – "not legible".] Signed: Rob. Burnet. Ackn.: 7 Dec 1706, Robert Burnet apprd. bef. Francis Davenport, Majesty's Council.

Pg 159. 22 Jun 1724. Peter Vannesse, the Elder, of Somerset Co., East NJ, yeoman, sells to Peter Vannesse, the Younger, of the afsd. place, yeoman, for the natural love he has for his son and £200, for an undivided half of the below mentioned 600 a., and to be on the n. side and be divided by a line from the n. branch to the outside lines and now in the occupation of sd. Vannesse, the Younger. WITNESSETH, Andrew Hamilton and the Proprietors, by Patent dated 6 Jan 1697, confirmed unto sd. Vannesse, the Elder, land on the w. side of the north branch of the Rariton River, in Somerset Co., beg. at the e. corner of land of Hendrick Coursen on sd. branch, and 40 chains from the meeting of the s. & n. branches of the sd. Rariton and then 2 miles; bnd. e. by sd. branch, s. by sd. Coursen, w. & n. by unsurveyed land, being 600 a. Wits.: Michael Henry, Zachariah Weeks, Coeraet Ten Eyck. Signed: Pieter Vanneste. Ackn.: 27 Nov 1725, Peter Vanneste apprd. bef. Robert Lettis Hooper.

Pg 161. 22 Jun 1724. Peter Vannest, of Somerset Co., East NJ, yeoman, sells to his son, John Vannest, of the afsd. place, yeoman, for the natural love he has for his son and £150, for an undivided half of the below mentioned 600 a., and to be on the s. side and be divided by a line from the n. branch to the outside lines and now in the occupation of sd. John Vannest. [Relates the 600 a. in the absd. deed – Page 159, and indicates it is in Book F:518-19.] Wits.: Michael Henry,

Zachariah Weeks, Coeraet Ten Eyck. Signed: Pieter Van Neste. Ackn.: 25 Nov 1725, Peter Vanneste apprd. bef. Robert Lettis Hooper.

Pg 163. 21 Jan 1687/8. Samuel Dotey, of Piscataway, Middlesex Co., NJ, yeoman, sells to Henry Dorsey, of Rariton, NJ, for £35, for 104 a. of land on the Rariton River, beg. at a small brook and then running several courses to the beg.; bnd. n. by land form of Edward Slaters, s. by sd. brook and part by land form. of Mr. Higgens, w. by sd. Rariton, and e. by unsurveyed land, wch. land is in my Patent dated 10 Oct 1678. Wits.: Benia Hull, [FNU] Peyartt, Edward Slater. Signed: Samuel Dottey. Ackn.: 9 Oct 1725, Benja. Hull and Edward Slater, both of Piscataqua, Middlesex Co., NJ, apprd. bef. John Parker, Majesty's Council, and Benj. Hull stated that he was familiar with the handwriting of his father, Benjamin Hull, and that of Edward Slater and believes it to be their handwriting on the absd. document. And, Edward Slater stated that he has seen several letters to his mother by his father, and he is familiar with the handwriting of his father, Edward Slater, and believes it to be his father's handwriting.

Pg 165. 28 Nov 1718. Moses Burnett, of Brookhaven, Suffolk Co., Island of Nassau, NY, yeoman, sells to John Crane, of Newark, Essex Co., East NJ, for £50, for several tr. of upland & swamp within Newark on the n.w. of town near the mill tract on Long Hill; bnd. n. by Samuel Plum, w. by highway, s. by Stephen Davis, e. by unsurveyed land. ALSO, 20 a. in the mill brook swamp at the north branch; bnd. n. by Samuel Plum, e. by a highway, s. by Stephen Davis and w. by unsurveyed land. Wits.: Jno. Cooper, Robert Young. Signed: Moses Burnett. Ackn.: 29 Apr 1720, John Cooper apprd. bef. Joseph Harrison, Judge, Essex Co.

Pg 166. 31 Mar 1725. Richard Mount, Junr., of Middlesex Co., East NJ, cordwainer, & Rebeckah, his wife, sells to Stephen Warne, of the afsd. place, yeoman, for £270, for a tr. of land at Cranberry, Middlesex Co., beg. at the s.w. corner of land form. of Thomas Morford, dec'd, in the Division line that parts the dec'd Morford's land and Joseph Dennis' land being 37 chains on the same line above the place form. of Benjamin Applegate's s.w. corner, then several courses to Cranberry Brook and then up same to the line of land form. of sd. Applegate and now in the possession of Thomas Applegate, being the absd. Division line, then along same by the land form. Benjamin Applegate's & Thomas Morford's to the beg.; bnd. s. by Joseph Dennis' land, w. by Humphrey Mount's land, n. by Cranberry Brook, e. by the absd. land form. of Benjamin Applegate & Thomas Morford's; wch. land was given to Richard Mount by deed of gift from his father, Richard Mount, dated 12 Mar 1711. Wits.: Daniel Harkut, Junr., Myndert Johnson, Martha Hughes, made her mark. Signed: Richard Mount, Junr., Rebeckah Mount, made her mark. Ackn.: 3 Apr 1725, Richard Mount apprd. bef. Samuel Leonard, Esqr., Judge, Middlesex Co.

Pg 168. 25 May 1724. George Willocks, late of Perth Amboy, Middlesex Co., , now of Philadelphia, PA, Esqr., sells to George Leslie, of Perth Amboy, Middlesex Co., East NJ, Gent., and nephew of sd. Willocks, for the natural love and affection he has toward sd. Leslie, and for 5 shillings, a tr. of land in Middlesex Co., on the e. side of the Manalapan River by land form. of Andrew Jeffery now to John Johnston, being 294 a. , beg. at the n.e. corner of land sold sd. by Willocks to John Barclay, Junr., by deed dated 16 May 1724, and then numerous courses to sd. Johnston's corner in the Great Bog and then to John Barclay's corner in the sd. Bog, and then across same numerous courses to the beg. Wits.: John Johnston, Robt. King. Signed: Geo. Willocks. Ackn.: 27 May 1724, George Willocks apprd. bef John Hamilton, Esqr., Majesty's Council.

Pg 169. 2 Aug 1725. George Leslie, of Perth Amboy, Middlesex Co., NJ, Gent., sells to Charles Gordon, of Monmouth Co., NJ, Gent., for £420 , for 294 a. on the e. side of Manalapan River...being by the lot of George Willocks, late of Philadelphia, PA, now of London, Gent., sold to John Barclay, Junr. [wch. is the land described in the absd. deed – Page 168]. Wits.: Andw. Johnston, John Parker. Signed: Geo. Leslie. Ackn.: 2 Aug 1725, George Leslie apprd. bef John Parker, Majesty's Council.

Pg 171. 1 Aug 1722[?]. James Alexander, of NY City, attorney, sells to John Crane, of Newark, Essex Co., NJ, yeoman, for 1.9 a. to be taken up and surveyed in the unappropriated lands in East NJ, belonging to the thirteen-fortieths of a Proprietary form. of Sir Eugenious Cameron, of Lochiel and in part of that half of sd. undivided lands bot. by sd. Alexander of Evan Drummond, who was vested in it by sd. Cameron to his grandson, Donald Cameron and by another deed from sd. Donald Cameron to sd. Drummond; excep. one-third of all the mines & minerals. Wits.: Thos. Jackman, Isaac Stuckey. Signed: James Alexander. Ackn.: 25 Jun 1724, Josiah Ogden, Judge, Essex Co.

Pg 172. 29 Nov 1725[?]. John Hamilton, of NJ, Esqr., sells to Hendrick Reneerse, of Raritan River, NJ, for £71, 15 shillings, for 206 a. of land to be taken up and surveyed in the unappropriated lands in East NJ, wch. sd. Hamilton in Right of one-third of a Propriety form. of James Brain. Wits.: James Alexander, James Gillchrist. Signed: John Hamilton. Ackn.: John Hamilton, Esqr., apprd. bef. James Alexander, Majesty's Council.

Pg 173. 4 Sep 1722. John Throckmorton, of Shrewsbury, Monmouth Co., East NJ, Gent., son & heir of Job Throckmorton, dec'd, sells to William Leeds, Junr., of Middletown, Monmouth Co., afsd., yeoman, for a competent sum of money, for all the Rights of quit rents of two-thirds of the one half part of the one-tenth part of the absd. forty-eight part of East NJ. ALSO, the one-third of the quit rent arrearages on the one-half part of the sd. one-tenth part of the absd. forty-eight part of East NJ. WHEREAS, Joseph Throckmorton, of Middletown, form., dec'd, owned a full one-tenth of a forty-eight part of East NJ, by deed from his brother, John Throckmorton, dated 28 Mar 1688, and sd. Job Throckmorton was seized among several Rights to a Right of a half of all quit rents and arrearages due on the absd. forth-eight part as may further appear on a Release from John Stilwell and Rebekah, his wife; Moses Lipitt and Sarah, his wife; Thomas Stilwell and Alice, his wife; Hugh Coward and Patience, his wife; and Deliverance Throckmorton to the sd. Job Throckmorton, dated 19 Nov 1705. Wits.: [unreadable]. Signed: John Throckmorton. Ackn.: 7 Oct 1725, John Throckmorton apprd. bef. John Johnston, Junr., Majesty's Council.

Pg 174. 27 Feb 1723 English Style. Joseph Wakeham, of Boxhill, County of Sussex, England, yeoman, dec'd, was at the time of his death seized of certain estate or estates in New England and New York and East & West NJ, in America, and by his will, dated 6 Sep 1714, did devise his estate to be equally divided btw. his children and it appointed Elizabeth Wakeham, his wife, sole Exec., and she was so appointed when his will was probated on 23 Nov 1715 in the Per. Court of Canterbury. AND, WHEREAS, the sd. dec'd left behind at the time of his death, 4 children-Elizabeth, Hannah, Anne, and Mary Wakeham, his natural and lawful daughters. NOW, KNOW that the sd. Elizabeth Wakeham, the widow & relict & Exec. afsd., and Elizabeth Wakeham, spinster, one of the daus. of the sd. Joseph Wakeham, dec'd, for diverse causes appointed and by these presents appoints William Clark, of Sheffield, in Hampshire, in New England, husbandman, to be their lawful attorney in reference to and lands in the absd. places owned by sd Joseph Wakeham, dec'd, and to do whatever is necessary and to manage the same for their use. Wits.: George Christopher, Henry Gorham, Richard Quasie, made his mark. Signed: Elizabeth Wakeham, Elizabeth Wakeham, Junr. Ackn.: 23 Jun 1724, Henry Gorham apprd. and swore to same.

Pg 175. 3 Nov 1722. Richard Clarke, of Elizabeth Town, Essex Co., NJ, shipwright, for the natural love and affection he bears toward his grandchild, Daniel Hendricks, son of Abraham Hendricks, late of the afsd. place, dec'd, do grant and confirm to him all that land or part of salt marsh in Elizabeth Town at a place called Little Island Ridge, being 10 chains by 4 chains; bnd. e. by sd. Little Island Ridge, w. & n. by unsurveyed meadow and s. by meadow of Henry Norris, dec'd, being 4 a.; and wch. salt marsh was bot. by sd. Clarke by deed from Henry Norris, dated 22 Jan 1717/18. AND, if sd. Daniel Hendricks shall happen to die bef. 21 years and bef. being married that upon his death & under 21 years and bef. his marriage w/o issue lawfully begotten; Abraham Hendricks, Isaac Hendricks and Hannah Hendricks, the other two sons and one dau. of sd. Abraham Hendricks dec'd, shall stand seized of the absd. piece of salt marsh to be divided equally. Wits.: Samuel Whitehead, Elisha Whitehead. Signed: Richard Clarke. Ackn.: 21 May 1723, Samuel Whitehead apprd. bef. Joseph Bonnel, Judge, Essex Co.

Pg 177. 4 Jun 1722. John Brain, of London, mariner, son and heir of Thomas Brain, late of London, mariner, dec'd, leases to John Hamilton, of NY, in America, Esqr., for 5 shillings, for one-third of one half of one-twelfth of East NJ, for one year, under transferring uses into possessions. Wits.: Henry Holland, James De Lancey, John Midford. Signed: John Brain. Ackn.: 27 Aug 1723, Henry Holland apprd. bef. Lewis Morris, Esqr., Majesty's Council.

Pg 178. 5 Jun 1722. John Brain, of London, mariner, son and heir of Thomas Brain, late of London, mariner, dec'd, releases to John Hamilton, of NY, in America, Esqr., for 5 shillings, for one-third of one half of one-twelfth of East NJ, for one year, under transferring uses into possessions [and deed goes into all the transactions from King Charles II, etc. wch. has been recited elsewhere], for £166, 13 shillings, 4 pence, for one-third of one half of one-twelfth of East NJ, for one year, under transferring uses into possessions. Wits.: Henry Holland, James De Lancey, John Midford. Signed: John Brain. Ackn.: 27 Aug 1723, Henry Holland apprd. bef. Lewis Morris, Esqr., Majesty's Council.

Pg 184. 12 Feb 1719/20. Whereas, Elizabeth Drummond, widow & relict and Admin. of Captain Robert Drummond, late Commander of the ship *Caledonia*, dec'd, and Major William Drummond, eldest brother and her of sd. Robert Drummond, did by power of attorney, dated 26 Feb 1717, appointed Benjamin Funnele[?], of NY, to be their lawful attorney to recover & receive from whomever that wch. belongs to Captain Robert Drummond by virtue of 3 deeds, wch. sd. Elizabeth and Major William Drummond sent over with the absd. power of attorney-one dated 3 Jun 1684, betw. John Cambele and John Dobie and the last dated 7 Sep 1700 betw. sd. Dobie, of Scotland, and Captain Robert Drummond. AND, WHEREAS Since the items being sent sd. Funnele[?] is dec'd and the items are in possession of his widow or her agents. THEREFORE, we now appoint James Alexander of NY, in America, Esqr., to be our true attorney to do whatever is necessary to do acting in our place and in our name to recover the absd. lands plus one-forth of one-eight part of a full twenty-forth part of East Jersey. Wits.: Wm. Martincee, Archd. Blair. Ackn.: City of Edinburgh – 12 Feb 1720, Major William and Elizabeth Drummond apprd. bef. John Campbele, Tho. Fenton, James Laing.

Pg 187. 8 Mar 1726. John Hamilton, of NJ, Esqr., sells to Alexander Mackdowall, of Perth Amboy, NJ, trader, for £300, for 1,000 a. to be taken up & surveyed in the unappropriated lands of East NJ, wch. belong to sd. Hamilton in Right of one-third of a Proprietary of John Brains and now vested in sd. Hamilton. Wits.: Robert King, Phineas Mackintoshe. Signed: John Hamilton. Ackn.: 16 Apr 1726, John Hamilton apprd. bef. Robert Lettice Hooper, Esqr., Chief Justice.

Pg 189. 1 Jun 1703. John Harrison, of Middlesex Co., East NJ, sells to Peter Cortilleon, Stoffle Probasco, Theodorey Polhemus, Cornelius Wyckoff,

Hendrick Lott, Frederick Hendrickse, Jaques Cortilleau, and Denyse Tunisse, all of Nassau, NY Co. WHEREAS, there has been a mistake committed by sd. John Harrison in conveying a tr. of land in Middlesex Co., afsd. to sd. Peter Cortilleon and company absd. by deed, dated 7 Nov 1701, by naming and taking the wrong book, whereby disputes have arisen and claims and demands have been made. NOW, THIS INDENTURE, the sd. Harrison for better ascertaining the bounds of the sd. land and for a certain sum of money paid by the absd. persons, who are satisfied, has conveyed unto them all that land in Middlesex Co., beg. at the lodging brook and then n. along the Millstone Rivver to another small brook opposite Hans Tunisse's house and then e.s.e. for 248 chains and then to the beg. and the e.s.e. 248 chains. Wits.: Dereck Bensom, Andries Coeyemans. Signed: John Harrison. Ackn.: 1 Nov 1725, Andrew Coeymans apprd. bef. James Alexander, Esqr., Majesty's Council.

Pg 191. 17 Aug 1725. Christopher Gildermeester, of London, merchant, send greetings. WHEREAS, Peter Sonmans, of London, Esqr., by deed, dated 4 Aug 1724 granted unto me 2,000 a. of land in Middlesex Co., East NJ, being part of a tr. of 15,600 a. on both sides of Lawrence's Brook. AND, WHEREAS, Peter Sonmans has refused to admit my agents on my behalf to take possession of sd. land & premises. NOW, KNOW YE, that I have made by these presents and do make and appoint an attorney, agent, etc. for me in my name to do whatever is necessary to obtain & recover and take possession of the sd. 2,000 a. of land conveyed to me, and I appoint Captain Thomas Hopkins, of NY, my true and lawful attorney. Wits.: D. Downing, William Bale. Signed: Christopher Gildemeester. Ackn.: 27 May 1726, Dennis Downing apprd. bef. James Alexander, Majesty's Council.

Pg 192. 1 Apr 1726 – NY. I having often heretofore by virtue of a power of attorney from Christopher Gildermeester requested you to join me in the location of the 2,000 a. of land granted by you to him by deed of lease & release, dated 3 & 4 Aug 1724 in order to avoid any mistakes that may be committed in not exactly finding the lines of Osterland & Keyser upon wch. the sd. 2,000 a. in bound. [Letter is longer] Signed: Thos. Hopkins. Ackn: 1 Apr 1726 – We certify that we saw Captain Hopkins deliver to Peter Sonmans the absd. letter. Signed: Jer. Lattouch, Teleman Cruger. Ackn.: 27 May 1726, Teleman Cruger apprd. bef. James Alexander, Majesty's Council and stated that he, too, witnessed the delivery of the letter to Sonmans and found them to agree.

Pg 193. 27 May 1726. James Alexander, Surveyor General sendeth greetings. WHEREAS, by a Lease & Release, dated 3 & 4 Aug 1724, betw. Peter Sonmans of one part and Christopher Gildermeester, of London, sold to sd. Christopher 2,000 a. in Middlesex Co. East NJ. And, by his power of attorney, sd. Thomas Hopkins did obtain an Order & Warrant from the Government to direct me to survey run and ascertain the metes and bounds of the 2,000 a., dated 26 May 1725. Now, by virtue of the several writings by Thomas Hopkins, I and my

Deputy, Alexander Mackdowall proceeded to the location of the 2,000 a. pursuant to his notice given to Peter Sonmans and located, butted and bounded the same **[Page 194 is a full detailed map of the area and the adjoining lands, roads, etc. with names of land owners.]** as follows: beg. on the 3rd line of the large tr. of 15,600 a. and then numerous courses [wherein the following names are mentioned – Keyser & Osterland, John White's & Peter White's cleared land]. Signed: Ja. Alexander. I, Christopher Gildermeester by the sd. Thomas Hopkins, my attorney, do hereby declare that I have accepted the locating and the bounding of the sd. 2,000 a. Wits.: James Gillchrist, John Revell. Signed: Christopher Gildermeester by Thomas Hopkins, his attorney. Ackn.: 30 May 1726, Thomas Hopkins apprd. bef. James Alexander, Majesty's Council, and acknowledged that he signed the above instrument as the land deed for sd. Christopher Gildermeester.

Pg 196. 22 Mar 1722. I, Nathan Allen, Monmouth Co., NJ, Esqr., sells to Thomas Gordon, of the afsd. place, for £140, for a tr. of land in Amwell Twp., Hunterdon Co., near the great swamp beg. at the n. corner of [can't read] land and then several courses to the n.w. corner of B.F.'s land and then along same to the beg. ALSO, another tr. on the Delaware River on a hill called by the Indians pinnungging, being 200 a. and to be surveyed by sd. Gordon excep. only th eland sold by me to Lawrence Vanhook and Joseph Allin, wch. both date bef. this deed. Wits.: Joseph Hind, Anne Dudin. Signed: Nathan Allen. Ackn.: 9 May 1723, Joseph Hands apprd. bef. Richard Saltar, Majesty's Council.

Pg 197. 12 Apr 1726. WHEREAS, James Miller, of Highberry, Great Britain, yeoman, was seized in his lifetime of diverse tr. of land in NJ, wch. at his decease were vested one-third in Mary Miller, relict of the sd. James, for her life and the residue by decent to James Miller, son & heir of the sd. James Miller, dec'd. AND, WHEREAS, Mary Miller, widow, with her son, James, gave to James Kinsey, Junr., their Power of Attorney, dated 13 Dec 1725. NOW KNOW YE, that James Kinsey, attorney for Mary Miller and her son, James, quit claimed unto John Anderson, of Freehold, Monmouth Co., East NJ, Esqr., for £100, the 500 a. of land in Monmouth Co., East NJ, beg. where a small run comes into Clear Brook, and is so called because it surrounds the s. & e. sides of the clear fields of Manalapan, near or below the head of the sd. Brook & the Lower End of the meadow and then runs numerous courses to the beg. Wits.: John Read, John Bray. Signed: James Miller, Mary Miller, both were signed by their attorney. Ackn.: 12 Apr 1726, John Kinsey, for Mary Miller and James Miller, apprd. bef. John Hamilton, Esqr., Majesty's Council, and acknowledged that the release on this property was voluntary.

Pg 198. 13 Dec 1726. James Miller, of Highberry, Great Britain, yeoman, was seized of diverse lands in NJ at his death and one-third went to Mary Miller, his widow, with the rest to their son, James Miller, and the both of them appointed John Kinsey, Junr. to be their true and lawful attorney to act on their behalf and

to sell the above sd. lands. Wits.; Geo. Leslie, Wm. Tidmarsh, Wm. Powell.
Signed: James Miller, Mary Miller, made her mark. Ackn.: 12 Apr 1726,
George Leslie apprd. bef. John Hamilton, Esqr., Majesty's Council.

Pg 199. 13 Jan 1723. Thomas Davis, of Newark, Essex Co., East NJ, yeoman,
sells to Cornelius Thomsen, of the afsd. place, for £115, for several tr. of land &
meadow called Pine Meadow on the n.w. side of Second River, one certain tr. of
fresh meadow for 12 a. ; bnd. w.s.w with my own land, n. by Daniel Dod, e.
partly by John Cockborn and part by unsurveyed land, w. by my own land.
ALSO, another tr. adjacent to the one absd., being 10 by 13 chains; bnd. on n.w.
by the afsd. tr., s. by the head of a swamp, e. & w. by land unsurveyed being 12
a.. ALSO, a tr. of land by the last mentioned one, beg. at Daniel Dodd's s.e.
corner, then to the Second River and then along same to John Cockborn's corner
and then along his line; bnd. n. by sd. Dod, e. by my own land, s.e. by sd.
Cockborn, w. by part by Second River and part by land form. of John Gardner.
Wits.: John Cooper, Thomas Sargint. Signed: Thomas Davis. Ackn.: 24 Feb
1723/24, Thomas Davis apprd. bef. Jonathan Crane & John Cooper, two Judges,
Essex Co.

Pg 201. 24 Feb 1723. John Crane, of Newark, Essex Co., East NJ, yeoman, and
Mary, his wife, sell to Cornelius Thomsen, of the afsd. place, yeoman, for a
valuable sum of money, for a tr. of land within Newark in the branches of
Second River, beg. at the s.e. corner of Thomas Davis and then along the branch
to another branch and as it runs; bnd. e. by the branches, n. by Thomas Davis,
and unsurveyed land, and w. and s. to the bounds of my Patent. Wits.: Saml.
Farrand, Thomas Huntington. Signed: John Crane. Ackn.: 24 Feb 1723, John
Crane apprd. bef. Jonathan Crane & John Cooper, two Judges, Essex Co.

Pg 202. 14 Apr 1726. James Miller, son & heir of James Miller, late of
Highberry, Great Britain, dec'd, and Mary Miller, widow of James Miller sell to
Tunis Dennis, of New Utruckt, Kings Co., Nassau Island, NY, by their attorney
John Kinsey Junr., for a tr. of land in Freehold, Monmouth Co., beg. by lands of
Robert Ray and then several courses to land of Thomas Comb's corner and then
along his line to a ditch in Spotwood's Middle Brook and then down same to
Ray's Run and then up same to Robert Ray's line and then along same to the
beg.; bnd. n. & e. by Ray's Run & Spotwood's Middle Brook, s. by land form.
of Thomas Combes and John Reid's, w. by land form. belonging to David
Hamton. ALSO, into & out of another tr. of land in sd. county, beg. at the head
of Spotwood's Middlebrook by Burlington Path and s.w. along Burlington Path
to a corner of land form. sd. Hamton's, then along his line to a ditch that parts it
from John Wycoff's land, then along the ditch & John Wycoff's line to the beg.;
bnd. s.e. by Burlington Path, w. by land of sd. David Hamton, n. by John
Hamton's land, n.e. by the ditch & John Wicoff's land. Wits.: John Anderson,
John Reid. Signed: James Miller and Mary Miller by their attorney John

Kinsey. 14 Apr 1726, John Kinsey on behalf of James Miller & Mary Miller apprd. bef. John Hamilton, Esqr., Majesty's Council.

Pg 204. 12 Apr 1726. James Miller, son & heir of James Miller, late of Highberry, Great Britain, dec'd, and Mary Miller, widow of James Miller, sell to John Bray, late of Middletown, Monmouth Co., NJ. WITNESSETH that John Bray late of Middletown, afsd., dec'd, was seized in his lifetime was possessed of a tr. of land in Middletown being 130 a., beg. at the meeting of a small run with Hop River (wch. bounds land of William Lawrence on the west) & the to the Hop River, s. by the small run and w. by unappropriated land. AND, being so possessed, he died and since that time to the present has been possessed by his son & heir, John Bray, and wch. lands did of Right belong to the afsd. of James Miller, the elder, dec'd and at the time of his death vested one-third in his relict, Mary Miller and the rest to his son, James Miller. NOW THIS INDENTURE, James Miller, son & heir of James & Mary Miller, his relict, sell for £40, have released and quit claimed unto John Bray the absd. land. Wits.: John Anderson, John Reid. Signed: James Miller & Mary Miller, by their attorney, John Kinsey. Ackn.: 12 Apr 1726, John Kinsey apprd. bef. John Hamilton, Esqr., Majesty's Council.

Pg 206. 3 Dec 1725. Jurya Westervelt, of Bergen Co., NJ, Icuman[?] and Cornelius, his wife[?], sell to William Provoost, of NY City, merchant, for £68, for a lot of land on the w. side of the Hackensack River near the Dutch Church in the Precinct of New Barbadoes, Bergen Co, East NJ, being 4.25 a. on the w. side of the road, beg. at the e. corner of land of John Wright, and then along sd. Wright's & Gerritt Van Dien's line, and then several courses to the road and then along same to the beg. Wits.: Egbert Ackerman, Jan. Roomign. Signed: J. Westervelt, Cornelias Westervelt made her mark. Ackn.: 11 May 1726, John Romaine & Egbert Ackerman apprd. bef. Robert Lettis Hooper, Esqr., Chief Justice.

Pg 207. 4 Apr1726. James Wilson, of Middlesex Co., East NJ, yeoman, son & heir of James Willison, late of Monmouth Co., East NJ, yeoman, dec'd, for the natural love & affection he has for his brother, Walter Wilson, quit claims unto him the two tr. of land and half parts of the two tr. of meadow described below. WHEREAS, James Willson, dec'd, father of sd. James Willson, by his last will, dated 2 Aug 1718, gave unto his son, Walter Willson, part of those tr. of land and meadow, wch. he bot. from Jedidiah Allen and Cornelius Thompson, in Monmouth Co. (on part of wch. the sd. James Willson in his lifetime did dwell). AND, there having been some contest abt. the intent of the testator in his will, the sd. James Willson and his brother, Walter Willson, have agreed that the lines of the sd. land & meadow be run beg. at a point in the line of Peter Wilson and then along the middle of the hallow to the e. side of the bog, and long the bog to a branch and across the branch to the brook and then as the brook runs to where two bogs meet and along the s. side of the w. bog to Shaddock's line and then along same to the Burlington Path and then along same to Peter Willson's line and to the beg.; bnd. n. by James Wilson's part of the tr., w. by Shaddock's line, s. by Burlington Rd & e. by Peter Willson's land. ALSO, one half of 14 a. of bog meadow in the meadow of sd. Allen abt. a mile s. of the Great Meadow in the Pines; beg. by a brook and bnd. of both sides by the Barrens. ALSO, a part of the tr. bot. from Cornelius Thompson on the s.e. side of the bog next to the Burlington Path; bnd. s.e. by sd. Path, n.w. by James Wilson's part of sd. tr., s.w. by Nathaniel Parker's land, n.e. by William Shaddock's land. ALSO, one half of 3.5 a. of meadow in the Great Meadow being 22 chains by 7 rods; bnd. n. & s. by upland, e. by meadow of sd. Shaddock, w. by meadow of Thomas Cook. Wits.: James Cox, Wm. Madock. Signed: James Wilson. Ackn.: 26 Apr 1726, William Madock apprd. bef. Robert Lettis Hooper, Esqr., Chief Justice.

Pg 209. 4 Apr 1726. James Wilson, of Middlesex Co., East NJ, yeoman, son & heir of James Willison, late of Monmouth Co., East NJ, yeoman, dec'd, for the natural love & affection he has for his brother, Peter Wilson, has quit claimed unto him his estate Right to one-half of the land described below. WHEREAS, James Willson, dec'd, father of sd. James Willson, by his last will, dated 2 Aug 1718, gave unto his son, Peter Wilson one half of a tr. of land he bot. of Samuel Hophmire lying at Amwell, Hunterdon Co., being 300 a. lying above the Falls of the Delaware in West NJ; bnd. n. of land of Peter Wilson's, w. by land of Lawrence Van Hook, s. & e. by lines of the Society's land and being part of a tr. wch. the sd. Hophmire bot. from Benjamin Field, by deed dated 14 Nov 1701 and from sd. Hophmire to James Wilson, dec'd, on 11 May 1709. AND, there having been some contest abt. the intent of the Testator. Wits.: James Cox, Wm. Madock. Signed: James Willson. Ackn.: 26 Apr 1726, William Madock apprd. bef. Robert Lettis Hooper, Esqr., Chief Justice.

Pg 212. 2 Mar 1723. Benjamin Fitz Randolph, of Middlesex Co., NJ, Esqr., sells to his son Benjamin Fitz Randolph, Junr., of the afsd. place, single man, for £100, for a tr. of land in Somerset Co., being 100 a., beg. at the n.w. corner of Isaac Fitz Randolph's land, and then running n.n.w. of the absd. line parallel to sd. Isaac's line to the e. of sd. Benjamin's land and then to the n.e. corner of sd. Isaac's land and then as his line runs to the beg.; bnd. s. by land of Isaac, n. by land of Benjamin, w. by land of Joseph Stockton, e. by land of Thomas Leonard. Wits.: Robert Stockton, Joseph Stockton. Signed: Benjamin Fitzrandolph. Ackn.: 27 Mar 1724, Benjamin Fitz Randolph apprd. bef. Thos. Leonard, Esqr., Judge, Somerset Co.

Pg 213. 22 May 1702. William Dockwra, of London, merchant, by his attorney, Richard Saltar, of Freehold, Monmouth Co., NJ, and with the consent of Andrew Bown, of the afsd. place, sells to Richard Davis, Senior, of Middletown, Monmouth Co., NJ, for £34, for a tr. of land on the s. side of Raritan River, being 140 a., beg. at the s.e. corner of Richard Davis, Junr.'s land and then several courses to the beg., bnd. w. by Vanwick's land & Bohart's land, s. & e. by sd. Dockwra's land, n.e. by sd. Dockwra's land. Wits.: Andrew Bown, John Royse, Obadiah Holmes, William Hodgson, Jonathan Holmes. Signed: William Dockwra by Richard Saltar, his attorney. Ackn.: 8 May 1723, Richard Saltar apprd. bef. David Lyell, Esqr., Majesty's Council.

Pg 214. 16 Nov 1725. Abraham Tappen, of Woodbridge, Middlesex Co., NJ, weaver, sells to William Bunn, of the afsd. place, yeoman, for £4, 10 shillings, for two little pieces of landing Woodbridge and part of the Sixth Division laid out to sd. Tappen in Right of his father, Isaac Tappen, dec'd, at a place called the Cornfield near the landing place. THE FIRST piece beg. at the n.e corner of the Fifth Division laid out for sd. Bunn and then several courses by the salt meadow and as it runs to the s.e. corner of sd. Bunn's land and then along his line to the s.e. corner of the sd. Bunn lot as then as the line runs to the beg. ALSO, land beg. at the n.w. corner of Bunn's Fifth Division and then several courses to a place by the meadow and then as the meadow runs to the s.e. corner of Bunn's lot and then n. as the line runs to the beg. Wits.: John Heard, Saml. Rolfe, Ichabod Smith. Signed: Abraham Tappen. Ackn.: 16 Nov 1725, Abraham Tappen apprd. bef. Adam Hude, Esqr., Judge, Middlesex Co.

Pg 216. 7 Dec 1723. John Gordon, of Perth Amboy, Middlesex Co., East NJ, cordwainer, sells to Stephen Warne, of the afsd. place, yeoman, for £55, for all the bank lot of land in Perth Amboy on s.e. side of Water Street and then along same to low water mark on the Sound, wch. lot is parallel to and opposite to the most s.w. lot of the two lots of land on wch. St. Peter's Church is now built[?]; wch. land was granted unto John Gordon by his father, Thomas Gordon, dec'd, by deed dated 1 May 1699. Wits.: John Barclay, Junr., Mary Gordon. Ackn.: 8 Aug 1726, John Gordon came bef. John Parker, Majesty's Council.

Pg 217. 22 Jul 1726. Francis Elrington, of Somerset Co, NJ, Gent., sells to Thomas Gordon, for £50, for 15 a. to be taken up & surveyed in the unappropriated lands of East NJ with a Warrant on the hands of Alexander Mackdowall, Deputy Surveyor, NJ. Wits.: Christopher Wiser, Elizabeth Wiser made her mark. Signed: Fran. Elrington. Ackn.: 30 Jul 1726, Christopher Wiser apprd. bef. Thomas Leonard, Esqr., Judge, Somerset Co.

Pg 218. 4 May 1691. Agreement btw. Richard Baker, the Younger, of Elizabeth Town, yeoman, of the one part and Lydia, the widow and relict of John Toe, late dec'd, of the other part bef. the day & time of their marriage. WITNESSETH, that FIRST sd. Baker grants to sd. Lydia Toe that he sd. Baker does convey a piece of land by these Presents. AND, if he, the sd. Baker shall die bef. the sd. Lydia, that the sd. Lydia shall hold & possess and enjoy all his land, etc that he shall possess at the time of his death including his gift from his father, John Baker, Gent., of the afsd. place. AND, if she should die then the lands to be possessed by heirs of her body begotten by sd. Baker. AND, both parties agree that if she should die bef. sd. Baker then sd. Baker shall have and possess all the sd. lands, etc. given to sd. Lydia by her father, Robert Mosse, or by any other means during her natural life, sd. Baker is to enjoy and then at his death to go to the heirs of his body begotten by sd. Lydia. Wit.: Nathaniel Tutle made his mark, Edward Guy. Signed: Lydia Toe made her mark, Richard Baker. Ackn.: Essex Co. 14 Feb 1725/6, the within named Richard Baker & Lydia Toe apprd. bef. Joseph Bonnel, Judge, Essex Co.

Pg 219. 23 Nov 1725. Stephen Warne, of Perth Amboy, Middlesex, East NJ, yeoman, sells to John Covenhoven, of Freehold, Monmouth Co., East NJ, yeoman, for £29, for all the Bank lot in Perth Amboy on the s.e. side of Water Street and along same to s.e. side of sd. street to the low water mark on the Sound; it being the n. half of a bank lot bot. of John Gordon, and as may appear in sd. deed from sd. Gordon, dated 7 Dec 1723; bnd. w. by sd. Street, n. by a Bank Lot form. of Thomas Gordon, brother of sd. John Gordon, e. by the Sound, s. by the sd. Warne lot and also partly opposite to St. Peter's Church in sd. Perth Amboy. Wits.: Richard Akeman, made his mark, Rachel Lawrence. Ackn.: 23 Nov 1725, Stephen Warne apprd. bef. William Lawrence, Judge.

Pg 220. 20 May 1723. Stephen Warne, of Perth Amboy, Middlesex, East NJ, yeoman, releases to Samuel Leonard, of the afsd. place, Gent., for a competent sum of money, for one-half of his Proprietary Right in the undivided lands of East NJ, being one-sixth of a twenty-forth part & quit rents. Wits.: John Hamton, John Lorton. Signed: Sten. Warne. Ackn.: 6 Jan 1724, Stephen Warne apprd. bef. John Parker, Majesty's Council.

Pg 221. 24 Nov 1725. Stephen Warne, of Perth Amboy, Middlesex Co., East NJ, yeoman, sells to Jacob Polhemius, of Kings Co., NY, carpenter, for £30 paid by John Covenhoven, of Freehold, for sd. Jacob, for a Bank Lot in Perth Amboy of the s. side of Water Street, being the lot bot of John Gordon by deed, dated 7 Dec 1723; bnd. w. by Walter Street, n. by John Covenhoven's lot bot. from sd. Warne, e. by the Sound. Wits.: Roeliph Covenhoven, William Covenhoven. Signed: Sten. Warne. Ackn.: 23 May 1726, Steven Warne apprd. bef. Adam Hude, Judge, Middlesex Co.

Pg 222. 31 Mar 1720. John Morford, of Cranberry, Perth Amboy Twp., Middlesex Co., East NJ, yeoman, sells to Mindert Johnson, of the afsd. place, weaver, for £100, for a tr. of land at Cranberry, being 200 a., beg. in the e. line of sd. Morford's land, wch. he bot. from John Harrison, at the s.e. corner of land already granted by sd. Morford to his two grandchildren, John & Thomas Morford, and then several courses to the Millstone River and then up same to the bound line first mentioned, and then a few courses to the beg.; bnd. n. by the land of the two children above, w. by sd. John Morford's land, s. by Millstone River, e. by the afsd. bound line and wch. the 200 a. being part of the land granted to sd. John Morford by deed of John Harrison, dated 3 July 1710. Wits.: Elias Stonbury made his mark, William Saltar, Richd. Saltar. Signed: John

Morford made his mark. Ackn.: 15 Feb 1723, John Morford apprd. bef. John Johnston, Junr., Esqr., Majesty's Council.

Pg 224. 23 Jul 1722. John Jaques, of Woodbridge, Middlesex Co., NJ, yeoman, sells to Moses Rolfe, of the afsd. place, Esqr., for £100, for several tr. of land and meadow in Woodbridge, and also all other lands and meadow that are due or shall become due to sd. Jacques in the Woodbridge Commons. Wits.: Benjamin Rolfe, Matthias Swayze. Signed: John Jaques. Ackn.: 4 Mar 1725/6, Benjamin Rolfe apprd. bef. Adam Hude, Esqr., Judge, Middlesex Co.

Pg 225. 17 May 1722[?]. James Alexander, of NY City, Gent., sells to Thomas Emmerson, of Middlesex Co., carpenter, for £10, for 25 a. to be taken up & surveyed in the unappropriated lands of East NJ, being part of the thirteen-fortieths of a Propriety form. of Sir Eugenius Cameron, of Lochiel, and part of the one-half of land from Evan Drummond who was vested in land of Cameron's grandson, Donald Cameron and by another conveyance from sd. Donald to sd. Evan; excep. one-third of all mines and minerals to sd. James Alexander. Wits.: Thos. Jackman, Zachari Weeks. Signed: Ja. Alexander. 31 Jul 1725, James Alexander apprd. bef. John Parker, Esqr., Majesty's Council.

Pg 226. 7 Jul 1726. James Alexander, Esqr., NY City, sells to John Walls, of Newark, Essex Co., NJ, for £7, 14 shillings, for 22 a. of land to be taken up & surveyed in the unappropriated lands of East NJ, being part of the thirteen-fortieths of a Propriety form. of Sir Eugenius Cameron, of Lochiel, lately bot. by sd. Alexander being the one-half of land from Evan Drummond who was vested in land of Cameron's grandson, Donald Cameron and by another conveyance from sd. Donald to sd. Evan; excep. one-third of all mines and minerals to sd. James Alexander. Wits.: Adam Hay, Ja. Gillchriste. Signed: Ja. Alexander. Ackn.: 8 Jul 1726, James Alexander apprd. bef. John Parker, Majesty's Council.

Pg 227. 10 Sep 1723. John Johnston, of Perth Amboy, Middlesex Co., East NJ, Esqr., sells to James Grover, in Middletown, Monmouth Co., East NJ, yeoman, for a tr. of land in Middletown Twp., beg. on the bank of Swimming River and then to Little Falls Brook and then along same to the bank of sd. river and then along same to the beg.; bnd. s. by sd. River, n. by sd. Falls Brook, e. & w. by unsurveyed land, being 90 a.; wch. land was bot. by sd. Johnston from John Brown, of Middletown, dated 13 Dec 1692. {Lib. C:277, 278}. Wits.: John Barclay, Joseph Jackson. Signed: John Johnston. Ackn.: 10 Sep 1723, Joseph Jackson apprd. bef. John Parker, Majesty's Council.

Pg 228. 11 Mar 1717. Capt. Richard Stout, of Middletown, Monmouth Co., East NJ, Gent., son and heir of John Stout, of the afsd. place, late dec'd, for diverse good causes and valuable considerations, quit claims unto Elisha Lawrence, of Freehold, Monmouth Co., yeoman, for 50 a. described below. WHEREAS my father, the sd. John Stout, was entitled to 50 a. on the w. side of

the Waycake Creek within Middletown, beg. at the lower corner of land form. of
Jarat Walls on sd. creek and then to the line of Zebulon Clayton and along his
line to land form. of William Lawrence and then along his line to the edge of the
meadow form. of sd. Clayton and then along the sd. edge to the sd. creek and
long same to the beg., as may appear to a survey now on record. Wits.: Wm.
Lawrence, Junr., Hugh Hartshorne. Signed: Richard Stout. Ackn.: 24 Aug
1721, Hugh Hartshorne apprd. bef. John Reid.

Pg 229. 7 Apr 1715. John Ruckman, Junr., of Middletown Twp., Monmouth
Co., East NJ, yeoman, sells to Jonathan Ruckman, of the afsd. place, yeoman,
for £230, for several tr. of land & meadow lying within Middletown, beg. by the
street and then numerous courses to a cartway and then along the n. side of sd.
cartway and then to the beg., being 60 a.; bnd. n. by James Grover, w. by land of
John Wilson, s. by the way, and e. by the road, wch. land was granted to John
Ruckman by his father, John Ruckman, on 22 Mar 1702. ALSO, land in the sd.
town; bnd. s. by 9 a. form. of John Wilson, Junr., e. by the absd. tr., n. by land
form. of Robert Hamilton, w. by Mohoras Brook, wch. land was granted to sd.
Ruckman by deed from John Reid, dated 9 Jun 1692. ALSO, meadow of 6 a.
within Middletown; bnd. w. by Shoal Harbour Creek, e. by upland, n. by an acre
lot of Thomas Cox, s. by meadow form. of John Ruckman, Senr., wch. sd. 6 a.
of meadow was granted to sd. Ruckman by deed from Mordecai Gibbons, dated
8 Dec 1690. Wits.: [FNU] Pintard, Edward Wolle, Samuel Pintard. Signed:
John Ruckman. Ackn.: 29 Aug 1726, John Ruckman apprd. bef. Wm.
Lawrence.

Pg 231. 27 Jul 1726. John Johnston, of Amboy, Middlesex Co.,, NJ, Esqr., sells
to Elizabeth Lyon, widow of Thomas Lyon, late of Newark, dec'd, for 5
shillings, for 6 a. in East NJ being part of land belonging to me and not yet taken
up and surveyed in the unappropriated lands of East NJ. Wits.: James Johnston,
Lewis Johnston. Signed: John Johnston. Ackn.: 27 Sep 1726, John Johnston
apprd. bef. John Parker, Majesty's Council.

Pg 232. 26 Jul 1726. John Hamilton, of Perth Amboy, Middlesex Co., East NJ,
Esqr., sells to Francis Elrington, of Somerset Co., East NJ, Gent., for £60, for
200 a. to be taken up and surveyed in the unappropriated lands of East NJ.
Wits.: Robt. King, John Chapman. Signed: John Hamilton. Ackn.: 9 Aug 1726,
John Chapman apprd. bef. John Parker, Majesty's Council.

Pg 233. 2 Aug 1726. Capt. Hugh Hartshorne, of Middletown, Monmouth Co.,
East NJ, and Cathrine, his wife, sell to Joseph Morgan, of Freehold, in the afsd.
place, Minister, for £480, for several tr. of land & meadow in Middletown on
Waycake Neck, being 215 a. on the n. side of Pine Neck on the border of a
swamp and then through Poly Pod Swamp and along a small brook to a tree that
parts sd. Neck from Little Neck and then along sd. creek as it runs to the head of
Waycake Neck. ALSO, several pieces of meadow on the n. side of Pine Neck

joining sd. Creek that parts sd. Neck & Waycake Creek and all the meadow on the s.w. side of sd. Waycake; bnd. s.e. by fresh brooks, being 16 a. ALSO, 2 tr. of land being 100 a., beg. at the N. end of sd. Waycake on the w. side of sd. Creek and then as it runs several courses and being a Neck of land called Pine Neck; bnd. e. & w. by two creeks, s. by land unsurveyed, n. by sd. Creek. ALSO, a tr. beg. at a tree on the Little Neck in the line of land form. of Richard Hartshorne on the w. side of a run of water wch. sd. Little Neck lies w. of sd. Waycake Creek Neck and runs by the w. side of a run of water, etc.; bnd. by same and all other sides of the mouth of Waycake Creek in Middletown. ALSO, 17 a. of upland on the w. side of sd. Creek and along the line of one of the absd. tracts from the Creek and then several courses. AND, all of the absd. Tracts of land & meadow was granted to me by deed from John Stout, late of Middletown, dec'd, dated 12 Dec 1724. Wits.: Robt. White, Junr., John Stout, Yesbrant Van Clef. Signed: Hugh Hartshorne, Katherine Hartshorne. Ackn.: 20 Aug 1726, Isabrant Van Cleave apprd. bef. John Johnston, Junr., Majesty's Council.

Pg 235. 2 Nov 1725. Richard Dockwra, of Epsom, County of Surray, Great Britain, Gent., son and heir of William Dockwra, late of London, merchant, dec'd; William Dockwra, of Christ Church College in Oxford, clerk, another son of sd. William, dec'd, and Admin. of the annexed will of sd. Dockwra, dec'd; Mary Freeman, of London, widow; Margaret Bowels, of Parish of Lambeth, County of Surray, widow; Thomas Warburton, of Tunershall, County of Hertford, Gent., and Ann, his wife; and Andrew Nicolls, of NJ, in America, Gent., and Rebecca, his wife (wch. sd. Mary Freeman, Anne Warburton, Margaret Bowells and Rebecca Nicholls are the daus. of sd. William Dockwra, dec'd) by their attorney Thomas Humphreys, late of London, Gent., sell to Andrew Hay, of Perth Amboy, Middlesex Co., NJ, periwig-maker, for £50, for a lot of land in Perth Amboy on Water Street; bnd. s. by the Bank lot of John Stevens (lately bot. of Thomas Humphrey, w. by Water Street, n. by Smith Street, e. by the low water mark. Wits.: John Barclay, Robt. King. Signed: Thomas Humphreys, attorney, for Mr. Dockwra'a assigns. Ackn.: Perth Amboy, 12 Nov 1726, John Barclay apprd. bef. John Parker, Esqr., Majesty's Council.

Pg 238. 18 Nov 1626 [1726?]. Benjamin Force, of Woodbridge, Middlesex Co., NJ, clothier, and Elizabeth, his wife, sell to Solomon Hunt, of the Borough Town of West Chester, West Chester Co., NY, yeoman, for £221, for several pieces of land & meadow in Woodbridge, beg. at a corner of a lot of Thomas Gach and then to a highway and e. on same to the beg.; bnd. e. by Gach, n. by Isaac Tappen, w. by Robert Wright, and s. by sd. highway. ALSO, upland of 60 a. being a First Division Lot and is the 3rd lot in the 4th tier and drawn in the Right of Jonathan Kinnes. ALSO, a piece of meadow in Rahway Meadows on a small island of meadow adjoining meadow form. of John Cromwell. ALSO, 5 a. of meadow on the sd. small island, beg. at the side of a crk. that makes sd.

island and then by sd. crk. several courses to Rahway River and then as the sd. River runs to the mouth of the afsd. crk., being 10.5 a. Wits.: Samuel Jaques, Thomas Force, Junr. Signed: Ben. Force, Elizebath Force, made her mark. Ackn.: 18 Nov 1626[1726?], Benjamin Force & wife, Elizabeth apprd. bef. Adam Hude, Judge, Middlesex Co. Memorandum - Personally came bef. sd. Hude and Josiah Hunt ackn. the same freely to his son, Solomon Hunt, the whole premises to him as his free act & acknowledged & a deed taken & acknowledged on 18 Nov 1726 bef. me, Adam Hude.

Memorandum - This is to certify to all person to whom it may concern that Josiah Hunt, of West Chester Borough, West Chester Co., NY, having bot. of Benjamin Force of Woodbridge, many years ago all of the absd. several parts of land and meadow contained in the absd. deed, and the sd. Josiah Hunt in order to save charges freely gave all of the absd. land & meadow to his son, Soloman Hunt, for the parental and natural love he has toward him. AND, it is continued in the absd. deed that the sd. Josiah Hunt hath prevented with the above named, signing and sealing, Benjamin Force to grant one deed for the whole absd. lands, meadows and premises to his son Solomon Hunt for the saving charges wch. the sd. Benjamin Force complied with upon the Condition that the deeds he had given to be compelled bef. the signing & sealing and delivery of the absd. deed, wch. the sd. Hunt promised and performed bef. the absd. deed & further the sd. Josiah Hunt by these presents does convey & confirm freely and clearly to his well beloved son all the whole land and meadow & premises contained in the absd. deed to him my sd. son, Solomon Hunt. I the sd. Josiah Hunt have hereto set my hand that date & year above written. Wits.: Samuel Jacques, Thomas Force, Junr. Signed: Josiah Hunt.

Pg 241. 8 Oct 1726. Enoch Freeland, of New Brunswick Twp., Middlesex Co., East NJ, yeoman, & Mary his wife, sell to Thomas Leonard, of Somerset Co., afsd. place, Esqr., for £52, for a piece of land in New Brunswick, beg. at John Vanhorn's s. corner and then down his line to low water mark and then down the Raritan River to the lot of Darby Standland's, then up his lot's line to Burnet St., and by sd. street to the beg.; bnd. e. by sd. River, w. by the street, n. by sd. Vanhorn's. Wits.: Samuel Smith, Henry [LNU], made his mark. Signed: Enoch Freland, Mary Freland, made her mark. Ackn.: 17 Nov 1726, Samuel Smith apprd. bef. John Parker, Majesty's Council.

Pg 243. 15 Nov 1726. James Miller, son & heir of James Miller, late of High Berry's, Great Britain, dec'd, and Mary Miller, widow of the sd. James Miller (by James Kinsey, Junr., their attorney to this purpose) as well as certain Articles of Agreement expressed in a pair of Indentures dated 12 Apr 1726, betw. Jams & Mary Miller of the one part & John Reid, of Hortencie, Monmouth Co., NJ, son and heir of John Reid, late of the afsd. place, dec'd, , and also for other diverse good reasons, do quit claim by these Presents to sd. John Reid all their Right that they have or might have to all lands, etc in NJ by the sd. John Reid, the father in his lifetime had surveyed & laid out for James Miller, dec'd, in the First Dividend, Second Dividend and the Second Dividend of the share of the Proprietary bot. by him of Robert Burnet, as much hath already been conveyed to the tenants in possession by consent of the sd. john Reid, Junr., always excepted. Wits.: Timothy Evans, P. Kearny. Signed: James Miller and Mary Miller by their attorney, James Kinsey. Ackn.: 25 Nov 1726, John Kinsey apprd. bef. John Parker, Majesty's Council.

Pg 244. 23 Mar 1719/20. John Jaques, of Woodbridge, Middlesex Co., NJ, yeoman, sells to John Willson, [name also spelled Wilcoson in the deed but is probably Wilkison] of the afsd. place, mason, for a certain sum of money for a certain tr. of land in Woodbridge, being part of the farm where the sd. Jaques now lives, beg. at the n.w. corner of land lately bot. by John Allston and in the line n.w. to the county road, then several other courses to the beg.; bnd. w. by the absd. farm form. belonging to Joseph Rolfe, n. by the sd. road, e. by land of Ezekiel Bloomfield, s. by land of sd. Allston. Wits.: Jno. Alston, Dabara Moore made her mark. Signed: John Jaques. 31 Dec 1722, John Alston apprd. bef. Adam Hude, Judge, Middlesex Co.

Pg 245. 13 Jan 1722[3?]. John Wilkison, of Woodbridge, Middlesex Co., NJ, mason, sells to Benjamin Force, of the afsd. place, clothier, for 36, for a tr. of land in Woodbridge, being a part of the farm given to John Jaques by his father & grandfather, dec'd, beg. at the n.w. corner of land lately bot. by John Allston but now in the hands of Isaac Thoren, and in the line betw. the land claimed by Joseph Rolph and then to the county road and then to Ezekiel Bloomfield's corner and then several other courses to the beg.; bnd. w. by the absd. farm form. belonging to Joseph Rolfe, n. by the sd. road, e. by land of Ezekiel Bloomfield, s. by land of sd. Thoren [possibly Tappen]. Wits.: John Bell, Wright Skinner, Thomas Force. Signed: John Wilkison. Ackn.: 1 Dec 1722[?], Thomas Force, son of Thomas, apprd. bef. Adam Hude, Judge, Majesty's Council.

Pg 247. 18 Feb 1724. Richard Dockwra, of Epsom, County of Surray, Great Britain, Gent., eldest son and heir of William Dockwra, late of London, merchant, dec'd; William Dockwra, of Christ Church College in Oxford, clerk, another son of sd. William, dec'd, and Admin. of the annexed will of sd. Dockwra, dec'd; Mary Freeman, of London, widow; Margaret Bowels, of Parish of Lambeth, County of Surray, widow; Thomas Warburton, of Tunershall, County of Hertford, Gent., and Ann, his wife; and Andrew Nicolls, of NJ, in America, Gent., and Rebecca, his wife (wch. sd. Mary Freeman, Anne Warburton, Margaret Bowells and Rebecca Nicholls are the daus. of sd. William Dockwra, dec'd) by their attorney Thomas Humphreys, late of London, Gent., sell to John Stevens, of Perth Amboy, Middlesex Co., NJ, tavern keeper, for £50, for the Bank Lot or slip of land in Perth Amboy; bnd. n. by one of sd. William Dockwra's [dec'd] bank lots, e. by low water mark, s. by Andrew

Johnston's bank lot form. Michael Hawdon's, w. by Water Street; beg. at Water Street opposite the s.e. corner of sd. Stevens lot, form. Marian Campbell's lot 6 chains from Market Street on the s. side of sd. lot and 1 chain from Smith street on the n. side of sd. lot; wch. land is described below. WHEREAS, the Proprietors by Patent, dated 2 Aug 1699, granted unto William Dockwra, of London, merchant, and one of the Proprietors, several slips of land in Perth Amboy, Middlesex Co., NJ in the e.s.e part of sd. town towards the Sound, one side being bnd. by intended street and the other with low water mark, beg. opposite the s.s.e. corner of James Armour's lot and then to the s.s.e. corner of Robert Burnet's lot (excep. the part fronting the lots of Peter Sonmans and the street that goes along John Carrington's lots, dec'd, and Robert Burnet's lot to the sound {Lib. G: 80,81}, and wch. the sd. slips of land are contained in the Bank Lot slip of land directly opposite the land form. Patented to Marian Campbell, widow (on wch. she lived) in Perth Amboy and is now in the occupation of John Stevens, wch. is hereby intended to be bot. by sd. Stevens by these Presents. AND, WHEREAS, sd. Dockwra's land was left to his children and they gave power of attorney to Thomas Humphreys to sell land in NJ, in America. Wits.: Lancaster Symes, Hendrick Hendrickson made his mark. Signed: Thomas Humphrey, attorney, signed for the granting parties. Ackn.: 18 Feb 1724, Thomas Humphreys, attorney, apprd. bef. John Hamilton, Esqr., Majesty's Council.

Pg 251. 12 Jul 1722. Benjamin Tappen, of Woodbridge, Middlesex Co., NJ, shoemaker, and Sisell, his wife, sell to Robert Hude, of the afsd. place, yeoman, for £108, for several tr. of land in Woodbridge, beg. at the s.e. corner of Edward Crowell's land where Adam Hude's land joins Crowell's and along sd. Hude's line and then several courses to a outlet and then joining the country road and then to the beg.; bnd. n. by sd. Hude, e. by Abraham Tappen, s. by the sd. Road, w. by the sd. outlet, being 10 a. ALSO, a piece of meadow in Papiak Meadows beg at sd. country road and then several courses to Papiake Creek and then up same to a small branch of sd. Creek and then up the Creek to a bridge and then e. as the highway runs to the beg.; bnd. n. by sd. highway, e. by sd. meadow of sd. Abraham Tappen, s. & w. by sd. Creek, being 4 a. ALSO, half of a small island of meadow s.w. of absd. meadow, being 3 a., wch. half is to be taken at the n. end of sd. island and wch. half being the home accommodations form. of Isaac Tappen, dec'd, and by his will, dated 8 Aug 1710[?], was bequeathed to his sons, Abraham & Benjamin Tappen. ALSO, 11.25 a. of land in Rahway Neck adjoining Robert Gillchrist's land, beg. at the n.w. corner of sd. Gillchrist's land and n.n.e. on a highway and then to the line of Andrew Brown and them to the s.s.w. corner of Brown's land and then to the n.e. corner of sd. Gillchrist's land and then to the beg.; bnd. n. by Abraham's land, e. by Brown's land, s. by Gillchrist's land, w. by sd. highway, wch. land being one half of sd. Isaac Tappen's Second Division lot in Woodbridge Commons. ALSO, 10 a. in Woodbridge Neck, beg. in the line of Capt. John Bishop's Second Division lot and then to his n.e. corner and then to the lone of Job Conger's land and along his line to his s.w. corner and along his line to Frances Evert's n.w. corner and along his line to n.e. corner of Edward Crowell's land (part of his Third Division) and then along his line to the beg. ALSO, 8 a. of land at Metuchen being part of the Fourth Division in absd. Commons beg. at the n.e. corner of Samuel Ayres' Third Division and then several courses to the n.e. corner of William Sharp's land, s. to the n.w. corner of sd. Ayres' land and then to the beg. Wits.: Edwd. Crowell, David Tappen, Jas. Gillchrist. Signed: Benjamin Tappen, Sicell Tappen. Ackn.: 2 Feb 1722/23, Benjamin and Sisel Tappen apprd. bef. John Parker, Majesty's Council.

Pg 253. 3 Jun 1715. John Marsh, of Elizabeth Town, Essex Co., NJ, yeoman, for the love and affection he bears to his son, Joshua Marsh, of the afsd. place, yeoman, grants unto him a tr. of land in absd. place, beg. at a tree and then numerous courses to the beg., being 57 a. ; bnd. s.e. and n.e. by Richard Clarkson's land, s.e. by unsurveyed land, s.w. by Joseph Kellsey in part & part by unsurveyed land, n.w. by unsurveyed land and n.e. part by land of Thomas Clarke and part by unsurveyed land. ALSO, a tr. of salt marsh within Elizabeth Town, beg. at Frazer's Creek and then up a small crk. and then numerous courses to the beg., being 4 a.; bnd. w. by meadow of Samuel Mills, and n., e. , s. by creeks. Wits.: John Harriman, Nathan Whitehead. Signed: John Marsh. Ackn.: 6 Sep 1717, John Marsh apprd. bef. Isaac Whitehead, Judge, Essex Co.

Pg 254. 1 May 1711. Francis Letts, of Perth Amboy, Middlesex Co., NJ, yeoman, and his wife, Mary, sell to Peter Buckaliew, of the afsd. place, yeoman, for a competent sum of money for a tr. of land in the afsd. place at the head of Cheesquack Creek, beg. at a corner of land lately belonging to Thomas Lawrie now of Frederick Buckaliew, being 14 chains by 12 chains; bnd. s.e. by head of sd. Creek, n.e. by sd. Frederick, n.w. and s.w. by unsurveyed land, being 100 a. Wits.: Alex. Walker, Jannet Gordon. Signed: Francis Letts, Mary Letts, with both making their marks. Ackn.: 8 May 1711, Francis Letts and Mary, his wife, apprd. bef. Thomas Gordon, Esqr., Majesty's Council.

Pg 255. 26 Mar 1726. Jedediah Higgins [no location] sells to Daniel Hollinshead & James Alexander [no location], for £22, 10 shillings, for with one-tenth of a twenty-fourth part of East NJ. ALSO, the first, second and addition to the Second Dividend as yet not located being 200 a. and to all further dividends and part of the quit rents, etc. WHEREAS, Jedediah Higgins is vested by several conveyances through Sir John Gordon, Charles Armston & others with one-tenth of a twenty-fourth part of East NJ, wch. form. belonged to Thomas Cooper. Wits.: Phillip Cox, Thomas Wiggins. Signed: Jediah Higgins. Ackn.: 29 Jan 1726, Jediah Higgins apprd. bef. John Parker, Esqr., Majesty's Council.

Pg 257. 9 Dec 1725. Francis Elrington, of Rocky Hill, Somerset Co., NJ, Gent. releases and confirms to John Parker, of Perth Amboy, Middlesex Co., NJ,

merchant, for £6, for 200 a. of land to be taken up & surveyed in the
unappropriated lands of East NJ. Wits.: Ursula Parker, Andrew Johnston.
Signed: Francis Elrington. Ackn.: Andrew Johnston apprd. bef. John Hamilton,
Esqr., Majesty's Council.

Pg 258. 20 Apr 1724. James Alexander has granted and conveyed on this date
to Josiah Ogden, 500 a. to be taken up and surveyed in the unappropriated lands
of East NJ, and sd. deed was granted on the Conditions that sd. Ogden is to grant
& sell same & with one-half of the price shall begot for sd. Alexander, and if
ready money is not paid to take a Bond or penal bill in the name of sd.
Alexander for his half. Wits.: Daniel Martin, Ja. Gillchrist. Signed: Jos. Ogden
Ackn.: 29 Mar 1727, James Gillchrist came bef. John Hamilton, Majesty's
Council.

Pg 258. 31 Jul 1722. Colonel Josiah Ogden, of Newark, Essex Co., NJ, sells to
James Alexander, of NY City, Gent., for £20, for ten-sixtieth parts of six-
sevenths of the tr. of land now called the Blewmine on the brook wch. runs into
the North Branch of the Rariton River and on wch. Peter Keightly's Mill stands,
beg. at a remarkable place below the sd. mill abt. a half mile at the foot of a
steep hill wch. lays round a short bend in sd. brook, and then numerous other
courses to the beg., being 100 a. Wits.: Thomas Jackman, Isaac Stuckey.
Signed: Jos. Ogden. Ackn.: Thomas Jackman apprd. bef. John Hamilton, Esqr.,
Majesty's Council.

Pg 259. 21 May 1726. Daniel Hollinshead, Esqr. [no location] sells to James
Alexander, [no location] of the other part, for £65, for one-third part of the tr. of
land described below. WHEREAS, sd. Hollinshead by Indenture dated 17 May
1726, is seized of two-thirds of a tr. of land on the South Branch of the Rariton
River, being 375 a., beg. at a tree in the meadow near the river and then running
several courses to the river and then as it flows to the beg.; bnd. s.e. by the
River, n.e. by John Campbell's land, n.w. & s.w. by unappropriated land. Wits.:
Ja. Gillchrist. Signed: Daniel Hollinshead. Ackn.: 29 Mar 1727, James
Gillchrist apprd. bef. John Hamilton, Esqr., Majesty's Council.

Pg 260. 1 Sep 1718. John Johnston, of NY City, Esqr., sells to Thomas Lyon,
of Newark, Essex Co., East NJ, for a competent sum of money, for 100 a. of
land in East NJ, wch. is part of other land to be taken up and surveyed in the
unappropriated lands of East NJ. Wits.: Patrick Macknight, James Nutman.
Signed: John Johnston. Ackn.: 1 Jan 1720[22?], James Nutman apprd. bef,
Joseph Harrison, Judge, Essex Co.

Pg 261. 10 Mar 1691. Richard Stout, Junr., of Manasquan, Monmouth Co.,
East NJ, planter, sells to Hannanias Gifford, of Shrewsbury, in the afsd. place, ,
for £110, for all those tr. of land on the n. side of the Manasquan River, beg. at a
tree on a bank and then several courses to the beg., with a piece of lowland

lying n. of the sd. tr. betw. the bank of the river; bnd. n.e. by the River, and with unsurveyed land on all other sides, being 200 a. ALSO, another tr. of land being 50 a. at the afsd. Manasquan adjoining the sd. Stout's plantation upon the sd. River betw. him & Job Throckmorton's land. AND, wch. land was conveyed to sd. Stout by Samuel Leonard on 3 Dec 1687; by James Johnston on 18 Jul 1690. Wits.: Nicholas Browne made his mark, Nathaniel Chammake made his mark, Samuel Dennis, Clement Masters. Signed: Richard Stoutt made his mark. Ackn.: 8 Jun 1725, Samuel Dennis, Esqr. apprd. bef. Richard Saltar, Esqr., Judge, Monmouth Co. and declared that he was well acquainted with the writing of Samuel Dennis, his father, and that he verily believes that his father signed the document and wrote the entire document.

Pg 263. 1 Jan 1715. Effingham Townley, of Elizabeth Town, Essex Co., NJ, Gent., and Sarah, his wife, sells to William Lucar, of the afsd. place, Gent. WITNESSETH, that John Bayley, of Nassau Island, Long Island NY, by his instrument dated 1676[?] {Lib. 1:2}, when James Boullen, Esqr, the recorder, the sd. Bayley conveyed unto Phillip Carterett, Esqr., what he had in Elizabeth Town by wch. the sd. Effingham became seized for 5 shillings and discharged William Lucar by these Presents, with his wife, Sarah, and confirmed unto him William Looker two tr. of land in Elizabeth Town beg. at the s. corner of a tr. lately belonging to William Lucar and then along his line, and then to a brook and then several courses to the beg., bnd. e. & n.e. by land late of sd. Lucar and the brook, n. w. by the South mountain called Elizabeth Town South Mountain, w. by common land and s.e. by land of one Wintrup, being 50 a. ALSO, another tr. of upland adjoining the afsd. tr., beg. by a brook and then several courses to the beg.; bnd. n.e. by afsd. tr., s.e. by sd. Wintrup's Common land, s.w. by Common land and n.w. by afsd. South mountain, being 56 a., the contents of both tr. being 108 a. Wits.: John Osborne, Daniel Osborne, Wm. Dagworthy. Signed: Effingham Townley, Sarah Townley. Ackn.: 13 Feb 1726/7, Daniel Osborn apprd. bef. Joseph Bonnel, Judge, Essex Co.

Pg 265. 1 Jun 1686. We have released & confirmed by these Presents unto John Dobbie, Scotland, who has a Right to one-sixteenth of a Propriety bot. from John Campbell, Gent., who bot. it from John Drummond, of London, Esqr., one of the Proprietors, being all that land on the south branch of the Raritan River, Middlesex Co., being 404 a., beg. at a tree in a meadow near the sd. River and then several courses to the beg..; bnd. s.e. by the River, n.e. by sd. Campbell's land, n.w. & s.w. by unappropriated land. TO HAVE and to hold 300 a. as share in the afsd. Propriety and the other 75 a. being granted to sd. Dobbie for head land for 3 Servants imported into this Province in October. Signed: John Berry, Saml. Winder, Thomas Gordon. Gawen Laurie, Wm. Sandford, Ja. Johnstone, Isaac Kingsland, Ben Price, John Barclay, Jno. Campbell.

Pg 266. 27 Apr 1722. Jonathan Peirson, son & heir of Theophilus Peirson, of
Newark, Essex Co., dec'd, sells to James Alexander, of NY City, for a
competent sum of money, for all that undivided one-thirtieth of a Propriety in
the West NJ (the first & second dividend being already taken up with the town
lots and town land) wch. land sd. Theophilus died seized of by several
conveyances from William Perkins, of England. Wits.: John Walls, Joseph
Tuttle. Signed: Jonathan Peirson. Ackn.: 10 May 1722, John Walls apprd. bef.
William Eier, Judge, Middlesex Co.

Pg 267. 1 Dec 1719. Donald Cameron, of Lochell, grandchild and heir to Sir
Evan (alias Eugenius) Cameron, of Lochell, knight, dec'd, was seized as a
Proprietor of thirteen-fortieths of one-twenty fourth of a tr. of land in East NJ, in
America, by two Indentures and grants; one dated the 2nd and the other dated
the 3rd of April 1685 from Thomas Cox, of London, Gent., in favor of Sir Evan
and also by a Patent to my sd. grandfather, dated 24 May 1690. BY THESE
PRESENTS, I appoint my loving friend and cousin, Evan Drummond, merchant,
to be my true & lawful attorney and to act in my name and do whatever is
necessary regarding the lands in NJ that belonged to my Grandfather. Wits.: Ja.
Taylor, Pat. Campbell. Signed: Donald Cameron.

Pg 268. 1 Dec 1719. Donald Cameron, of Lochell, grandchild and heir to Sir
Evan (alias Eugenius) Cameron, of Lochell, knight, dec'd, presented a Letter of
Attorney, apprd. with James Taylor, Writer and Patrick Campbell, Writer, who
all swore to the documents presented, and further indicated that they know
Donald Cameron to be the eldest son of John Cameron, late of Lochiell, procreat
betwixt him and Mrs. Isabell Campbell, his spouse, wch. John Cameron was the
eldest lawful son of Sir Evan, alias Eugenius Cameron, of Lochiell, Knight,
dec'd, and they gave cause of this knowledge, by having frequent business with
them – Sir Evan, sd. John, his son, and the present Donald his grandson. Wits.:
Ja. Taylor, Pat. Campbell. Signed: Jo. Campbell, Provost, Robert Wrightman,
Bailie, James Laing, Baillie, Ja. Newlande, Jun. Baillie.

Pg. 269. 30 Jul 1716. Sir Evan, alias Eugenius Camerone, of Lochiell,
Scotland, Knight, grants unto Donald Camerone, younger, of Lochiell, grandson
to sd. Sir Evan, for the love and affection he bears unto him, all the thirteen-
fortieths of a twenty-fourth part of a tr. of land in East NJ, in America. Wits.:
Major Donald Camrone, Lieutenant General Murray his Regiment, Robert
Mackey, vintner in Carrmdaille, John Camerone, servitor to sd. Sir Evan and
Alexander Cumming, Notary. Ackn.: 1722, Alexander Cumming, Notary, in
Lochabber, apprd. bef. the Magistrates of Edinburgh and swore that he was the
writer and Adam Watt, Clerk, signed the Presents at Edinburgh on 24 Mar 1724.
Signed: Alexander Cumming, [FNU] Fergussone, Bailie, Alexr. Wilson, Bailie,
Adam Watt, clk., [?] Bailie. [Also, includes another document dated 24 Oct
presented to John Finlayson, Commissary of Dunblane.]

Pg 271. 20 Jan 1710. John Cramer, of Wopening, West NJ, yeoman, sells to Theophilus Peirson, of Newark, Essex Co., East NJ, yeoman, for a valuable sum of money, for an undivided parcel of land or meadow of reversion of one-thirtieth of a Propriety in West NJ, the first & second dividend form. belonging to the sd. one- thirtieth of a Propriety with the town lots and other land being already taken from and therefore is excepted, wch. sd. Reversion of a one-thirtieth of a Propriety the sd. Thomas Brion bot. of Thomas Roper and Abigal, his wife, dau. of William & Mary Perkins, late of the Kingdom of England, dec'd, by Indenture, dated 1 Jun 1703, wch. sd. one- thirtieth of a Propriety is part of a one-fourth of a seven and a half parts of a Propriety that was bot. of sd. William Perkins and John Pentard and given among his three children after the death of his wife as follows: one-half to his son, Thomas Perkins, and the other half to be equally divided betw. his two daus., Mary & Abigal, by a deed dated 27 Oct 1677 and recorded in West NJ at Burlington on 1 Aug 1682. Wits.: Jeremiah Osborn, Twain[?] Ogden. Signed: John Cramer. Ackn.: 20 Jan 1710, John Cramer apprd. bef. Samuel Alling.

Pg 273. 20 Feb 1725. Thomas Houghton, of Stony Brook, Middlesex Co., East NJ, yeoman, and Mary, his wife, sell to Joseph Burleigh, of the town & county of Burlington, of West NJ, merchant, for £480, for all of their farm and plantation in Middlesex Co., being 200 a., beg. at a corner near Stony Brook near the mouth of a small run and then as it runs w. to the Province line and then along sd. line to the corner of Joseph Worth's land and then along same e. at right angles from the sd. Province line and then to a corner where two ditches meet, and then along sd. Worth's land to the sd. Brook and then down same to the beg.; wch. came to sd. Houghton by the will of his father, John Houghton, dated 24 Jan 1709, wherein he gave the above to his son, and wch. 200 a. was bot. by John Houghton from Thomas Warne, by a deed dated 11 Jan 1696 {Lib. F:171-172}. Wits.: Benjamin Clark, John Tantum, Thomas Scattergood, Margret Powell, made her mark. Signed: Thomas Houghton, Mary Houghton made her mark. 24 th day of 12th month 1725. 28 Feb 1725/6, Thomas Scattergood apprd. bef. John Wills, Majesty's Council.

Pg 276. 7 May 1722. John Dagworthy, of Elizabeth Town, Esqr., sold to James Alexander, of NY City, for a competent sum of money, for one-twelfth part of a tr. of land in Essex Co., beg. at a tree s.w. of a small brook called Rattle Snake Brook on the s. side of the south mountain n.e. of Green Brook falls and then by numerous courses per a survey to Dagworthy, dated 2 Apr last past. Wits.: Moses Rolfe, Hugh Dunn. Signed: John Dagworthy. Ackn.: 18 May 1727, Moses Rolfe apprd. bef. John Parker, Majesty's Council.

Pg 277. 17 May 1726. Elizabeth Drummond, widow and relict and Admin. of Captain Robert Drummond, late Commander of the ship, *Caledonia*, dec'd and Major William Drummond, eldest brother and heir of the sd. Robert Drummond by James Alexander, their attorney, sell to Joseph Murray and Daniel

Hollinshead, Esqr., for £195, the tr. of land as described in the Dobie Patent below; with one-third of same to Joseph Murray and the remaining two-thirds to Daniel Hollinshead. WHEREAS, Elizabeth Drummond and William Drummond by a power of attorney, dated 12 Feb 1719/20, appointed James Alexander to be their true attorney and to act on their behalf to sell one-fourth of one-eighth of a one-twenty fourth of a Proprietary of East NJ, wch. was form. sold by John Campbell to John Dobie and by sd. Dobie to Capt. Robert Drummond. AND, the sd. Patent dated 1 Jun 1686 confirmed to sd. Dobie was for a tr. of land on the south branch of Rariton River, being 404 a. down to 375 a.; bend. s.e. by the river, n.e. by John Campbell's land, n.w. & s.w. by unappropriated lands. Wits.: Ja. Gillchrist, Humphrey Clay. Signed: James Alexander, their attorney signed for Elizabeth Drummond and William Drummond. Ackn.: 18 May 1727, James Gillchrist apprd. bef. John Parker, Esqr., Majesty's Council.

Pg 279. 20 May 1727. Elizabeth Bass, sold Exec. of the will of Jeremiah Bass, late of the town & county of Burlington, West NJ, Esqr., dec'd, for diverse causes, appointed Samuel Bustill, Esqr., to be my true attorney for me in my name and to do whatever is necessary to recover whatever for the estate. Wits.: Daniel Meslayer, Kathe Talbot. Signed: Elizabeth Bass. Ackn.: 30 May 1727, Elizabeth Bass apprd. bef. James Smith, Esqr., Majesty's Council.

Pg 280. 25 Jul 1719. Tripartite Deed. [Three page document setting the north Division Points of NJ & NY] Robert Walters, of NY City, NY and Isaac Hicks of Queens Co., NY, Esqrs.; and Allan Jarret, of NY City, NY, Esqr., surveyor, for and in behalf of NY Province, of the one part, and John Johnston and George Willocks, of East NJ, Esqrs. and James Alexander, Surveyor General of East NJ, of the second part; and Joseph Kirkbride and John Reading, of West NJ, and James Alexander, Surveyor General of West NJ, of the third part. WHEREAS, the sd. Commissioners and surveyors, as well as NY and NJ have carefully inspected and informed themselves wch. of the respective branches is the northernmost branch of the Delaware River, and therefore by these Presents do Certify & Declare that the river called the Fishkill to be the bigger and swifter stream that forms the sd. Delaware River....Therefore they Certify & Declare that the North Partition of Division point on the northernmost branch of the Delaware River betw. NY & NJ, wch. is also the North Partition Point betw. East & West NJ, is latitude 40 degrees and forty minutes....Wits.: John Harrison. Signed: R. Walter, John Johnston, Joseph Kirkbride, Isaac Hicks, Geo. Willocks. Jno. Reading. Allane Jarratt, and Ja. Alexander on behalf of East & West NJ Divisions. Ackn.: Province of NJ -10 Aug 1719, John Harrison, of Perth Amboy, Middlesex Co., NJ, Esqr., apprd. bef. John Parker, Esqr., Majesty's Council. Province of NY – 10 Aug 1719, John Harrison, of Perth Amboy, Middlesex Co., NJ, Esqr., apprd. bef. Lewis Morris, Esqr., Chief Justice, NY.

Pg 283. 27 Oct 1717. Samuel Smith, of Woodbridge, Middlesex Co., NJ, yeoman, confirms unto my son, Samuel Smith, of the afsd. place, for the love and affection I bear toward him, a meadow and a tr. of land being 41 a., within Woodbridge Twp., on the e. side of the road to Elizabeth Town, being part of 60 a. of land mentioned in my Patent together with a small piece of land on the s. side of the sd. Patent land with another piece adjoining to the e. end of the first land mentioned, wch. was laid out to me by the Freeholders of Woodbridge, being part of a Second Division in Woodbridge Commons, the whole being 41. a.; beg. at a stake on the e. side of the absd. road, then to the n.w. corner of Samuel Moore's land, then to the w. corner found marked of Bald Hill land, then along the sd. Hill line to the n. corner and then numerous courses to the beg. Wits.: J. Kinsey, Junr., Thomas Pike. Signed: Samuel Smith made his mark. Ackn.: 27 Feb 1718, Samuel Smith, Senr. apprd. bef. Adam Hude, Judge, Middlesex Co.

Pg 284. 27 Apr 1724. Margaret Rolph, widow and devisee of Henry Rolph, of Elizabeth Town, and John Rolph, eldest son & heir, sell to James Alexander, for sd. Alexander delivering up to them and releasing a Bond granted by sd. Henry Rolph, dec'd, to the sd. Alexander for £120, dated 28 Oct 1720, wch. Bond & 6 pence they accept as payment in full for the below mentioned land of 200 a. AND, also the sd. 85.5 a. surveyed as part of the 200 a. below. WHEREAS, James Alexander by deed, dated 28 Oct 1720 {Lib. C-2:85} conveyed to Henry Rolph, 200 a. of land, being part of 300 a., wch. sd. Alexander bot. of Donald Cameron, of Locheil, in East NJ, and wch. was surveyed to sd. Rolph a tr. in Elizabeth Town, beg. of the e. side of the Great Stone Brook near the w. side of Thomas Hart's land, and then several courses to a point of the s.e. side of sd. Brook and then down same as it runs to the beg., being 82 a. ALSO, a tr. of land on Elizabeth Town bounds, beg. on the s. side of a branch of Rahway River called Robisones Branch to the w. of Edward Frazey's now dwelling house, and then several courses to the Woodbridge line and then w. along sd. line to sd. Branch and then down same to the beg., being 8 a.; wch. two tr. of land remain as 85.5 a. by the Survey {Lib. 2:222} and {Lib. S:22}. AND, WHEREAS, the sd. Henry Rolph, made his will on 27 Feb [1722/3] devised to Margaret Rolph and empowered his lands to be sold, and he died and his will was proved 13 Aug 1723. Wits.: Wm. Robison, James Gilchrist. Signed: John Rolph, Margaret Rolph made her mark. Ackn.: 28 Apr 1724, James Gilchrist apprd. bef. David Lyell, Majesty's Council.

Pg 285. 15 May 1722. Charles Dockmininque, Esqr.; Edward Richier; Sir John Bennett; John Darnell, Esqr.; Thos. Skinner, Esqr.; Sir William Hammond; Robert Mitchell; Charles Mitchell; Obadiah Burnet; John Bridges; Joseph Brooksbank, Esqr; John Whiteing; John Child; & Robert Allen, all of London, Great Britain & other Proprietors of East NJ, known by the name of the East NJ Forty and Lewis Morris, Esqr., their attorney, of one part and James Alexander, of NY City, of the other part. WHEREAS, the absd. first part by Letters of

Attorney authorized sd. Lewis Morris to act on their behalf to grant and sells lands in NJ as he should think proper. WITNESSETH, that for consideration of £100 paid by the sd. James Alexander, the party of the first part by Lewis Morris releases and confirms unto sd. Alexander 500 a. of land in East NJ part of their dividend in East NJ, to be taken up and surveyed in the unappropriated lands. Signed: The grantors names were signed by their attorney Lewis Morris in the presence of Cadwallader Colden.

Pg 287. 27 Dec 1721. John Budd, of Philadelphia, PA, sells to James Alexander, [no location] for £200, for a half part of a tr. of land on Pasaick River, in Somerset Co., beg. at the upper corner of a tr. surveyed for William Penn on sd. River at a corner and then along the line of sd. Penn to another corner of Penn's and then numerous courses to a brook falling into the sd. River and then to the beg., being 1,036.5 a. ALSO, one half of a tr. of land beg. on the n.w. side of the absd. brook and then several courses to the beg., being 84.55 a. Wits.: Fen. Lyell, Isaac Stuckey. Signed: Jno. Budd. Ackn.: 18 May 1727, Fenwick Lyell apprd. bef. John Parker, Esqr., Majesty's Council.

Pg 289. 14 Aug 1722. John Ayers, of Woodbridge, Middlesex Co., NJ, yeoman quit claims unto Joseph Ayers, his brother, of the afsd. place, [painter/printer?] all his Right to several parcels of land and meadow wch. was form. given unto my absd. brother by our father, Obadiah Ayres, form. of Woodbridge, dec'd, being 50 a. of upland bot. by our father from Jonathan [LNU] and 60 a. of the First Division in the Woodbridge Commons. ALSO, 7 a. of meadow being the remainder of his absd. 30 a. in his Patent wch. he had given in his will to my self and my brother, Samuel, all of the absd. upland & meadow. Wits.: Robert Gillchrist, Tho. Pike. Signed: John Ayers. Ackn.: 24 Jul 1727, Robert Gillchrist apprd. bef. Adam Hude, Judge, Middlesex Co.

Pg 289. 29 Oct 1725. James Moore, of Woodbridge, Middlesex Co., NJ, yeoman, for the parental love and affection I bear unto my second youngest son, James Moore, of the afsd. place, weaver, have conveyed unto him, all my lands whereon I now live being known by the name of James Moore's farm, beg. at the n.e. corner of the 60 a. I gave unto my son, Samuel Moor, wch. I bot. from Mathew Moore and then along the line of the 60 a. and then several courses to a brook and then several more courses to the beg. ALSO, 25 a. lying in Raritan Meadows, being wch. consists of 15 a. of meadow in part of 30 a. contained in honored Father Matthew More, dec'd, his Patent, wch. all land and meadow is lying within Woodbridge. Wits.: Samuel Moores, Ad. Hude. Signed: James Moore. Ackn.: 2 Nov 1725, James Moore apprd. bef. Adam Hude. Judge, Majesty's Council.

Pg 290. 13 Sep 1723. Isabella Davis, of Perth Amboy, Middlesex Co., NJ, widow, grand-daughter and heir of Gawen Lawrie, form. of London, merchant, and afterwards Dep. Gov. of East NJ, leases to Henry Lane, of NY City, merchant, for 5 shillings, for one year the one-half of a full undivided twenty-fourth part of East NJ, wch. is still to be share-divided amongst the NJ Proprietors, by transferring uses into possessions. Wits.: Rebecca Davis, Eliza. Swift, John Chambers. Signed: Isabella Davis. Ackn.: 18 May 1727, John Chambers apprd. bef. John Parker, Majesty's Council.

Pg 291. 14 Sep 1723. Isabella Davis, of Perth Amboy, Middlesex Co., NJ, widow, grand-daughter and heir of Gawen Lawrie, form. of London, merchant, and afterwards Dep. Gov. of East NJ, releases to Henry Lane, of NY City, merchant, for £60, for land now in is possession under transferring uses into possessions, all that equal half part of one full twenty-fourth part of East NJ, still remaining to be share-divided among the Proprietors and all appurtenances re: what is described below. WHEREAS, Gawen Laurie was seized in his lifetime of a one-twenty-fourth part of East NJ and the Proprietors abt. 1684 agreed that there should be a survey and a Patent to each Proprietor that held a full 10,000 a of land and sd. Gawen procured 5,000 a. and his proportion of the land and town lots in Perth Amboy to be surveyed and after his death the Proprietors concluded it should be set forth as a one-twenty-fourth part; being 1,200 a. of meadow at Barnagate, 5,000 a called the Second Division and 2,500 a. being the addition to the Second Division all of wch. was set in East NJ as the proportion of said moiety of a twenty-fourth part besides the land & lots in Perth Amboy. Wits.: Rebecca Davis, Eliza. Swift, John Chambers. Signed: Isabella Davis. Ackn.: 18 May 1727, John Chambers apprd. bef. John Parker, Majesty's Council.

Pg 294. 23 Sep 1725. Henry Lane, of NY City, merchant, leases to James Alexander, Esqr., for 5 shillings, for a one-half of an undivided one-twenty-fourth part of East NJ, wch. is still remaining to be divided among the Proprietors, under the transferring of uses into possessions. Wits.: Ja. Gillchrist, James Adames. Signed: Henry Lane. Ackn.: 24 Sep 1725, Henry Lane apprd. bef. John Hamilton, Esqr., Majesty's Council.

Pg 295. 23 Sep 1725. Henry Lane, of NY City, merchant, releases to James Alexander, Esqr., for a competent sum of money, for a one-half of an undivided one-twenty-fourth part of East NJ, wch. is still remaining to be divided among the Proprietors, under the transferring of uses into possessions [re: the absd. deed – Page 294 and this again describes the whole area of NJ and amount of acres, etc.]. Wits.: Ja. Gillchrist, James Adames. Signed: Henry Lane. Ackn.: 24 Sep 1725, Henry Lane apprd. bef. John Hamilton, Esqr., Majesty's Council.

Pg 298. 19 Feb 1724. John Johnston, of Perth Amboy, sells to Alexander Carns, of the afsd. place, tailor, for £30, for a lot of land in Perth Amboy, Middlesex Co., East NJ, on Smith Street being 10 chains by 1 chain; bnd. e. by John Colllin's lot, s. by sd. Street, w. by Hodgon's lot, n. by a street; wch. land was granted to sd. Johnston by Patent, on 17 Jun 1701. Wits.: Geo. Leslie,

James Johnston. Signed: John Johnston. Ackn.: 19 Feb 1724, John Johnston
apprd. bef. John Parker, Majesty's Council.

END OF BOOK D-2 DEEDS

[Note: The remainder of the pages in Book D-2 contain the recorded
records of the Chancery Court of East NJ, 1683-1702, wch. were sewn in,
upside down. These records were published by Preseton W. Edsall, ed., in
1937, by the American Legal History Society, Philadelphia, PA, under the
title *Journal of the Courts of Common Right and Chancery of East New
Jersey, 1683-1702.*]

"CALEDONIA", Majesty's Ship, 19, 82, 100
"WHITE", sloop, 36

[

[?ARNS], Thomas, 28
[LNU], Benjamin, 72
  Derick, 72
  Derick, yeoman, 72
  Gilbert, "the butcher", 60
  Henry, 93
  Joannah, 8
  John, 35
  Jonathan, 103
  Robert, 72
[ROLF/ROSE?], Samuel, 26

A

AARISON, Art, 64
ABENAKER, Elias, 65
  Elias, merchant, 64
ACKERMAN, Egbert, 86
ADAMES, James, 104
AEDIE, George, 57, 58
AERTSEN, John, 29
AERTSON, John, yeoman, 29
AIKMAN, William, dec'd, 16
AKEMAN, Richard, 89
ALEXANDER, Ja., 14, 31, 34, 46, 59, 60, 84, 90; Ja., Surveyor General, 67, 78; James, 3, 12, 13, 19, 26, 31, 34, 46, 72, 96, 97, 99, 100, 101, 102, 103; James, attorney, 80; James, Esqr., 4, 23, 65, 67, 82, 104; James, Esqr., Majesty's Council, 77, 83; James, Gent., 8, 12, 58, 59, 60, 74, 78, 90, 97; James, Majesty's Council, 44, 47, 52, 68, 69, 70, 80, 83, 84; James, Surveyor General, 14, 17, 65, 72, 83, 101
ALLEN, Annanias, 55; Annanies, 56; Jedidah, 86, 87; John, 10; Nathan,

Esqr., 84; Robert, 102; Robert, Gent., 68; Robt., 68; Samuel, 76
ALLIN, Joseph, 84
ALLING, John, 27; Saml., 67; Samuel, 26, 100; Samuel, Judge, Essex Co., 65
ALLSTON, John, 94
ALLWOOD, Henry, dec'd, 34
ALORD, Henry, 5
ALSTON, Jno., 94; John, 10, 21, 46
AMERICAN LEGAL HISTORY SOCIETY, 105
ANDERSON, Jan, 32; John, 14, 85; John, Esqr., 84; Wm., 8
ANDREWS, Ephraim, 8; John, 73
ANERSON, John, 86
ANGELE, May, 45
APPLEGATE, Benjamin, 79; Joseph, 40; Thomas, 79
ARENTS, J., 9Jacob, doctor, 23; Jacob, physician, 18, 20, 24
ARKING, Robert, 69; Robt., 68, 69, 70
ARMOUR, James, 95; James, Gent., 69, 70
ARMSTON, Charles, 96
ASHLEY, Isaac, 69, 70; Isaac, merchant, 67, 68
ASTON, Ralph, 69
ATKINS, Edward, Sir, 61; Robert, Sir, 61
AYERS, John, 30; John, yeoman, 103; Joseph, 103; Obadiah, 30, 42; Obadiah, planter, 30; Obediah, 8; Samuel, 30, 103
AYRES, John, 8, 9; Obadiah, dec'd, 103; Samuel, 96
AYREST, Gunsley John, 24

B

BAILY, Elias, 73

BAKER, Agnes, 20; Daniel, yeoman, 45; John, Capt., dec'd, 48; John, Gent., 20, 88; Richard, 89; Richard, the Younger, yeoman, 88

BALDWIN, Elnathan, 46; John, 24; John, Junr., school master, 23

BALE, William, 83

BALL, Edward, 26; John, yeoman, 65; Moses, 23

BANISTER, Edmund, 60, 61

BANKS, James, 35

BARCLAY, Jno., 34; John, 3, 4, 8, 9, 18, 28, 34, 44, 48, 67, 90, 92, 98; John, Gent., 52, 60, 64; John, Junr., 80, 88; John, Junr.[?], Gent., 77; Robert, 13, 44; Robert, Esqr., dec'd, 73, 77; Robert, yeoman, 41, 45

BARD, Peter, 14
Peter, Esqr., 37
Peter, Esqr., Majesty's Council, 38

BARKELY[?], John, Baron, 17

BARKER, Martha, 8; Martha, widow, 8; Richard, 20; Thomas, 12, 29, 59; Thomas, merchant, dec'd, 8

BARTOW, John, 13

BASS, Elizabeth, 101; J., 12; Jeremiah, Esqr., 12, 101

BAYLEY, John, 98

BAYLY, Daniel, 40

BEAKMAN, Jacobus, 25; Jacobus, surgeon, 25; Martin, 52

BEEJMAN, Gerardus, Capt., 32

BEEKMAN, Adrian, 29, 32; Adrian, yeoman, 29; Charles, 40; Chrest., 32; Christopher, Esqr., 32; Gerradus, 29; Gerrardus, 46; Heecke[?], 52;

Henry, 32; Jerard, 32; Mag., 32; Magdelena, 32; Martin, blacksmith, 52; Noocka, 52; William, 32; William, Gent., 29

BELL, John, 94

BENNETT, John, Sir, 102

BENSON, Dereck, 83; Derick, 73; Derick, Gent., 72; Direck, 73; Maritie, 31; Sampson, inn holder, 31

BENSORTIS[?], William, 9

BENTHALL, Walter, 14, 24, 29, 33

BERE, Charles, Esqr., 68

BERRY, John, 98

BILLING, Edward, Gent., 61

BINGLA, William, 8

BINGLEY, William, 13

BIRD, Grantham, 38; Josiah, 73, 74

BISHOP, Freelove, 15; John, 8, 9, 10, 46, 64, 70; John, Capt., 95; John, Esqr., 14, 21; John, Esqr., Majesty's Council, 64; John, Junr., 14, 21; John, Junr., yeoman, 15; John, Justice, Middlesex Co, 46; Mary, 21; Moses, 21; Noah, 15, 21; Noah, blacksmith, 2; Richard, 12, 23; Richd., 23; Richs., 30

BISHOP[?], Moses, 15

BLACK, George, 63; Wm., 50

BLACKWOOD, James, 69; James, merchant, 68; Jas., 69; Rob., 49; Robert, 69; Robert, merchant, dec'd, 68

BLAIR, Archd., 82

BLAKE, John, 37; John, Junr., 37

BLANCHARD, Anne, 72
John, merchant, 72

BLOMFIELD, Thomas, Senr., dec'd, 57

BLOOMFIELD, Benjaman, cordwainer, 43; Ezekiel, 10, 94; John, 1, 43; Joseph, weaver, 43

BLUMFIELD, Timothy, 8

BOBIN, Js., Dep., Sec., 22

BOCKE, Abraham, yeoman, dec'd, 31

BOCKEE, Abraham, cooper, 31; Abraham, dec'd, 31; Isaac, cooper, 31; Sarah, spinster, 31

BOCKIN, Thomas, 65

BOHART, [FNU], 87

BOLEINES, Peter, 72

BOLLEN, James, 72

BOND, Hanna, 23; Joseph, 23

BONDS, Mrs., 26

BONNEL, Joseph, Judge, Essex Co., 31, 35, 70, 72, 81, 89, 98

BONNELL, Joseph, Judge, Essex Co., 48

BONSON, Catalina, 31; Dirk, yeoman, 31

BORDEN, Banjm., 38; Benjamin, yeoman, 37, 38; Benjm., 37; Mary, 38; Richard, 38; Safety, 37, 38

BOREM, Area, 77

BOREN, Are, yeoman, 77

BORROW, John, 37

BORROWE, John, 1

BORROWES, John, merchant, 65

BOUGHTON, Jo., 68; John, 69; John, Gent., 68

BOULLEN, James, Esqr., 98

BOURDET, Samll., Junr., 54

BOWELLS, Margaret (Dockwra), widow, 38, 74

BOWELS, Margaret (Dockwra), widow, 92, 94

BOWLES, Margt., 38; Phineas, merchant, 38

BOWN, Andrew, 87, 88; Andrew, Capt., 35; John, 71

BOWNE, Andrew, 35; Andrew, Capt., 59; Anne, 51, 52; Frances, 51, 52; James, 51, 52; John, 12, 51, 52; John, cordwainer, 12, 66, 67; Lydia, 51, 52; Obadiah, 51, 52; Wm., 35

BRADFORD, Will., Senr., 13, 48; William, 13

BRADLEY, Samuel, 62

BRAGARD, Bragoon, 56

BRAGHAR, Bragoon, 35

BRAID[?], William, 26

BRAIN, Benjamin, 60, 63; Benjamin, merchant, 61; Elizabeth, 62; James, 80; James, Junr., 60; James, Junr., Gent., 61; James, merchant, 62; James, Senr., Gent., 61; James, Senr., merchant, 60; John, mariner, 82; John, yeoman, 27; Joseph, yeoman, 27; Thomas, mariner, dec'd, 82

BRAINS, Benjamin, 62; Benjamin, merchant, 63; John, 62, 82; Thomas, 62

BRANT, William, 46

BRAY, John, 84; John, dec'd, 86

BRECKAER, Bargoon, 56

BRIDGES, John, 102

BRION, Thomas, 100

BRITTAIN, Daniel, 14, 15, 70; Daniel, cordwainer, 15; John, 66; Thomas, 28

BRITTEN, Daniel, 2

BROCKAW, Cataline, 39

BROCKE, Jameke, widow, 31

BRODERWUK, Tho., 46

BROECKAER, Ketlyeu, 56

BROKAR, John, 54

BROOKSBANK, Joseph, Esqr., 102

BROTHERTON, Henry, 6

BROWN, Andrew, 95; George, 6, 8; James, Major, 59; James, 41; John, 13, 64, 90; Joseph, 24; Thomas, 18
BROWNE, Nicholas, 98
BRUIN, John, 27; Joseph, 27; William, 27
BUCKALIEW, Frederick, 96; Mary, 96; Peter, yeoman, 96
BUCKINGHAM, Jedediah, 16
BUDD, Jno., 103; John, 19, 103; John, Gent., 20
BUES, Alexander, 78
BUISAS, Jacob, 64; Jacob, yeoman, 63
BUISE, Jacob, yeoman, 64
BUN, William, 8
BUNN, Mary, 42; Miles, 42; William, yeoman, 88
BURGESS, Robt., scribe, 38
BURLEIGH, Joseph, merchant, 100
BURLING, Edward, merchant, 28
BURNET, John, 26,50; John, Gent., 25; John, grocer, 49; John, merchant, 31; Obadiah, 102; Rob., 78; Robert, 11, 19, 28, 34, 59, 94, 95; Robert, Gent., 63; Robert, Gent. & Proprietor, 78; William, Esqr. Gov., 22; William, Esqr., Gov., 28
BURNETT, Andrew, 13; John, grocer, 50; Moses, yeoman, 79
BURRELL, John, 15
BURWELL, John, 15; Joseph, cooper, 23; Zach., 23
BUSTILL, Samuel, Esqr., 101
BYSE, John, 77

C

CAMERON, Donald, 8, 12, 74, 80, 90, 99, 102; Donald, Major, 57; Donald, younger, 57; Eugenius, 57, 67, 99;

Eugenius, Sir, 12, 58, 74, 78, 80, 90; Evan, 74; Evan, Sir, 57, 72, 99; John, 57, 58, 99
CAMERONE, John, servitor, 99
CAMERSON, Donald, 78
CAMFIELD, Mathew, freeholder, 27
CAMPBELL, Archd., 69; Archibald, 69; Archibald, dec'd, 68; David, 19; Isabell, Mrs., 99; Ja., 58; Jno., 98; Jo., 58; Jo., Provost, 99; John, 4, 9, 97, 101; John, dec'd, 2; John, Esqr., Sheriff, 9; John, Gent., 98; Marian, widow, 95; Mary, 9; Neil, Lord, 69; Neil, Lord, dec'd, 5; Pat., 99; Patrick, 99
CAMPYON, John, 36
CAMRONE, Donald, Major, 99
CANNESTE, Pieter, 78
CARDALE, Thomas, 32; Thos., 29
CARHART, William, 44, 45
CARHARTT, Robt., 18
CARMUCHULL, Wm., Justice, 50
CARNS, Alexander, tailor, 104
CARRINGTON, John, dec'd, 95
CARSEN, Cornelius, Gent., 55
CARTER, Samuel, 72
CARTERET, Elizabeth, 61 Elizabeth, Baroness, 72 George, Knight, 17; George, Sir, 60, 77; Ph., 72; Philip, Esqr., Gov, 72; Phillip, Gov., 77
CARTERETT, Elizabeth, Lady, 73; Phillip, Esqr., 98
CAZIE, Philip, 43; Phillip, 36

CAZIER, Phillip, Gent., 36
CHAMBERS, John, 28, 104
CHAMMAKE, Nathaniel, 98
CHANCERY COURT RECORDS, 105
CHAPMAN, John, 91; John, merchant, 47; Mary, 47
CHEESMAN, William, cordwainer, 45
CHEYNE, Ja., 50
CHILD, Elizabeth, 63; Tho., 63
CHILDS, Elizabeth, 63; Thomas, inn holder, 63
CHRISTOPHER, George, 81
CHURCH, Thos., 55
CLARK, Benjamin, 72, 100; Elizabeth, 20; Ephraim, 20; John, yeoman, 70; Joshua, yeoman, 43; Phebe, 70; Richard, 70; Richard, shipwright, 70; William, husbandman, 81; William, tailor, 48
CLARKE, Benjamin, 75; Benjamin, dec'd, 75; Elizabeth, 21; Ephraim, 21; Ephraim, planter, 20; Ephraim, yeoman, 20; Richard, shipwright, 81; Thomas, 96
CLARKSON, Ja., 39; James, 8; James, yeoman, 39; John, 6; Richard, 96
CLAWSON, John, bricklayer, 20; Mary, 77; William, 64; William, dec'd, 77
CLAY, Humphrey, 101
CLAYTON, Zebulon, 91
CLEMENT, Jonathan, dec'd, 63
CLIZLE[?], James, 15
COANRAATS, Octavo, 31
COBUS, John, 39
COCK, John, 10
COCKBORN, John, 85
COCKBURN, John, 26
CODRINGTON, Margaret, 53, 54; Thomas, 54; Thomas,

Captain, Esqr., 53; Thomas, Gent., 53
CODWISES, John Conrad, Junr., 73
CODWISES[?] MILL, 73
CODWISS, Conrad, 9
COEYEMANS, Andries, 83
COL[?]ON, John, Junr., 23
COLDEN, Cadwallader, 103
COLER, thomas, 8
COLLENS, John, 60
COLLIER[?], Thomas, 42
COLLINS, John, 104; Moses, 64
COMB, Thomas, 85
COMBES, Thomas, 85
COMBS, Robert, planter, 57
COMPTON, Elizabeth, 6; John, 8; John, blacksmith, 6; Wm., dec'd, 5
CONGER, Job, 95; John, 9; Joseph, 8
CONINE[?], Derick, 74
CONONIS[?], Derick, 72
CONVERS, Samuel, 77
CONYERS, Gerrard, Sir, 60
CONYNAFORES[?], Derick, 72
COOK, John, 35; Thomas, 87
COOPER, Jno., 23, 27, 79; John, 15, 24, 26, 35, 79, 85; John, Judge, Essex Co., 85; Thomas, 96; Thomas, merchant, dec'd, 73
CORLELYOU, Peter, 25 Pieter, 25
CORTILLEAU, Jaques, 83
CORTILLEON, Peter, 82, 83
COSENS, Sarah, 33
COUERSON, John, 35
COUPER[COOPER?], Thomas, merchant & Proprietor, 55
COURSEN, Hendrick, 78
COURTLAND, [FNU], 10
COUZARD, David, 76

COUZENS, Sarah (Dennis), 33;
Sarah, seamstress, 33
COVENHOVEN, John, yeoman,
89; Roeliph, 89; William, 89
COVERT, John, yeoman, 56
COVINGTON, Sarah, 27
COWARD, Hugh, 81; Patience, 81
COWPERTHANTE, Grace, 28
COX, Charles, 57; James, 87;
John, 66; Phillip, 96; Thomas,
91; Thomas, Gent., 57, 58, 99
CRAIG, Archibald, yeoman, 6;
John, 4, 6, 7
CRAMER, John, yeoman, 100
CRANE, John, 79; John, yeoman,
80, 85; Jonathan, 23;
Jonathan, Judge, Essex Co.,
85; Jonathan, Justice, Essex
Co., 24; Mary, 85; Widow, 46
CREED, William, 29;
William, yeoman, 29
CREMER, Thomas, 61
CREW, Lord, 61
CROMWELL, John, 92
CROMWELLE, Benjamin, 39
CROSHLIE, Adam, 75
CROSLEY, Henry, 40
CROWEL, Edward, 8
CROWELL, Edward, 9, 95, 96;
Edwd., 39, 96
CRUGER, Teleman, 83
CRUMWEL, Benjamin, 8
CU[?]INGGAME, Thomas, 67
CUMING, Alexander, 57
CUMMING, Alexander, notary, 99
CURTIS, John, 26, 27; John,
Justice, 26
CUTCHINSONE, Ja,. Sr., 70;
Ja., Sr., 69
CUTHANS, John, 64

D

D'NIGHT, Matthias, 5
DAGWORTHY, John, 12;
John, Esqr., 100; Wm., 98
DARNELL, John, Esqr., 102

DAVENPORT, Francis,
Majesty's Council, 78
DAVES, Isabella, 4
DAVIES, Isabella, 7
DAVIS, Elijah, cordwainer, 12,
31; Henry, yeoman, 30;
Isabella, 13, 14, 19, 23, 34;
Isabella, widow, 7, 103, 104;
John, 26; John, yeoman, 27;
Rebecca, 104; Richard, 59;
Richard, Junr., 87; Richard,
Senior, 87; Ro., 69; Stephen,
79; Stephen, dec'd, 26;
Thomas, 26, 27, 46; Thomas,
yeoman, 85; Wm., Gent.,
dec'd, 7
DAY, John, 24
DE LANCEY, James, 82
DE LOUZADA, Jacob, 65
DE LOZADA, Aaron, 64;
Jacob, merchant, 64; Moses,
64; Rachel, 64
DE MARREE, Mary, 37
Samuel, 37
DE MORRAIS, David,
lapidary, 64
DE MORRAY, David, 65
DEARE[?], Wm., 4
DEGRAW, Gerredt, 52; Gerret,
52
DEHART, Mathias, Capt., 31
DEHLERICH, Daniel, 37
DELPEET, Isaac, 63
Jabus, 63
DENNIS, John, weaver, 33;
Joseph, 46, 52, 79; Joseph,
cooper, 39; Samuel, Esqr., 98;
Sanuel, 98; Tunis, 85
DES MAREST, Mary, 37;
Samuel, yeoman, 37
DEWSBERRY, Benjamin, 74
DICK, Tho., Justice, 50
DIN, John, 57
DISBROW, Benjamin, 73, 74
DIXON, William, 63; Wm., 63
DOBBIE, John, 98

DOBIE, John, 19, 82, 101
DOBIE PATENT, 101
DOCK, Joseph, 27
DOCKININIQUE, Paul, Esqr., 34
DOCKMININQUE, Charles, Esqr., 102
DOCKMINIQUE, Charles, 31; James, 31
DOCKWRA, [FNU], 74; Rebecca, 38; Rich., 38; Richard, Gent., 38, 74, 92, 94; William, 44, 45, 47, 69, 88; William, clerk, 38, 92, 94; William, dec'd, 38, 94; William, merchant, 35, 59, 74, 87, 92; William, Proprietor, 75, 95; Willm., 38; Wm., 35, 44
DOD, Daniel, 85
DODD, Daniel, 27, 85
DOLLY, John, 10
DORSEY, Henry, 79
DORUES, Cornelius, 65
DOTEY, Samuel, yeoman, 79
DOTIE, Samuel, 63
DOTTEY, Samuel, 79
DOUGHTY, Amie, 28; Amy, 28; Charles, 28; Jacob, 23; Jacob, yeoman, 28
DOVE, John, 42
DOW, Johannes, 33
DOWNING, D., 83; Dennis, 83
DRAKE, Abraham, carpenter, 1; Deliverence, 1; Francis, Captain, 42
DREW, Buthbert, 62
DREWITT, Benjamin, 10
DRINKWATER, Edward, dec'd, 56
DRUMMEY, John, 72; John, shop keeper, 71; Mary, 71
DRUMMOND, Anne, 43; Ed., 57; Elizabeth, 100, 101; Elizabeth, widow, 19, 82; Evan, 34, 58, 74, 78, 80, 90; Evan, Gent., 12, 59, 60; Evan, merchant, 12, 57, 58, 59, 67, 99; Jo., 57; John, Esqr., 98;

John, of Lundie, 2; Js., 57; Robert, Capt., 101; Robert, Captain, 82, 100; Robert, Captain, dec'd, 19; Robert, dec'd, 43; Robert, vintner, 43; William, 101; William, Major, 19, 82, 100
DUBRIES, John, 10
DUDIN, Anne, 84
DUKE OF YORK, James, 60
DUMONT, John, 75; Peter, 54, 75
DUNDAS, James, dec'd, 19
DUNHAM, David, 35; David, blacksmith, 41
DUNN, Hugh, 41, 100
DUNNIDGE, Jabus, 63; James, notary, 63
DUNSTAR, Charles, 69; Charles, Gent., 70; Charles, merchant, 68

E

EARL, John, 61
EARL OF PERTH, James, 69
EARL OF SANDWICH, Edward, 61
EAST NEW JERSEY FORTY, Proprietors, 102
EDSALL, Preston W., ed., 105
EIER, William, 28, 44; William, dec'd, 47; William, Esqr., Middlesex Co., 99; William, Judge, Middlesex Co., 14, 18, 39; William, Mayor, Perth Amboy, 19, 20, 56; William, Judge, Essex Co., 11; Wm., 4, 12
EIGHTMAN, Robert, 58
EIRE, Mary, 47; William, 47; William, Esqr., Judge, Middlesex Co., 3; William, Esqr., Majesty's Council, 12; William, Judge, Middlesex Co., 15; William, Mayor, Perth Amboy, 14; Wm., Judge, Middlesex Co., 9

ELBERSON, John, 22

ELISON, Seth, 20, 74; Thomas, 20, 44

ELLISON, Mary, 23; Seth, 44; Thomas, husbandman, 44; Thomas, yeoman, 45; William, 2

ELLSWORTH, Clement, shipwright, 56

ELMORE, George, carpenter, 5; Union, 5

ELRINGTON, Fran., 88; Francis, 24, 33; Francis, Gent., 88, 91, 96

ELSTON, John, 14; Peter, 8

ELSTONE, John, 15; Peter, Junr., 64; William, turner, 64

ELSWORTH, Clement, 39

EMLEY, William, surveyor, 78

EMMERSON, Thomas, carpenter, 90

EMOTT, James, Gent., dec'd, 18; Mary, 18

ESTAUGH, John, Gent., 8

EVANS, Timothy, 94

EVERET, Abraham, 64

EVERSON, John, 32

EVERT, Frances, 96

EWBANKS, George, school master, 41

F

FARMER, Thos., 44

FARMER[FARMAR?], Thomas, Judge, Somerset Co., 55

FARRAND, Saml., 85

FEARNE, Richard, Gent., 38; Richd., 38

FENTON, Tho., 82

FERGUSSONE, [FNU], bailie, 99

FEURT, Peter, 51

FFARMER, Tgo., 5

FIELD, Benjamin, 87; John, 54, 73

FILKIN, Henry, J.P., 32

FINLAYSON, John, 57; John, commissary, 99

FITCH, Tho., 47, 63; Thomas, 47

FITZ RANDOLPH, Benjamin, 46; Benjamin, Esqr., 87; Benjamin, Junr., single man, 87; Benjamin, yeoman, 76; Isaac, 87; Nathaniel, 8; Samuel, 9; Thomas, 41

FITZRANDOLPH, Benjamin, 87; Thos., 34

FOLKER, Dirick, 39

FORBES, Alexander, 50

FORCE, Ben., 93; Benjamin, 11, 64, 93; Benjamin, clothier, 92, 94; Elizabeth, 92, 93; Mathew, planter, 70; Thomas, 94; Thomas, cordwainer, 70;Thomas, Junr., 93

FOREMAN, John, 42 John, dec'd, 41; Thomas, 4

FORMAN, [FNU], 13

FORREST, Mathew, 57

FORSTER, Mary, spinster, 54; Miles, dec'd, 59; Miles, merchant, 7; Wm., 54

FOSTER, Anne, 37; Josias, 37

FOSTER[FORSTER], William, 54

FOURTER, Nathaniel, 65

FRANCURT, Benj., Junr., 2

FRAZEE, Elisha, house carpenter, 42

FRAZEY, Edward, 102

FRAZIER, Edward, 11; Elias Pelle, 35

FREELAND, Enoch, yeoman, 93

FREEMAN, Bernard, minister, 25; Margareta, 25; Mary (Dockwra), 38, 94; Mary (Dockwra), widow, 74, 92

FREENCH, John, 64

FRELAND, Enoch, 93; Mary, 93

FRENCH, Anne, 54; Elizabeth, 54; John, 64; Madame, 54, 76; Margaret, 54; Philip, 54; Phillip, Gent., 53; Susanna, 55
FULLERTON, Thomas, 45
FUNNELE[?], Benjamin, 82

G

GACH, Thomas, 92
GAGE, Thomas, 70
GALLOWAY, Andrew, 58
GANDY, Peter, mariner, 35, 36
GARDNER, John, 24, 26, 27, 85
GARWAY'S COFFEE HOUSE, 57
GAUNET, Rohobath, 77
GERRITSON, S., 22
GIBBINS, Mordciai, 66; Rebecca, 66
GIBBONS, Modecay, 66; Mordecai, 91; Mordicay, 66; Rebecca, 66
GIBSON, Samuel, 13
GIFFORD, Hannanias, 97
GILBERT, John, 23
GILCHRIST, James, 102
GILDERMEESTER, Christopher, 84; Christopher, merchant, 71, 83
GILDERSLEEVE, Asa, yeoman, 48
GILES, James, 73
GILLCHRIST, Ja., 78, 97, 101, 104; James, 80, 84, 97, 101; Jas., 96; Ro., Judge, Middlesex Co., 35; Robert, 95, 103
GILLCHRISTE, Ja., 90
GILLMAN, John, planter, 40; Joseph, 10
GILMAN, John, 40; Jos., 24
GODDEN, John, carpenter, 46
GODDIN, Mary, 46
GODIN, John, 46
GOODEN, Charles, 18
GORDON, Alexr., 63; Andrew, 19, 33, 34, 74, 78; Andrew,

Gent., 40; Augustin, 49; Augustine, surgeon, 50; Augustus, 25; Augustus, surgeon, 49; Charles, dec'd, 13; Charles, Gent., 80; Eupem, 34; Euphaim, 27; Euphem, 34; Jannet, 33, 34, 96; John, 27, 28, 33, 34, 40, 89; John, cordwainer, 88; John, Sir, 96; Kenneth, 50; Margaret, 4; Margarett, 27, 34; Mary, 27, 34, 88; Robert, dec'd, 49, 50; Robert, Esqr., 25, 49; Thomas, 9, 12, 17, 18, 26, 27, 34, 76, 84, 89, 98; Thomas, dec'd, 88; Thomas, Esqr., 4, 25, 27; Thomas, Esqr., dec'd, 33; Thomas, Esqr., Majesty's Council, 96; Thomas, Gent., 34; Thomas, Junr., 4, 25, 41; Thomas, Majesty's Council, 8, 17, 19, 41; Thos., Esqr., Majesty's Council, 30; Thos., Majesty's Council, 2
GORHAM, Henry, 81
GOSNEY, John, 43; John, planter, 42
GOVERNEIR, Abrah., 32
GOVERNEUR, Abraham, 10
GRAHAM, James, Gent., 55
GRAME, Patrick, 69
GRAMe, Patrick, 70
GRANDENS[?], Amico, 41
GRANT, Pat., 50
GREEN, Henry, 72
GREENLAND, Henry, 33
GREENWICH, Bernard, Esqr., 61
GRIFFITH, John, 8
GROOM, Samuel, Junr., 60, 61; Samuel, Senr., 61
GROOME, Samuel, Senr., mariner, 60
GROOMS, [FNU], 38
GROVER, Elizabeth, 65; James, 91; James, yeoman, 90; Joseph, 65
GRUBB, Thomas, 52; Widow, 64
GUY, Edward, 89
GYLES, James, yeoman, 72

H

HAINDES, John, dec'd, 31
HALE, George, 10; George,
  yeoman, 9; Samuel, 1;
  Samuel, Justice, 10;
  Thomas, 9
HALL, John, 25; Joseph, 26
HALLINBECK, John, 11;
  John, yeoman, 11
HALSTEAD, Caleb, 35;
  Timothy, 35
HAM, Antho., 29;
  Anthony, Gent., 29
HAMELL, Elias, 66
HAMILTON, Agnes, 47;
  Andrew, 51, 78; Andrew,
  Esqr., 47; Andrew, form. Gov.,
  75; Andrew, Gent., 50; Doctor, 25;
  George, Esqr., Majesty's
  Council, 3; James, Esqr.,
  Majesty's Council, 84
  John, 13, 14, 16, 19, 23, 34,
  63, 69; John, Coll., 76;
  John, Esqr., 17, 23, 82, 91;
  John, Esqr., Majesty's Council,
  4, 5, 7, 36, 37, 51, 71, 73, 80,
  85, 86, 95, 97, 104; John,
  Majesty's Council, 97; Robert,
  91
HAMMERTON, Jos., 69
HAMMOND, William, Sir, 102
HAMOCK, Sandy, 13
HAMPTON, John, 45
HAMTON, Andrew, 20; David, 85;
  John, 85, 89
HANCOCK, Edward, 46
HANDS, Joseph, 84
HANKINS, John, 76
HARISON, Fra., 7; Francis[?], 7
HARKER, Richard, 8
HARKUT, Daniel, Junr., 79
HARRIMAN, John, 96
HARRIOSN, William, 45
HARRIOTT, David, Junr., cooper,
  5
HARRIS, John, 62

Nicholas, 40
HARRISON, Benj., 30; Benja.,
  56; Captain, 59; Elisa, 47, 56;
  Elizabeth, 47; Ganata, 23;
  Gannatta, 23; Henry, 47; John,
  3, 6, 8, 24, 39, 40, 43, 48, 77,
  82, 83, 89; John, Esqr., 18, 40,
  65, 101; John, Gent., 28, 30,
  43, 46, 47, 73; John, Judge,
  Essex Co., 20, 23, 27; John,
  Major, 23; John, merchant,
  dec'd, 7; Joseph, 24;Joseph,
  Judge, Essex Co., 15,79, 97;
  Joseph, Justice, Essex Co., 24;
  William, 23; William, yeoman,
  22; Willm., 23
HARRISON'S MILL, John, 18, 33
HART, Thomas, 29, 102; Thomas,
  dec'd, 71; Thomas, merchant, 61;
  Thomas, merchant & Proprietor,
  29
HARTSHORNE, Cathrine, 91; Hugh,
  Capt., 91; Hugh, 91; Hugh,
  skinner, 61; Katherine, 92;
  Margaret, 51, 52, 66; Richard, 51,
  52, 59, 66, 92; William, 51, 52
HASKILE, John, Gent., 47
HASSING, Jarol, yeoman, 31;
  Jaromine, 31
HATCH, Tobias, 6
HATFIELD, Jos., 71
HAWDON, Michael, 95; Michael,
  Gent., 7
HAY, Adam, 90; Andrew, periwig
  maker, 92; Mary, 24, 75, 76;
  Robert, 1; William, 75, 76
HAYS, Robt., 23
HAYWOOD, John, skinner, 63
HEARD, John, 43, 88
HENDRICK, Daniel, 65; John, 8,
  21, 63
HENDRICKS, Abraham, dec'd, 81;
  Daniel, 81; Daniel, Captain, 74;
  Hannah, 81; Isaac, 81;
  John, 8
HENDRICKs, John, Gent., 70

HENDRICKSE, Frederick, 83
HENDRICKSON, Hendrick, 95
HENRY, Michael, 44, 78
HEPBORN, John, 28
HERRIMAN, Richard, 48;
  Stephen, 48
HERRING, Cornelius, Esqr., 37
HERRIOT, David, 13; David,
  Junr., cooper, 41
HEWIT, Jos., 61; Joseph, Gent., 60
HEYWOOD, John, skinner, 61
HICKLE, George, yeoman, 37
HICKS, Isaac, Esqr., 101; Jos., 35;
  Jos., Judge, Queens Co., NY, 35
HIER, Thos., 65
HIGBEE, Obadiah, 37
HIGGENS, Mr., 79
HIGGINS, Gershom, 31;
  Jedediah, 96; Jediah,
  96; Jediah, cordwainer,
  40; Mary, 40; Thomas,
  40; Thomas, dec'd, 16
HILL, John, 62
HIND, John, 20; Joseph, 84;
  Samuel, 13
HITON, George, 20
HNOLLINSHEAD, Daniel,
  merchant, 36
HOAGLAND, Richard, 10
HODGONS, [FNU], 104
HODGSON, Lydia, 28; William,
  28, 88; William, brick layer,
  44; William, bricklayer, 1
HOGELAND, [FNU], 10
HOLDEN, Richard, 16
HOLLAND, Henry, 82
HOLLAND'S BROOK MILL,
  25
HOLLEN, Nickolas, 30
HOLLINSHEAD, Daniel, 14, 37,
  96; Daniel, Esqr., 97; Daniel,
  merchant, 59; Daniel. Gent.,
  24; Daniel,Esqr., 101; Danl.,
  24
HOLMES, Jonathan, 88;
  Obadiah, 88

HOME, Alex., 49;Alexa., 57;
  Alexander, 57
HOMES, George, 54
HOOPER, John, 74; R.L., 76;
  Robert Lettis, 78, 79;
  Robert Lettis, Esqr., Chief
  Justice, 75, 82, 86, 87
HOPHMIRE, Samuel, 87
HOPKINS, Captain, 83;
  Thomas, 84; Thomas,
  Captain, 83; Thos., 83
HOUGHTON, John, 100;
  Mary, 100
HOUTON, Tho., Justice, 50
HOUYGHTON, Thomas,
  yeoman, 100
HOWEN[?], Robt., 8
HUBBARD, James, Judge,
  Monmouth Co., 66
HUDD [HUDE?], Adam, Gent., 3
HUDDLESTON, Wm., 28
HUDE, Ad., 103; Adam, 8, 9, 35,
  39, 95;Adam, Esqr., 16, 34;
  Adam, Esqr., Judge, Middlesex
  Co., 4, 5, 64, 88, 90; Adam,
  Judge, Middlesex & Somerset, 9
  Adam, Judge, Middlesex Co., 6,
  10, 11, 13, 14, 15, 16, 18, 21, 25,
  28, 30, 36, 39, 42, 43, 70, 77, 89,
  93, 94, 102, 103;Robert, yeoman,
  95;Robt., 39, 42
HUDGSON, William, brick layer, 28
HUDLESTON, Wm., 37
HUGHES, Martha, 79
HUGSON, Lydia, 28;William, brick
  layer, 28
HUKELLS, Thos., 51
HULL, Benia, 79;Benj., 16; Benja.,
  79; Benjamin, 1, 39, 52, 77, 79;
  Hopewell, 40, 41
HUMPHREY, Thomas, 92; Thomas,
  Gent., 75
HUMPHREYS, Thomas, 95
  Thomas, Gent., 92, 94; Thos.,
  Esqr., 75
HUMPHRY, Thomas, attorney, 95;

Thos., 38
HUNLOCK, Joshua, 63
HUNT, Josiah, 93; Solomon, 93;
 Solomon, yeoman, 92
HUNTER, Brigadier, 28; Jonathan,
 tanner, 45; Margery, 45; Robert,
 Esqr., Gov. NJ, 43
HUNTINGTON, Thomas, 85
HURLE, Henry, 19
HUTCHESONE, Wm., bailie, 49
HUTTON, John, 41, 45; John,
 cooper, 44
HYATT, John, 48

I

IEILEY[?], John, 8
ILESLEE, John, 30
INION, John, 32
INNES, Alexander, 34
IRELAND, John, 28, 41
ISELEE, Joseph, 39
ISELSEY, William, 9
ISLEAY, Wm., 6
ISLEE, John, 42
ISLEY, William, 39

J

JACK, Negro, 52
JACKMAN, Tho., 34; Thomas,
 25, 34, 43, 44, 97; Thos., 58,
 59, 80, 90
JACKSON, [FNU], 49, 60;
 John, 13; Joseph, 90; Mayor,
 London, 63
JACQUES, Henry, dec'd, 11;
 John, 8
JAFFRAY[?], Andrew, 77
JAMISON, David, Chief
 Justice, 10; David, Esqr.,
 Chief ; Justice, 1,2, 13, 29,
 32, 37 63; David, Esqr., 47;
JANSEN, Jahannos, 32;
 Johannis, 32
JANSON, William, 18
JAQUES, John, 11; John,
 yeoman, 46, 90, 94;

Samuel, 93; Stephen, 11
JAQUIAS, John, 46; Jonathan,
 10
JAQUISH, Henry, dec'd, 10;
 John, yeoman, 10;
 Jonathan, 11; Jonathan,
 laborer, 10; Jonathan, planter,
 10; Jonathan, yeoman, 10;
 Ruth, 10
JARRET, Allane, Esqr., surveyor,
 101
JARRETT, Allane, mariner, 29
JEFFRE, Free Negro, 64
JEFFREY, Andrew, 80
JEMISON, David, Esqr., Chief
 Justice, 73
JEWELS, George, 1
JOB, John, 42
JOBES[?], William, 66
JOHN REID'S LANDING, 71
JOHNSON, Edwd., 65; Elizabeth,
 62; John, 26; John, Junr., 26;
 Martha, 26; Mary, 62; Mindert,
 weaver, 89; Myndert, 79;
 Thomas, 20; Thomas, Justice,
 26; Thos., 20, 21; Tunis, yeoman,
 24
JOHNSTON, Andrew, 4, 17, 23, 95,
 97; Andrew, merchant, 3, 17;
 Andrw., 77; Andw., 80;
 Catherine, 3; Eugham, 16;
 Eupham, Junr., 16;; George, 11,
 31; James, 4, 6, 91, 98, 105;
 John, 16, 17, 33, 45, 47, 59, 73,
 77, 80, 104, 105; John, Esqr., 5,
 7, 16, 41, 44, 45, 71, 90, 91, 97,
 101; John, Junr., 5, 47, 74; John,
 Junr., Esqr., Majesty's Council,
 90; John, Junr., Majesty's
 Council, 19, 45, 76, 81, 92;
 Katherine, 3; Lewis, 44, 48, 66,
 91; Pat., 49
JOHNSTONE, Ja., 98; John, 12;
 John, Esqr., 66
JOLINE, Andrew, 35
JONES, Richard, 6, 59

JONS, Richard, 8
JOPLINE, Andrew, 43
JORDON, Jonathan, 16
JOUET, Elizabeth, shop keeper, 63

K

KAY, John, 8
KEARNY, [FNU], 67; Mich., 28;
    Michael, 25, 59, 60; Michael,
    Gent., 15, 18, 22; Michll., 15,
    59; P., 94; Tho., 12
KELLSEY, Joseph, 96
KELSY, William, 8
KENNEY, Samuel, 48
KENNYON, Roger, Gent., 65
KENT, David, yeoman, 30;
    Stephen, Junr., 5; Stephen, 6, 8,
    30, 34, 52; Steven, yeoman,
    30
KENYON, Roger, 65
KERUOHAUN[?], Andrew, 12
KETCHAM, Daniel, 40
KEYSER, [FNU], 83, 84; John,
    31, 32, 71
KICKS, Isaac, 101
KING, John, 15; Charles II, 77,
    82; John, 22; Robert, 82;
    Robt., 80, 91, 92
KINGSLAND, Edward, Capt, 9;
    Isaac, 98; Mary 9
KINKAID, Ja., 17
KINNES, Jonathan, 92
KINSEY, J., 59, 60; J., Junr.,
    102; James, 94; James, Junr.,
    84, 93; John, 2, 84, 86;
    John, Junr., 85
KIRKBRIDE, Joseph, 101
KURLTOWNE[?], Gilbert, 49

L

LA CANTE, [FNU], 35
LA FLORE, 52
LADD, Susanna, 30; William, 30,
    43; William, shipwright, 42;
    Wm., 30
LADNER, Absalom, sadler, 35;

Eliza., 35; Elizabeth, 35
LAING, James, 58, 82; James,
    bailie, 99
LANE, Adrian, 25; H., 8;
    Henry, 7; Henry, merchant, 103,
    104; Thomas, Sir, 34
LANGFORD, [FNU], 59
LANGSTAFF, John, 1
LANGSTAFF[?], JOHN, 9
LATHENBY, Henry, 6
LATTOUCH, Jer., 83
LATUT, Margaret, 44
LAURENCE, Willm., Junr., 40
LAURIE, Gawen, 98, 104
LAURIER, W., 16
LAWERY, Gawen, merchant, 60
LAWIE, Gawen, Proprietor,
    dec'd, 13
LAWRENCE, Elias, 67;Elisha, 67;
    Elisha, yeoman, 66, 90; James,
    72; James, yeoman, 66; Joseph,
    66; Joseph, yeoman, 67; Rachel,
    89; William, 7, 8, 52, 86, 91;
    William, Judge, 89; William,
    Junr., 40, 45, 74; William, Junr.,
    trader, 66, 74; William, Senr.,
    51, 72; Willm., 66; Wm., 91;
    Wm., Junr., 72, 91
LAWRIE, Gawen, 19, 34; Gawen,
    dec'd, 4, 14; Gawen, dec'd,
    Proprietor, 23; Gawen, Esqr.,
    dec'd, 7; Gawen, form. Gov.,
    51; Gawen, merchant, 103, 104
    James, 7; Mary, dec'd , 51;
    Thomas, 96
LE BOYLEAULA, Gabriel, 9
LE BOYTOULX, Gabriel, 52
LEE, David, yeoman, 40
LEEDS, Thomas, 72; Thos., 72;
    William, Junr., yeoman, 80
LEIGH, Joseph, 5, 43; Joseph,
    boatman, 30; Thankful, 43;
    Thankfull, 30
LENTINE, Abraham, 52
LEONARD, Anne, 19; John, 19;
    Nathall, 76; Nathaniel, 76;

Saml., 34, 66; Samll., 19;
Samuel, 98; Samuel, Capt., 19
Samuel, Esqr., 4, 40; Samuel,
Esqr., Judge, Middlesex Co.,
79; Samuel, Gent., 30, 89;
Samuell, Esqr., 4; Susana, 76;
Susannah, 76; Thomas, Esqr.,
Judge, Somerset Co., 88; Tho.,
46; Thomas, 87; Thomas, Esqr.,
23, 76, 93; Thomas, Gent., 33;
Thos., 33; Thos., Esqr., Judge,
Somerset Co., 87
LESENBY, Henry, planter, 17
LESLIE, Geo., 17, 44, 56, 85,
104; George, 85; George,
Gent., 80
LETTS, Francis, yeoman, 96;
Mary, 96
LEVENTHORP, Lydia, 54
LINDSLEY, John, 24;
John, Senr., wheelwright, 23
LINSLY, John, 23
LIPITT, Moses, 81; Sarah, 81
LISLE, Maurie, 69
LOCKHART, Goven, 8; Samuel,
42
LOCKHEART, James, dec'd, 34;
Samuel, merchant, 34
LOCKHERT, Gawen, 5; James,
yeoman, 5
LONG, John, 40; Thomas, 37
LONGFIELD, Cornelius, 8, 73,
77; Cornelius, Gent., 7
LONGSTAFFE, John, yeoman, 16
Sarah, 16
LOOFBURROW, John, 8
LOOKER, William, 98; William,
yeoman, 43
LORD BERKLEY, John, 60
LORTON, John, 89
LOTT, Hendrick, 83
LOURIER, Michael, carpenter,
73; Susannah, 73; William,
16
LOUZADA, Aaron, yeoman &
merchant, 77; Moses,

merchant, 77
LOVERIDGE, William, dec'd, 75
LOVING, Thos., 71
LOWRIE[LAWRIE], Mary, 51
LOYD, Timothy, 7
LUCAR, Sarah, 98; William, 98;
William, Gent., 98
LUCAS, Nicholas, Gent., 60
LUFBURROW, John, Junr.,
cooper, 45
LUFFBORROW, John, Junr., 3
LYELL, David, 8, 40, 44, 66, 67;
David, Esqr., 58, 59; David, Esqr.,
Majesty's Council, 33, 40, 45, 75,
88; David, Esqr., Proprietor, 30;
David, Majesty's Council, 26, 35,
67, 72, 74, 78, 102; Fen., 103;
Fenw., 19; Fenwick, 103;
Katherin, 33
LYNN, John, 6
LYON, Elizabeth, 91; Hannah, 15;
Henry, 15; Kenny, 23; Thomas,
97; Thomas, dec'd, 91; Thomas,
yeoman, 15, 16

M

M[?]LESS, Jno., 27
MAC CULLODY, John, 69
MACDOWALL, Alex., 11
MACKDANIEL, Daniel, 34
MACKDOWALL, Alex., 1
MACKDOWALL, Alexander, 39,
74, 84; Alexander, Deputy
Surveyor, 88; Alexander, Gent.;
75; Alexander, trader, 82; Alexr.,
59, 60
MACKDOWELL, Alexander, 54
MACKENSIE, Aeneas, 25
MACKEY, Robert, vintner, 57, 99
MACKINTOSHE, Phineas, 82
MACKNIGHT, Patrick, 97;
Patrick, merchant, 2
MADOCK, WM., 87
MAPLE, Benjamin, 40

MARSH, John, 28; John, yeoman, 96; Jonathan, mariner, dec'd, 20; Joshua, yeoman, 96; William, mariner, 20
MARTIN, Daniel, 97; James, 43, 44; James, Gent., 43; Thomas, 8
MARTINCEE, Wm., 82
MARTYN, W., 61
MARTYNE, John, 41
MASTERS, Clement, 98
MC CULLOCK, Colin, 69; Patrick, 70
MC KENZIE, George, Sir, 69
MC STANTONY, Arch., 57
MEEKER, Jos., Junr., 12; Joseph, Junr., Esqr., 12
MELVIN, John, 26
MENWELL, Richd., 36
MERLOT, Rebecca, 52
MERTTINS, George, Mayor, London, 76
MESLAYER, Daniel, 101
MESSLEAR, Evert, 73
MEW, Richard, merchant, 61
MIDFORD, John, 82
MILER, James, 4
MILLER, Henry, yeoman, 2; James, 6, 84, 85, 86, 93, 94; James, yeoman, 84; Mary, 84, 85, 86, 94; Mary, widow, 84, 85, 93
MILLS, Henry, 57; Samuel, 96
MITCHEL, Robert, 30
MITCHELL, Charles, 102; Robert, 102
MOMPESSON, Roger, Esqr., Chief Justice, NY, 16
MOOR, Mathew, 34
MOOR[E?], Samuel, 103
MOORE, Dabara, 94; James, 6 James Samuel, 6; James, weaver, 103; James, yeoman, 6, 103; John, 15; Mary, 2;

Mathew, 103; Samll., 2; Samuel, 70, 102; Samuel, Gent., 2
MOORES, James, yeoman, 6; Samuel, 103
MORE, Samuel, 70
MORE[MOORE?], Matthew, dec'd, 103
MORFORD, John, 39, 40, 46, 89, 90; John, yeoman, 89; Thomas, 39, 89; Thomas, dec'd, 39, 79
MORGAN, Joseph, 4; Joseph, 7, 33, 75; Joseph, clerk, 4; Joseph, Minister, 91 Nathaniel, 33
MORGAN, Andrew, 75
MORIN, Mary, 35; Samuel, 35
MORLET, Josias, yeoman, 52; Josyas, 52
MOROS, Mathew, 35
MORRIN, Samuel, 36
MORRINE, Samuel, 36
MORRIS, George, 57; John, 66; John, Capt., 4, 22; Lewis, 103; Lewis, East NJ Society, 34; Lewis, Esqr., 102; Lewis, Esqr., Chief Justice, 101; Lewis, Esqr., Majesty's Council, 8, 72, 82
MOSSE, Lydia, 89; Robert, 89
MOSSERAR[?], Johannes, dec'd, 73
MOTT, John, cooper, 66
MOULLON, Joseph, 11
MOUNT, George, 40; Humphrey, 79; Rebeckah, 79; Rebekah, 39, 40; Richard, 40; Richard, Junr., 39; Richard, Junr., cordwainer, 79; Richard, yeoman, 39, 46; Thomas, 7
MUDIE, David, 58
MUIR, Wm., 27
MURDOCK, Patrick, 60
MURRAY, Joseph, 100, 101

N

NEGRO MAN, Tom, 22
NEVINS, Peter, 22

NEWLAND, James, 58
NEWLANDE, Ja., Jun., bailie, 99
NEWMAN, Mary, 44; Walter, 45;
    Walter, planter, 44; William,
    dec'd, 76
NICCOLLS, And., 43; Rebecca, 38
NICHOLLS, Andrew, Gent., 39
NICHOLS, Mary, 71
NICKOLLS, Andrew, Gent., 38, 75;
    Rebecca (Dockwra), 38, 75
NICOLLS, Andrew, Gent., 92, 94;
    Rebecca (Dockwra), 92, 94
NINDS, John, dec'd, 31
NOKS, John, 8
NORRIS, Henry, dec'd, 81
NORTH, Wm., 65
NORTON, George, butcher, 45
NOTT, Francis, Gent., 68
NOWDON, Mich., 8
NUDIE, David, merchant, dec'd, 51
NUNES, Daniel, 37
NUNEZ, Daniel, 37; Mary, 37
NUTMAN, James, 97
NUWES, Daniel, merchant, 31

O

OGDEN, Banjamin, 48;
    Benjamin, 35;
    Benjamin, Senr., 63; David,
    67; Jos., 65, 67, 97; Josiah, 25,
    26, 43, 65, 67, 97; Josiah,
    Colonel, 97; Josiah, Esqr.,
    Judge, Essex Co., 31; Josiah,
    Judge, Essex Co., 33, 47 80;
    Thomas, 48; Twain[?], 100
OLDIN, William, 72
OLIVER, Samuel, yeoman, 31
ORMSTON, Joseph, merchant,
    67; Joseph, merchant, dec'd,
    68
OSBORN, Jeremiah, 100
OSBORNE, Daniel, 98; John, 98
OSTERLAND, [FNU], 83, 84;
    Jacob, 31, 32, 71

OULDEN, William, 74

P

PACHEO, Rodrigo, merchant, 37
PAER, Tunis, 24
PALMER, John, Capt., Esqr., 77;
    John, Captain, 53
PARKER, Coll., 42; Elisha, 39, 43;
    Elisha, dec'd, 64; Elisha, Majesty's
    Council, 41; Elisha, merchant, 9,
    63; Elisha, merchant, 63;
    Elizabeth, 64; Jennet, 17; John, 4,
    64, 80; John, Esqr., 14; John,
    Esqr., Majesty's Council, 31, 90,
    92, 96, 101, 103; John, Majesty's
    Council, 1, 2, 16, 17, 21, 23, 24,
    28, 30, 33, 34, 37, 40, 41, 45, 46,
    47, 48, 52, 54, 57, 59, 65, 74, 77,
    79, 80, 88, 89, 91, 93, 94, 96, 100,
    104, 105; John, merchant, 36, 96;
    Nathaniel, 87; Thomas, Esqr., 28;
    Ursula, 97
PARLER, Elisha, 8
PARMYTER, Par., 26, 31
PARSETT, J., 50; J., clerk, 49
PATTERSON, William, 43, 44;
    William, Gent., 43
PAYNE, Edward, 62
PEACOCK, Thomas, 61
PEARSE[?], [?]anneke, 31; Hendrick,
    turner, 31
PEARSON, Thomas, yeoman, 18
PEECHECO, Rodrigo, merchant, 37
PEIRSON, Jonathan, 99; Theophelias,
    23; Theophilus, 27; Theophilus,
    dec'd, 99; Theophilus. yeoman,
    100
PENN, William, 33, 103; William,
    Esqr., 60, 61; Wm., Junr., 69
PENNANT, Edward, 1, 2
PENNY, John, 68
PENTARD, John, 100
PERKINS, William, 99, 100
PETER KEIGHTLY MILLS, 97

PETERS, J.B., 50; J.B., attorney, 49; John Baptest, 50; Martha, widow, 50
PETIS [?], Thos., 5
PETTERSON, Abraham, 71; John, dec'd, 73; Mary, 73
PETTINGER, John, 36
PEYARTT, [FNU], 79
PEYSTER, J.D., 16
PHILIPS, Adolph, 54
PICKE, Mary, 48; Phillip, tailor, 48
PICKLE, Jabus., notary, 68
PIDGEON, Jos., 62
PIER, Abraham, 24; Tunis, 24; Tunis Johnson, 24
PIERCE, Francis, 7
PIERSON, Jonathan, 46; Theophilus, 47
PIKE, Jeannet, 42; Jno., 42; John, 8, 9, 42; John, Capt., dec'd, 42; John, dec'd, 42; Joseph, 42; Nathall., 42; Phillip, 48; Thomas, 2, 6, 8, 9, 42, 102; Thos., 9; Thos., Judge, Middlesex Co., 35; Zebulon, 42; Zebulon, yeoman, 41
PINTARD, [FNU], 91; Samuel, 91
PLACE, John, 30
PLUM, Samuel, 26, 79
PLUMSTEAD, CLEMENT, 24; Clement, merchant & Proprietor, 55; Clement, skinner, 61
POLHEMIUS, Jacob, carpenter, 89
POLHEMUS, Theodorey, 82
PONDIX, john, 9
POPE, John, yeoman, 72
PORTER[?], Robert, 11
POTTER, Henry, 42; Samuel, 1, 16
POWELL, Margret, 100; Richard, 42; Wm., 85
PRICE, Ben, 98; Benjamin, 35;

Benjamin, J.P., 20; Daniel, 18; Thomas, 48
PRIDMORE, Benjamin, 30
PRINCE, Elizabeth, Mrs., widow, 2; Henry, merchant, dec'd, 2
PRINGLE, Walter, 16
PRITCHARD, Aaron, turner, 50
PROBASCO, Stoffle, 82
PROVOOST, David, Judge, Bergen Co., 26
PROVOST, John, 13; William, merchant, 86
PRUDDEN, John, 47; John, Senr., 46
PUCK, Thos., notary, 76
PURSELE, Thomas, 8
PURSELL, Thomas, 57; Thomas, yeoman, 59

Q

QUASIE, Richard, 81
QUIMBY, Jonathan, 44, 45

R

RAINE, Rowland, 62
RANDOLPH, Benjamin, 30
RASORTSALIN, Lringna[?], 55
RAY, Robert, 85
READ, john, 84
READE, Anne, 54; Anne (French), 54; Jos., 55; Joseph, 55; Joseph, merchant, 54
READER, Eliz., 42; Elizabeth, 42; Jeremiah, 42; Jeremiah, planter, 42
READING, Jno., 101; John, 101
REDER, Jeremiah, 42
REDFORD, Thos., 78
REGINER, Jas., 8
REID, John, 5, 7, 8, 11, 12, 13, 66, 73, 75, 85, 86, 91, 93, 94; John, dec'd, 93; John, Esqr., 75; John, Gairdner, 17; John, Gent., 17; John, Judge, Monmouth Co., 52;

John, Junr., 94; John, Surveyor
General, 7
REIDES, John, 31
REMSER, Rem., 35
RENEERSE, Hendrick, 80
RESCARRICK, George, 18, 32;
George, dec'd, 18, 19; Mary,
19; Mary, widow, 18
REVELL, John, 84
REYNOE, John, 11
RICHARDS, Paul, 2
RICHARDSON, Robert, 77
RICHIER, Edward, Esqr., 34,
102
RICHMOND, John, 69, 70
RIDDEL, Walter, Esqr.,
Proprietor, 17
RIDDELL, Walter, Gent., 16
RIGG, Ambrose, Gent., 61
RIGGOZ, [FNU], 20
RIGGS, Edward, 27
RINDESAY, O., 57
ROBARDS, Amos, 15
ROBBENSON, James, yeoman,
6
ROBERTS, Hugh, 67
ROBESON, Andrew, blacksmith,
43; John, dec'd, 55; William,
64
ROBESON'S SAW MILL,
William, 46
ROBINSON, Deborah, 8; James,
6; John, dec'd, 6; John, weaver,
6; William, 10, 24; William,
Gent., 8
ROBISON, Deborah, 11; John, 21;
William, Gent., 11; Wm., 11,
102
ROCKERDS, Edward, 31
ROGERS, Elizabeth, 41; Robert,
dec'd, 6; William, school
master, 41; Wm., 2
ROLESON, Andrew, 23
ROLFE, Benjamin, 90; Henry,

Esqr., 8; Joseph, 94; Moses, 57,
100; Moses, Esqr., 21, 90; Saml.,
88
ROLPH, Henry, dec'd, 102; John,
102; Joseph, 94; Margaret,
widow, 102; Moses, 8; Moses,
Esqr., 64
ROMAINE, John, 86
ROMEYN, Jacobus, 4
ROMINE, Jacobus, 7; Jacobus,
yeoman, 6; Mary, 6
ROMMIGN, Jan., 86
ROPER, Abigal, 100; Abigal
(Perkins), 100; Thomas, 100
ROSE[Ross?], John, 31
ROSS, Alexander, 67; Daniel, 70;
George, dec'd, 70
ROUSE, Samuel, 73
ROUSET, D., 33
ROYCE, Samuel, Gent., 39
ROYSE, John, 41, 52, 53, 55, 88;
John, dec'd, 55, 56; John,
merchant, 53; Samll., 45;
Samuel, 56; Samuel, Gent., 31,
52, 55
RUCK, Thos., 63
RUCKMAN, John, 91; John, Junr.,
yeoman, 91; John, Senr., 91;
Jonathan, yeoman, 91
RUDGERS, Major, 54
RUDYARD, Deborah, 76; John, 14,
73; John, Esqr., 76; Thomas, 47;
Thomas, Gent., 61
RUNION, Peter, yeoman, 3
RUST, John, 62
RUTHERFORD, Richard Strachant,
49

S

SALTAR, Deborah, 51, 52, 67;
Ebenezer, 51; James, 51; John,
52, 67; Richard, 35, 51, 52, 59,
87, 88; Richard, Captain, 51
Richard, Esqr., Judge,

Monmouth Co., 98; Richard, Judge, Monmouth Co., 67; Richard, Majesty's Council, 84; Richd., 89; William, 51, 67, 89

SANDFORD, William, 11; Wm., 98

SANDILAND, James, dec'd, town clerk, 63; Robert, 63, 76

SARGINT, Thomas, 85

SARJANT, Jonathan, 26

SAUNDERS, William, 62

SAVAGE, James, 65

SAVERY, Peter, 14

SCATTERGOOD, Thomas, 100

SCHENCK, Gerret, 5

SCHUYLER, Arent, 9

SCHYLER, Arent, Gent., 22 Casparus, 22

SCOBIE, Alexander, yeoman, 19

SCOREY, Guil., 65

SCOT'S PROPRIETORS, 44, 45, 74, 75

SCOTT, John, 69

SEAMAN, Rachel, 28

SELLWOOD, John, 62

SEYMONDS, Michael, 1

SHADDOCK, William, 87

SHARP, John, carpenter, 13; John, Junr., 13; William, 96;

SHAW, Rob., 65

SHEPARD, Moses, 12

SHERD, Thos., 78

SHIPMAN, Benjamin, yeoman, 65

SILKES, Lawrence, 20

SIMONS, Sarah, widow, 48

SINCLAIR, Will., 69, 70

SKINER, John, 10

SKINNER, John, 10; Thos., Esqr., 102; Wright, 94

SLATAR, Oliver, 51

SLATER, Edward, 40, 79

SLATERS, Edward, 79

SLAUGHTER, Edward, 77

SLON, Samuel, 8

SMACK, [?]ndert, 77

SMALLEY, Isaac, 1

SMALLY, John, 64 Joshua, 31

SMITH, Able, yeoman, 35; Deborah, 35; Desior, 5; Ichabod, 8, 88; James, 28; James, Esqr., Majesty's Council, 101; Jekabods, 6; Jno., 30; John, 5; John, yeoman, 5; Joseph, 66, 67; Sam., 6; Samuel, 93; Samuel, Junr., 64; Samuel, Senr., 102; Samuel, yeoman, 102; Shobal, 6; Tho., 63; Thomas, 63, 65; Thomas, cordwainer, 11; Thos., 71

SMOCK, Johannes, 45

SMYTH, Lawr., 75

SOAPER, Elizabeth, 6; Richard, yeoman, 6

SONMAN, Peter, 13, 76

SONMANS, Arent, dec'd, 38; Peter, 32, 38, 44, 59, 95; Peter, Esqr., 31, 71, 83; Peter, Gent., 69; Peter, Majesty's Council, 44

SOOY, Joseph, 71

SOPER, Elizabeth, 6; Richard, 6, 8

SOPPER[?], Richard, 39

SOYES, Joseph, 71

SPEAR, Hance[?], 24

SPERLING, John Michael, 73

SPINING, Ebenezer, 20

SPREED, John, 39

ST. PETER'S CHURCH, 88, 89

STANDLAND, Darby, 93

STANDLY, Richard, 66

STELLE, Gabriel, 75

STEVENS, J., 31, 44, 75; John, 22, 23, 27, 28, 33, 43, 77, 92, 95; John, tavern keeper, 94;

Joseph, 10; Joseph, yeoman, 9
STEVENSON, John, Gent., 73
STEWARD, John, 10
STILL, Ambrose, 71
STILLWELL, Daniel, 46;
  Elizabeth, 65; Elizabeth
  (Grover), 65; Gershom, 65;
  Thos., 66
STILWELL, Alice, 81; John, 81;
  Rebekah, 81; Thomas, 81
STOCKTON, Benjamin, 76;
  John, 76; Joseph, 87; Richard,
  76; Robert, 87; Thomas, 76
STONBURY, Elias, 89
STONE, Samuel, 60, 64
STONE[?], Margaret, 42; William,
  39
STOUT, John, 59, 92; John, dec'd,
  90, 92; Richard, 91; Richard,
  Capt., Gent., 90; Richard, Junr.,
  98; Richard, Junr., planter, 97
STOUTT, Richard, 98
STRAYHEARN, William, 24
STRUMENTREMD, Jn., 73
STRYKER, Peter, 32
STUCKEY, Isaac, 19, 31, 78, 80,
  103; Israel, 13; John, 26
STUCKY, Isaac, 58, 59
SUMMER[?], George, 35
SUTTON, Richard, 3; Thomas,
  16
SUTTUN, Thomas, 16
SUYLER [Schuyler?], Arent, Gent.,
  15
SWAYZE, Matthias, 90
SWIFT, Eliza., 104
SYMES, Lancaster, 95
SYMONDS, Wm., 35
SYMS, Catherine, 29; Lancaster,
  Gent., 29

T

TALBOT, Kathe, 101
TANTUM, John, 100

TAPPEN, Abraham, 36, 42, 95;
  Abraham, weaver, 88; Benj., 36;
  Benjamin, 36, 96; Benjamin,
  shoemaker, 95; David, 36, 39,
  42, 96; Isaac, 92; Isaac, cooper,
  39; Isaac, dec'd, 36, 88, 95;
  Jacob, 39; Mary, 36; Sicell, 96;
  Sisel, 96; Sisell, 95
TAPPEN[?], Isaac, 94
TAPPIN, Isaac, 1
TAYLOR, Henry, 1, 2; Henry,
  turner, 1, 2, 64; Isaac, Esqr., J.P.,
  45; Ja., 57, 58, 99; James, writer,
  99; Jno., 45; John, 30, 57; Mary,
  45; Thomas, 51, 52, 72
TEN EYCK, Coeraet, 78, 79
TERHUNEN, Aeltie, 21, 22;
  Albert, 21, 22; Anne, 21;
  Gerritt, 21, 22; John, 21, 22
  Roeloff, 22; Sarah, 21;
  Williamtie, 21
THARPE, Joseph, 64
THOMAS, Dally, 57; James, 69
THOMASON, James, 24
THOMPSON, Azubah, 24;
  Cornelius, 86, 87
THOMSEN, Cornelius, 85;
  Cornelius, yeoman, 85
THOMSON, James, 35;
  Margaret, 28; Martha, 57;
  William, 60, 67
THONG, Walter, merchant, 1, 22
THOREN, Isaac, 94
THORNALL, [FNU], 35
THORNELL, Israel, 11
THROCKMORTON, Deliverence,
  81; Job, 37, 38, 81, 98; Job, dec'd,
  80; John, 81; John, Gent., 80;
  Joseph, Dec'd, 80
TIDMARSH, Wm., 85
TILTON, Daniel, 66
TOE, John, dec'd, 88; Lydia, 89;
  Lydia, widow, 88
TOOKER, Charles, 20; Charles,
  dec'd, 20

TOWNLEY, Effingham, Gent., 98; Richard, Esqr., Judge, Supreme Court, 39; Sarah, 98
TOWNLY, Rich., Esqr., Majesty's Council, 34
TREMBLE, John, yeoman, 8
TRENT, William, Esqr., Chief Justice, 59, 60; Wm., 33
TRIGONA, Brians, 62; Elizabeth, 62; Elizabeth (Brain), 62; Henry, mariner, 62; Mary, 62
TUNISSE, Denyse, 83; Hans, 83
TURNBUCK, Thomas, Dec'd, 60
TURNER, Robert, 12, 66; Robert, dec'd, 20
TUTLE, Nathaniel, 89
TUTTLE, Joseph, 99; Timothy, 14, 15

V

VAIL, John, 6, 18
VAN BOSCERKT, Bister, 11
VAN BRUNT, Cornelius, 20
VAN CLEAVE, Isabrant, 92
VAN CLEF, Yesbrant, 92
VAN COURTLAND, Steph., 22
VAN DE WATER, Wappein, 52
VAN DIEN, Gerritt, 86
VAN DYK, John, 18
VAN HOOK, Lawrence, 87
VAN HORN, John, merchant, 57
VAN HORNE, Abraham, mercahnt, 31; Cor., Senr., 55; Cornelius, 55; Cornelius, Esqr., Judge, Somerset Co., 54; Cornelius, merchant, 54; Elizabeth, 54, 55; Elizabeth (French), 54; John, merchant, 31, 55; Routa, 55; Rutt, yeoman, 76
VAN KERK, Henry, 75
VAN NESTE, Pieter, 79
VAN NUYSE, Isaac, yeoman, 18
VAN QUILLAN, Robert, 55

VAN VEGHTEEN, Michael, 55
VAN VEGHTEN, Michael, Gent., 75
VAN VEGTEN, Michael, 54, 55
VANDAM, Rip, merchant, 29
VANDORN, Joseph, 5
VANGALEN, Lowrance, 8
VANHOOK, Lawrence, 84
VANHORN, Cornelius, 37; Garret, 76; John, 66, 76, 93; John, merchant, 33
VANHORNE, John, merchant, 39, 47
VANMATER, John, yeoman, 2; Margaret, 2
VANMETRE, John, 2; Margaret, 2
VANNESSE, Peter, the Elder, yeoman, 78; Peter, the Younger, yeoman, 78
VANNEST, Peter, yeoman, 78
VANNEST, John, yeoman, 78
VANNESTE, Peter, 79; Peter, Sr., yeoman, 1
VANNOICE, John, 25
VANQUELLIN, Robert, 72
VANWICK, [FNU], 87
VANWICKLAND, Evert, 35
VANWINCKEL, Joannis Jacobse, yeoman, 22
VAUGHAN, Edward, 2, 36, 45, 74 Edward, Rev[?], 18; Edwd., 37; Mary, 18
VERNON, Lydia, 54
VERPLANCK, Wm., 15
VIELL, John, 54
VILANT, David, 4, 51; David, Gent., 51; David, merchant, dec'd, 50 William, 51; William, goldsmith, 50; William., goldsmith, 51
VOLKERSE, Derick, 56; Derick, yeoman, 56
VOORHIES, Koert, 22; Koort, 22
VORTMAN, John, yeoman, 56
VROOME, Hendrick, 37

W

WAINWRIGHT, Nicholas, 67
WAKEHAM, Anne, 81; Elizabeth, 81; Elizabeth, spinster, 81; Elizabeth, widow, 81; Hannah, 81; Joseph, yeoman, dec'd, 81; Mary, 81
WALDREN, William, 52
WALDRON, Joseph, 52
WALKER, Alex., 96; Saml., 41; Samll., 1; Samuel, 16
WALL, Garret, 33; Garret, dec'd, 11, 12; Humphrey, yeoman, 11; Humphry, 11, 12; Jarat, 65, 66; John, 33, 66; John, yeoman, 12, 65; Mary, 65, 66; Wal., 11; Walter, 66
WALLING, William, 11
WALLS, Jarat, 91; John, 13, 14, 90, 99; John, carpenter, 14; John, joyner, 23
WALTER, R., 101
WALTERS, Robert, Esqr., 101
WARBURTON, Ann (Dockwra), 92, 94; Anne (Dockwra), 38, 75; Thomas, Gent., 75, 92, 94; Thos., Gent., 38
WARD, Anthony, 19; john, 35; John, Sir., 38;John, yeoman, 78
WARDEN, John, 6
WARNE, Joshua, 74; Mary, 44; Sten., 44, 45, 74, 89; Stephen, 74; Stephen, Gent., 74; Stephen, yeoman, 79, 88, 89; Tho., 18; Thomas, 44, 47, 75, 100; Thomas, dec'd, 74; Thomas, Gent., 20; Thomas, yeoman, 18; Thos., 20, 45
WARREN, John, dec'd, 48
WATSON, David, 72; John, 3, 4; Peter, Junr., 71; Wm., 44
WATT, Adam, clerk, 99; John, 58

WEBBSTER, Welford, 54
WEBSTER, Robert, yeoman, 9
WEEKS, Zachari, 18, 90; Zachariah, 44, 78, 79
WELLS, John, joiner, 34
WEST, John, Senr., 4; Robt., 60, 61, 69
WESTERVEILT, J., 86
WESTERVELT, Cornelias, 86; Cornelius, 86; Jurya, 86
WETSON[?], John, 47
WETTON, Ben., 60, 61
WEYNANK, Samuel, 35
WHITE, John, 84; John, Gent., 55; Peter, 84; Robt., Junr., 92
WHITEHEAD, Elisha, 81; Isaac, 21; Isaac, Judge, Essex Co., 8, 9, 16, 22, 23, 24, 63, 96; Isaace, Judge, Essex Co., 43; Joseph, dec'd, 48; Nathan, 96; Samuel, 20, 21, 31, 43, 81; Samuel, Judge, Essex Co., 20
WHITEING, John, 102
WHITELOCK, John, 33; John, yeoman, 11
WHITEN, Benjamin, Esqr., 68
WHITLOCK, John, yeoman, 12, 33; Mary, 33; Thomas, 11, 12; Thomas, yeoman, 33
WIES[?], John, 28
WIGGINS, Thomas, 96
WIGHTMAN, Jo., 57
WILCOSON, John, 94
WILCOX, Thomas, goldsmith, 61
WILIAM, Reice, 44
WILKISON, James, 30; John, mason, 94
WILLEMES, Lomons, 32
WILLET, Samuel, 51, 52
WILLIAMS, Amos, carpenter, 16; Benjamin, 48; Joseph, 48; Samuel, carpenter, 15
WILLIAMSON, John, 23; Wm., 12

WILLISON, James, dec'd, 87; James, yeoman, dec'd, 86
WILLOCK, George, 43
WILLOCKS, Geo., 5, 8, 25, 33, 37, 44, 80, 101; George, 2, 4, 36, 50, 59, 65, 66, 73; George, Esqr., 80, 101; George, Gent., 3, 13, 17, 25, 43, 44, 45, 51, 77; George, merchant, 7, 19; Margaret, 25, 45
WILLS, John, Majesty's Council, 23, 100
WILLSON, James, 87; John, 94; Peter, 87; Walter, 86
WILLSON[?], Andrew, 74
WILSON, Alex., bailie, 99; Ebenezer, 29; James, yeoman, 86, 87; John, 91; John, Junr., 91; Peter, 86, 87; Walter, 86; Wm., 57, 58
WINANCEZ, John, Junr., 70
WINDER, Saml., 98; Samuel, Gent., 55
WINERIGHT, Nicholas, 66
WININATNZ, Wm., 20
WINMAN, William, 20
WINTRUP, [FNU], 98
WISER, Christopher, 88; Elizabeth, 88
WISES, Richard, notary, 2
WITHERS, William, Sir, 65
WITHRINGTON, Oliver, 68
WOLLE, Edward, 91
WONDER, Margaret, 13
WOOD, Jonas, 24; Joseph, 23
WOODBRIDGE, Joseph, Mass. Bay Colony, 11
WOODRUFF, Jonathan, 20, 21; Joseph, 48; Thos., 35
WOODS, James, 1, 2
WOOGSA[?], Robert, 52
WORRILAW, Ann, 45
WORTH, John, 1, 8, 9; Joseph, 1, 100

WRIGHT, Antho., 76; Elizabeth, 15; John, 86; Robert, 92
WRIGHTMAN, Robert, bailie, 99
WYCKOFF, Cornelius, 82; Peter, 5
WYCOFF, John, 85; Pieter, 22
WYNKOOP, Abrahm., 47

Y

YARD, Willm., 23
YATES, Tho., 40; Thomas, 18; Thos., 18
YOUNG, James, writer, 17; Mary, 17; Robert, 65, 79
YOUNG[?], Robt., 26

Z

ZACHARY, Lloyd, 76
ZENGER, [FNU], 35

www.ingramcontent.com/pod-product-compliance
Lightning Source LLC
Chambersburg PA
CBHW071134280326
41935CB00010B/1216